W9-DCM-377

ADVANCE PRAISE FOR

201 GREAT IDEAS FOR YOUR SMALL BUSINESS

by Jane Applegate

"Give your business an extraordinary advantage—**buy this book**."

HARVEY MACKAY
Author of *Dig Your Well Before You're Thirsty* and *Swim With the Sharks*
CEO, Mackay Envelope Corporation

"As the guru to the millions of women-owned businesses nationwide, **Applegate's 'inside information' is like money in the bank**."

AMY MILLMAN
Executive Director
National Women's Business Council

"Great Idea Number 202: **Buy Jane's book and read it all!**"

PHYLLIS HILL SLATER
Entrepreneur & President
National Association of Women Business Owners

"Jane Applegate has done it again. In her uniquely approachable yet insightful style, she has assembled **an invaluable resource for any entrepreneur**."

TODD MCCRACKEN
President
National Small Business United

"Just one of these smart ideas can help boost your business. **Glean a dozen, and you'll cream your competition**."

MARTHA ROGERS
Coauthor of *The One to One Future* and *Enterprise One to One*

"Any idea from Jane Applegate is a good one. **'201' is a treasure!** Grab this book and use it often!"

JOLINE GODFREY
CEO
Independent Means, Inc.

"These are **great strategies** that anyone in small business can easily use to be more successful!"

BENNIE L. THAYER
President & CEO
The National Association for the Self-Employed

"*201 Great Ideas for Your Small Business* is **the most comprehensive book I've ever read for the owner of a small business**. If you are in business for yourself, make sure you get your personal copy. **It could prove to be your biggest asset**."

WALLY AMOS
Founder of Famous Amos Cookies
and Uncle Noname Company

"An Applegate a day will keep the business problems away. **A wonderful collection of practical solutions to everyday business problems**."

BOB ROSNER
Author of *Working Wounded: Advice that Adds Insight to Injury* and Nationally Syndicated Columnist

201 Great Ideas FOR YOUR Small Business

AVAILABLE FROM

Bloomberg Small Business

Where to Go When the Bank Says No
Alternatives for Financing Your Business
by David R. Evanson
(June 1998)

Small Business Legal Smarts
by Deborah L. Jacobs
(August 1998)

ALSO OF INTEREST FROM

The Bloomberg Personal Bookshelf

Smarter Insurance Solutions
by Janet Bamford

Smart Questions to Ask Your Financial Advisers
by Lynn Brenner

A Commonsense Guide to Your 401(k)
by Mary Rowland

Choosing and Using an HMO
by Ellyn Spragins

BLOOMBERG SMALL BUSINESS

Jane Applegate

201 Great Ideas for Your Small Business

BLOOMBERG PRESS
PRINCETON

First edition published 1998
1 3 5 7 9 10 8 6 4 2

Applegate, Jane
201 great ideas for your small business / Jane Applegate.
p. cm.
ISBN 1-57660-050-5 (alk. paper)
1. Small business - - Management. I. Title.
HD62.7.A64 1998
658.02'2 - - dc21 97-52249
CIP

ACQUIRED AND EDITED BY
Christine Miles AND **Jacqueline Murphy**

BOOK DESIGN BY **Don Morris Design**

THIS BOOK IS DEDICATED TO Joe, Jeanne, and Evan Applegate, who make my life worth living. Also to my parents, Sherrie and Marty Weisman, and grandparents, George and Jean Coan, who always encourage me to follow my dreams.

CHAPTER 6

CHAPTER 7

CHAPTER 8

CHAPTER 9

CHAPTER 10

ACKNOWLEDGMENTS

EVERY PERSON QUOTED IN THIS BOOK DESERVES HEARTfelt thanks for the many hours they spent being interviewed, fact-checked, and pestered by me and my former research associate, Mimi Schultz.

I couldn't have covered this much ground without Mimi's energetic and enthusiastic help.

Thanks, also, to Juliette Tracey Goldman for her expert help with the government resources section. She provided invaluable insights into the myriad of government services and resources available to entrepreneurs. Thanks to Nick Sullivan and Meg Whittemore for their reporting help and friendship. Thanks to Donna Buckley, my assistant, for keeping my office and life in order.

Every author needs a great agent and Dominick Abel is the best. He has given me great advice and counsel on every book I've written, and I intend to write plenty more.

Every writer needs great editors. My editors at Bloomberg Press, Jacqueline Murphy and Chris Miles, provided the perfect balance of hand-holding, clear direction, and moral support.

Special thanks to Michael Bloomberg for hiring me as a consultant and giving me challenging projects that allowed me to move to New York. He also contributed a great idea and, best of all, published this book.

Introduction

Man's mind, stretched to a new idea, never goes back to its original dimensions.

—OLIVER WENDELL HOLMES JR.

Why I wrote "201"

WITH SO MANY GREAT IDEAS FLOATING AROUND OUT there, you might wonder how I narrowed it down to 201 and what criteria I used to decide whether or not the idea was just average or really great.

Well, to me a great idea is one that is timeless. It's not a fad, buzzword, or trendy fix-all. It has to be useful and appropriate for a variety of small businesses, no matter what they do or where they are based. Universal appeal is a major requirement.

It also has to be something tried by a real business owner in a real small business. Everything in this book came from an interview I've conducted, a business owner I've met, a consultant I've quizzed, or a book or article written by a respected business reporter or author.

Credit is given where credit is due, whenever possible. If I've "borrowed" an idea, I'll tell you where it came from. Recognizing the people who came up with these ideas is a great way to encourage them to dream up more.

I solicited ideas from entrepreneurs in Bakersfield and Bali, Fargo and France. I scoured my database, Rolodex, and scraps of paper to track down consultants, trainers, venture capitalists, bankers, accountants, credit managers, money managers, and attorneys.

We were relentless in searching for the best ideas possible. We found all sorts of interesting people to press for inspiration and anecdotes. You'll meet restaurant doctors, telephone doctors, and real doctors called psychiatrists.

My search also inspired me to collect a few great ideas from some of the country's best-known entrepreneurs. Mail-order queen Lillian Vernon and Southwest Airlines chairman Herb Kelleher graciously shared their great ideas with me.

Management guru Tom Peters contributed one; so did Muriel Siebert, the first woman to own a seat on the New York Stock Exchange.

The number in the title was supposed to link it to my first book, *Succeeding in Small Business®*, which featured 101 problems and solutions. What's 201 ideas anyway, I thought? I collect great ideas from successful business people every day.

I admit, though, on one sweet, balmy July day, I called my editor and suggested we change the title to *67 Great Ideas*. It didn't fly, so I kept going, and I'm glad I did.

The 201 ideas are divided into themes to make it easy to find what you're looking for. Many ideas are cross-indexed to easily link you to additional information on a related subject.

This book, in its handy format, is meant to be read on the run. Read it front-to-back or back-to-front, it doesn't matter. But read it cover-to-cover, and tell your friends about it. I guarantee you won't be bored.

JANE APPLEGATE
Pelham, New York

CHAPTER 1

Management Strategies

INCE I BEGAN WRITING ABOUT THE entrepreneurial market in 1988, I've compared business owners to plate spinners in the circus. It seems like as soon as you get one plate spinning, another starts wobbling and crashes to the floor.

No matter what kind of business you're managing, you face big and small challenges every day. Hands-on managers wear many hats but rarely have time to hang any of them on a hat rack.

For instance, one morning when I arrived to have my hair cut at the Total Image salon in New Rochelle, New York, the owner, Frank Como, was already facing an enormous pile of wet towels because his clothes dryer wasn't working. A few minutes later, the real-estate broker working a few doors away ran into the salon in a lather because the basement of her building was filling up with water. That wasn't all. Between clients, Frank was soothing an upset hairdresser. Just a typical day, we agreed.

While Frank's business is tiny compared to some of the other business owners you'll meet in this book, you'll see that no matter what size your company is, you can *always* use a few fresh management strategies.

One of the most successful entrepreneurs I know has bigger headaches than Frank's. In recent years, she's dealt with the unionization of her assembly line workers after a very nasty battle. During that incredibly stressful time, she was being wooed by one of the biggest corporations in her industry to possibly serve as manager of their West Coast manufacturing center.

Although she's one of my closest friends, we communicate mainly via voice mail, exchanging detailed messages at odd hours because she rarely has five minutes free for a live conversation. But, like Frank, she loves being an entrepreneur.

It doesn't matter whether you're running a fast-growing factory or a cozy suburban beauty salon—I have great ideas for you.

In this chapter, you'll learn how to woo clients and find great places to meet with them, even if you don't have a fancy office. You'll find out how to set up an informal advisory board to help solve tough problems and how to streamline your meetings so you have more time to work.

You'll learn how to hire great attorneys, accountants, and consultants, and how to create a safer workplace so you stay out of trouble with health and safety authorities.

You'll be inspired to plan a company retreat to rethink your priorities, move your business from home into a business incubator, invest in good office furniture, and improve your telephone skills.

Maybe you're feeling lost and want to find a mentor? I'll tell you how.

I've also included some thought-provoking ideas on dealing at a higher, less stressful level, and why it's so important to tell the truth and have more fun despite the incredible demands on your time.

I've been an affordable management consultant for years. For the price of a newspaper, you can get a weekly dose of practical advice in my syndicated column. Or you can check out the Web sites where I operate in cyberspace, including my own site, **www.janeapplegate.com**. But for now, you can have my greatest management ideas in one place—right here.

Always Deal with Decision Makers

THE ENTREPRENEUR'S CHALLENGE IS TO ALWAYS operate at the highest level possible; present proposals to the top decision maker, not the gatekeeper; elicit a prompt response; and move on quickly if the answer is "no."

Even when our company was based in the den of my suburban Los Angeles home, and later in a converted garage, we always resolved to deal directly with the very top people. Sure, it raised eyebrows because most of our consulting clients were Fortune 100 companies, but they wanted to work with us because they were anxious to sell into the fast-growing entrepreneurial market.

I am convinced we have been so successful because we've insisted on dealing with the top decision makers or managers with high-level access. No matter who you are, you can practice this approach. You can write directly to the president or chairman. Briefly outline your product and what you can do for his or her company. In many cases, the top person, or an assistant, will make a note on the letter and direct it back down through the ranks. That notation carries weight.

There are, of course, other ways to make the initial contact. Voice mail is a terrific tool for getting through to the person in charge. Most executives have a direct line. Ask to be put through by the receptionist. Call early in the morning or late in the evening—they often work longer hours than their secretaries. Try phoning during the lunch hour, too.

I should warn you that the "easier at the top" strategy *does* have pitfalls. Even if the top person signs off on your project, middle managers will sometimes exercise their powerful veto power. And at times they'll try to sabotage you.

After one project I had nurtured nearly to completion died a slow death from lack of middle management support, I learned that any outsider proposing a new idea to a major corporation must be very aware of the "not invented here" syndrome. It's a deadly corporate virus that can wipe out a good idea in no time. I share that not to discourage you, but to emphasize how critical it is to have solid support from the decision makers.

That said, be persistent—call the top managers, leave them a voice mail message describing your project. I'm living proof that it pays to start at the top and deal with whoever is signing the checks.

Don't Be Afraid to Recreate Your Business

WHEN ANTHONY'S FISH GROTTO DROPPED THE zabaglione cake from its menu, Rick Ghio feared his dear, departed grandmother, Catherine, would send a lightning bolt down from heaven in protest.

"But we were throwing away more cake than we were selling," said Ghio of the traditional sponge cake served with a rum custard sauce. Now Anthony's serves trendier tiramisu and fresh fruit tarts.

After 50 years, Anthony's also dropped rosé from the wine list, switching to white Zinfandel. These menu changes are just part of the major facelift under way at the famous San Diego–based restaurant chain.

Today Rick, a co-owner, manages the financial aspects of the company. His brother, Craig, and three other family members are the third generation to run the family-owned business founded by their grandparents.

Rick and his counterparts are giving the business a total makeover, inside and out. But why would a famous San Diego institution like Anthony's reinvent itself?

"We were losing our market share," he said. "Our reputation was still strong, but people were not dining at Anthony's as frequently as they did in the past."

Families still booked tables for major celebrations and holidays, but the younger, twenty- and thirty-something crowd did not consider Anthony's a hip place to eat.

"Competition is fierce, relentless, and unforgiving," said Craig Ghio, who oversees seafood purchasing and recipe development. "Diners have more choices than ever, and tradition is no longer enough to keep them coming back."

At first they changed advertising agencies, updated the menu, and did a little remodeling, but sales stayed flat.

The company, which started out in 1946 with one 18-seat diner, decided to completely rethink its purpose. The family hired two respected restaurant consultants who urged them not only to remodel their La Mesa location but also to turn the management of the company upside down.

The family had always made all the key decisions. Now Anthony's is managed by interdisciplinary teams, led by 21 trained "integrators" who conduct frequent discussions about everything from service to what kind of food and drinks to serve. The company's 400 employees all serve on one or more of the teams.

Everything at Anthony's has dramatically changed in the past year or so, Rick said. For example, "You always paid your bill at the cash register on the way out," he said. "Now you pay your server, which slows down turnover, but on the upside, it gives the server an excellent way to close out the meal."

They spent $1.3 million turning the lakeside La Mesa location into a fantasy grotto, complete with a video game arcade built on a 36-foot Criscraft boat, a trellis-covered patio, and cascading waterfalls.

They created two new characters for kids: "Sandy the fish" and "Diego the octopus." Kids have their own menu and a free beverage cup to take home.

"We learned to scan the environment," said Rick. "To stay in front of current trends. For the first time, we extended our hours. We are now open until 10 PM on weekdays and 11 PM on weekends."

Sales increased 35 percent shortly after the remodeled La Mesa restaurant opened. "People of all ages love it," Rick said.

While retooling the management and remodeling, they also worked hard to control food costs and boost profits. "For every dollar we took in, we used to spend 44 cents on food," he said. "Now it's down to 36.5 cents, and we've become more profitable." Anthony's, which is privately held, has revenues of about $18 million a year.

Although it has taken thousands of hours and more than a million dollars, Rick said the total revitalization program was worth it.

"It is the scariest darn process," he admits. "We literally had to reexamine things that were done the same way for 50 years. There's a huge risk in saying goodbye to some of the things we had been doing . . . but we are truly blessed by the initial response."

Check out Anthony's Web site at **www.gofishanthonys.com**.

Hire a Great Lawyer

WHEN YOU'RE STARTING A BUSINESS, IT'S natural to try to save money at every turn. But it doesn't pay to scrimp when it comes to getting solid legal advice.

Most business owners' first encounter with legal forms comes with a DBA, which means "doing business as" and is legally known as a *fictitious name statement*. After this first step, you'll need good legal advice to buy or sell real estate, form a partnership, create job applications, and write employee handbooks.

A good small-business attorney will protect you and your business from legal troubles involving staff, vendors, and customers. He or she can also help when you are looking for investors or dealing with bankers.

Finding a good attorney is not as challenging as you may think. According to Brad Carr, spokesman for the New York State Bar Association, there are about 729,000 practicing attorneys in this country, with three out of four working for themselves or for a small firm. The best way to find a good lawyer is to ask other small-business owners if they would recommend their own attorney. Your banker and your accountant may have some recommendations; ministers and rabbis are also good sources of referrals because they know so many people in the community.

Another way to find one is through legal directories. The reference section of most larger public libraries should have the *Martindale-Hubbell Law Directory*. This directory provides brief biographical information about lawyers in your area. Some listings also include the names of their clients, so you can call for references.

Most state bar associations offer free referral services. Call the bar association in your state for information. Most lawyers listed through the referral service charge a modest fee for an initial consultation.

Remember, hiring an attorney is a very personal thing. Be sure to choose someone you can confide in, who makes a good impression, and who has experience in your industry.

Some good news: A glut of attorneys, especially in big cities, has forced many to reduce their fees to beat the competition. Most are happy to work by the project and do not expect to be put on a monthly retainer. Some attorneys who specialize in working with entrepreneurs will take you on as a client in exchange for stock in your company or profit-sharing down the line. If an attorney is willing to work on this basis, consider making him or her a part of your strategic team.

The hourly fees you'll pay depend on where you live. For instance, business owners in New York City and Los Angeles generally pay higher legal fees than those living and working in Omaha, Nebraska.

When you are interviewing prospective attorneys, here are the questions to ask to get you started:

- Are you a member of the state bar and licensed to practice law in this state? (If your company does a lot of interstate commerce, you might want to hire an attorney who can practice in the federal courts as well.)
- What kinds of small businesses do you represent?
- How long have you been practicing law?
- Who can I call for a reference?

Hire an Infopreneur

YOU DON'T NEED TO SPEND ENDLESS HOURS IN front of your computer cruising the information superhighway. Here's a better idea: Hire someone to do it for you.

Savvy "infopreneurs" are selling everything from sources of alternative capital and high-level market research to celebrity fan-mail addresses. Most companies selling data specialize in providing a particular kind of valuable information to clients.

For nearly 20 years, for instance, Seena Sharp has been

digging up what she calls "competitive intelligence" for big and small clients.

"Small businesses don't have the financial cushion that large companies have for making mistakes," said Sharp, founder of Sharp Information Research in Hermosa Beach, California. Sharp works on a project basis, charging from $500 to $5,000 depending on the amount of work.

"Businesses constantly need to update their perspective," said Sharp. "The right information allows a business owner to identify the changing dynamics that impact his or her company."

Financing is another area in which small-business owners are constantly searching for new and better information. Businesses looking for alternatives to bank loans can turn to DataMerge Inc. in Denver. The company's Financing Sources Databank software features thousands of nontraditional lenders and equity investors interested in serving the entrepreneurial market.

Spencer Kluesner, DataMerge's owner, started the company in 1989 when he was 26. He was working in a securities law firm, helping small companies put together initial public offerings (IPOs), when he realized what a challenge it was to keep track of financial sources. The proprietary software product was initially developed for clients, but Kluesner said he saw much wider potential for selling the information to a range of entrepreneurs.

"I took $3,000 out of my bank account to do a direct mailing, then I prayed," said Kluesner. Within two weeks, he had $15,000 worth of orders for the company's software. In 1997, sales reached $1.75 million.

To find a match, users enter the type of financing they need, the type of lender they are looking for, their industry, geographical location, and how much money they require. The software searches the database to come up with a list of lenders fitting the request.

DataMerge's Entrepreneur version features 4,000 nationwide sources and sells for $139. The professional version, with 10,000 sources, sells for $499. The menu-driven software also has the ability to print mailing labels, do a mail merge, and issue simple reports.

If you don't have the time or expertise to research the business information you need, try hiring an infopreneur to do it for you. I think you'll find that having the best intelligence can save you money and help position your company as a market leader.

For more information, call Sharp Information Research at (310) 379-5197, and DataMerge at (800) 580-1188.

Solicit a Quick "Yes" or "No"

THROUGH THE YEARS, I'VE LEARNED THAT A quick and honest "no" is as important as a "yes" in many, many business situations. While we all love to sign on a new client or make a huge sale, too much time is wasted in discussion and negotiation because folks are afraid to just say "no."

If someone isn't interested in buying what you have to sell, it's painful but more efficient to know the truth and move on.

The challenge is this: Most people don't like to say no, so they waffle, stall, mumble, and don't return your phone calls, faxes, or e-mails. This adds to your frustration and wastes your time.

One strategy I've found to be extremely effective for getting a timely answer is setting a clear deadline. You may think this takes a lot of nerve, but it works very well in most situations. We set response deadlines on proposals submitted to even the biggest Fortune 500 companies.

This deadline policy is a very grown-up way to do business. It alleviates anxiety and stress. We ask our corporate clients, who usually take a long time to make decisions, to tell us where they are in the process. Keep us apprised—we cement the relationships by keeping the lines of communication open.

Of course, if someone asks for an extension because they can't schedule a meeting with colleagues or something vital arises, we'll wait for an answer.

The secret to setting deadlines is to do it in a very calm,

professional, and nonconfrontational manner.

Be very clear. Tell them that you truly want their business, but you believe a "no" is as important as a "yes." Try it. I guarantee it will change your life, and you'll never go back to waiting endlessly in limbo for an answer.

Tell the Truth—It's Critical

THIS IDEA MAY SEEM OBVIOUS, BUT TELLING THE truth is critical to business success.

Being truthful helps hone your vision for the company. While you may be tempted to hype sales figures or inflate projections to make yourself feel better, don't. These little untruths will come back to bite you.

Convincing yourself that things are great, or even okay, when they are really terrible creates serious trouble sooner or later. Successful business people admit they need help. They are willing to acknowledge mistakes and change direction, no matter how embarrassed or upset they may feel. They base their decisions on fact, not fiction, and take responsibility for their actions.

Telling the truth to your employees shows you care enough about them to share the good and the bad news. In most cases, keeping bad news secret backfires. Smart employees will eventually pick up on negative information and feel betrayed by your silence. If you are facing a cash-flow crunch or major crisis, rally the troops around you, ask for their help, and work together to turn things around.

Being honest with customers and suppliers is critical to forming strong relationships. If you make a mistake, quickly admit it and find out what it will take to remedy the situation. Making excuses, pointing fingers, and shifting blame will get you absolutely nowhere. Customers appreciate dealing with a company that admits it's not perfect but works hard to untangle problems.

Deal in an open and clear manner with all your vendors and suppliers. If your sales are slowing, and you know you won't be ordering as many cardboard boxes, yards of cloth, or other regular supplies, give your suppliers a heads-up.

They will appreciate your candor and, in many cases, stick by you if you are going into a temporary slide. If your business is seasonal, make sure they understand the fluctuations so they can serve you better.

Telling the truth in negotiation also has a powerful effect. This goes against most negotiating strategies, but I've found in my dealings with blue-chip corporations that being truthful works. If I want the deal to close, I tell my lawyer or agent to work out the details as quickly and as amicably as possible. We begin from a positive position and sort out the details. We are very clear about our expectations and how we like to do business.

I know people appreciate our straightforward approach. Down the line, if something doesn't feel right, I try to get out of it as smoothly and ethically as possible. Sometimes the chemistry isn't right, or you realize you've made a mistake by taking on a certain aspect of the project. Maybe you simply don't like dealing with the people you have to deal with.

So tell the truth and move along. People will respect you, and new opportunities will surely replace the ones you left behind.

Say Goodbye to Corporate Life

"I SUDDENLY REALIZED I WAS TAKING JUST AS BIG a risk staying in my corporate job as I would if I left," said Dairl Johnson, who was at the peak of his career and managing a product line with $1.5 billion in sales at IBM.

"With IBM cutting back, the whole idea of the company *being there* was no longer true," said Johnson. "It rocks your whole perspective, and you suddenly say, 'there's no such thing as job security. I would rather trust my own skills and abilities.'"

Stressed out from too many hours at the computer, Johnson had developed a painful "executive slouch." His back wasn't in great shape to begin with; he had been injured by an ejection seat when he was a Navy fighter pilot.

One day, his doctor sent him to Relax the Back, a small

store in Austin, to buy some products. Johnson forked out $5,000 for a recliner chair, lumbar supports, and other backsavers. Amazingly, his back pain eased.

Sensing a business opportunity, he checked out the franchise, cashed in his IRA, and maxed his credit cards to spend $184,000 on a Relax the Back franchise in Santa Monica.

"That business did $1 million in revenue in its first 10 months," recalls Johnson. "I knew there was really something going on here."

With Southern California sales soaring, he started thinking bigger.

"I said to myself, 'you know, I want to take this nationwide, and the only way I can do this is to purchase the entire company.'"

Turning to institutional investors, he raised $6 million to buy the operating company. The company owns 10 stores, with another 70 franchises across the United States. Sales are doubling every year, from $7 million in 1994 to $15 million in 1995 and $30 million in 1996. Sales in 1997 were $50 million.

Johnson is planning openings internationally and positioning Relax the Back as the largest retailer in the $2.5 billion back-care market.

Back care is a growing field, since most sufferers are 30- to 60-year-old baby boomers with high-stress jobs and money to spend on relief. Relax the Back stores sell 500 products ranging from inexpensive massage oils to high-end mattresses and reclining chairs.

Looking back at his life as an executive, Johnson said he has no regrets about leaving the corporate nest. He has this advice for other corporate types considering the entrepreneurial leap: "The most important thing is to be prepared for the risk," he advises. "It's a real free-fall, and sometimes you can't find the rip cord."

He said that once you do your research and decide what to do, you "have to launch. You can't put one foot on the boat and keep the other one on land. Failure is not an acceptable alternative. Doubt and fear are okay, but not failure."

Finding a business that really makes a difference is also critical to success, Johnson said. "Align yourself with something you really believe in."

Meanwhile, he's enjoying every minute in the back-care business. "Having a company is like having a sports car," he said. "If you step on the accelerator, the business accelerates. If you put your foot on the brake, everything stops. Everything that happens to the company is a direct result of what you do, and *not* what someone three rungs up the ladder did."

Before you take your job and shove it:

- Do extensive research on businesses and industries that appeal to you.
- Speak to as many entrepreneurs as possible to get a sense of what it's really like.
- Assess your family savings.
- Make sure you have the support of your spouse or significant other.
- Know that starting or buying a business is extremely stressful.
- Know that things usually take three times as long, and will cost you at least twice as much, as you expected.

Create an Informal Advisory Board

THE LARGEST COMPANIES IN THE WORLD HAVE all sorts of advisory boards, but entrepreneurs are often reluctant to ask outsiders for help.

An advisory board made up of industry leaders, deep thinkers, cutting-edge colleagues, and experts can steer you and your company through the choppiest waters—at very little cost.

Unlike a board of directors, which has legal and fiduciary responsibilities, advisory boards can be set up as formally or informally as you like. You should offer to pay people a modest sum, perhaps $500, to attend one meeting every quarter or at least twice a year.

Years ago I served on a small-business advisory board created by the American Express Corporate Card group. About a dozen movers and shakers in the small-business world met once or twice a year to brainstorm about new products and services, review existing products, and share our insights with company executives.

When the stock was soaring, we met in luxury hotels around the United States and were paid honoraria of about $1,000. After the opening-night dinner at one hotel, we found fluffy bathrobes and warm chocolate chip cookies and milk waiting in our rooms. A few years later, when Amex went through some belt-tightening, the meetings were held at a hotel across from their corporate headquarters in downtown New York City.

No matter where we met, we provided good consulting services for very little money. As board members, we did a lot of networking, learned about each other's companies and organizations, and enjoyed some very lively discussions.

I'm not saying you have to fly people around the country and put them up in fancy hotels to obtain free or affordable advice.

If you are in a manufacturing company, for instance, try to assemble a board with representatives from your major suppliers, a marketing expert in your field, a retired executive with experience in your industry, and perhaps your accountant or attorney.

Create an agenda, depending upon what you need to focus on at that time, but always start with a quick overview of what's happening at the company. Provide the details in writing, including a current balance sheet, new company brochures, and anything else that you think your advisers need to know.

After you've presented the facts, sit back and listen to their comments. Rely on your "kitchen cabinet" to keep you honest. They will certainly have a different perspective on your situation and often come up with objective solutions.

Look for advisers that will help you take the pulse of your industry and monitor your competition. There's nothing better than feeling supported by a group of people who believe in what you're doing.

We have always relied on a core group of advisers to keep The Applegate Group on track. My uncle, Steve Coan, a retired partner in a major Wall Street brokerage, is one of the smartest people I know. He's a whiz with numbers and terrific with personnel problems.

One of my best friends, Kathy Taggares, is one of the savviest business people I've ever met. She's my strategic adviser. Although she isn't an expert on the news business, she is incredibly street smart, and I never negotiate a deal without her input.

Jerry Gottlieb, a dear friend who is a highly respected entertainment lawyer, has been steering me in the right direction since 1988, when he crafted my first newspaper syndication deal. He is wonderful at looking at the big picture and has negotiated deals with some of the most stubborn people around.

These core advisers work very closely with me and my marketing consultant, Brooke Halpin, whenever it's time to redirect our efforts or forge new relationships.

My husband, Joe, my most trusted adviser, tackles the toughest problems. He's the ethical director, responsible for weighing the ramifications of every project we accept. Because I'm a working journalist, it's imperative that none of our other projects interfere or conflict with my day-to-day work.

While this kind of informal kitchen cabinet is essential, you might also consider establishing a customer advisory board.

Dr. Tony Carter, a professor of sales and marketing at Columbia University's Graduate School of Business, surveyed 70 Fortune 500 companies. He found that 21 of the companies surveyed had customer advisory boards, and 19 of those 21 said they were extremely useful.

For example, both Swissötel and Avis Rent-a-Car created women's advisory boards to help tap into the growing women's travel market.

Based on recommendations from its board, Swissötel is offering special services to women business travelers. They will be offered good seats in restaurants serving lighter, healthier spa-style cuisine, and the health clubs have extended their hours of operation to fit the women guests' busy schedules.

According to Susan Stautberg, a New York City consultant who helps companies create advisory boards, Avis is also trying to make women feel more welcome by lowering sections of the check-out counters and making the office areas bigger.

"Avis wants to stay ahead of where the customer has gone," said Ron Masini, vice president of product development. "If we hadn't used the women's advisory board as part of our process, we would have missed some important hot buttons regarding the best way for Avis to serve the female business traveler."

So think about inviting some savvy experts and customers to provide invaluable advice to you and your staff. It will be money well spent.

Move Your Business to an Incubator

IF YOU THINK INCUBATORS ARE JUST FOR CHICKS, think again. Incubators offer entrepreneurs orchestrated business support, including mentoring, financing programs, and a mix of compatible neighbors.

There are about 600 business incubators in 48 states, up from 400 in 1995, according to Dinah Adkins, executive director of the National Business Incubation Association, in Athens, Ohio.

"High-tech incubators usually have a university as the prime sponsor," said Adkins.

Ron Scovil, founder of Mixx Entertainment, moved into an incubator on the University of Southern California campus in 1997. "We hope to become a full-fledged film production company," said Scovil, who received start-up funds from Mitsui Venture and Nippon Venture in Japan.

Egg Company 2, or EC^2 as it is known at USC, has meeting spaces, offices, and an array of expensive, high-tech equipment, including AVID video editing systems. Scovil and his employees take advantage of the equipment, increasing their ability to grow.

"The most vital things about the incubator are the consultations and the meetings," said Scovil. "You save money on professional services. The people here are like angels with a lot of contacts."

Scovil admits that "the screening process to land a spot at EC^2 was pretty intense. We found out about this incubator from a friend who was one of the people who set up the high-tech equipment," he said. "We were trying to figure out our vision, and it just meshed with what Egg was doing."

While many incubators are hatched on college campuses, some are privately funded ventures. Foundation Capital in Menlo Park, California, for instance, invested $1 million on idealab!, a Pasadena incubator for Internet companies. idealab! attracted the funding in part because it was founded by Bill Gross, a veteran software entrepreneur.

There are a couple of dozen companies with idealab! now, and Foundation Capital expects to invest in some of them. Meanwhile, they have a safe and comfortable place to work.

To find out more about business incubators, check out the National Business Incubation Association's Web site at **www.NBIA.org**.

Overcome a Fear of Public Speaking

JOIN TOASTMASTERS

MANY ENTREPRENEURS HAVE TO BE THE COMPANY spokesperson, whether they like it or not. While public speaking can be terrifying, knowing how to make a clear, concise presentation can mean the difference between financial success and failure for many small firms.

You might want to join a group that has helped more than three million people around the world overcome their fear of speaking over the past 70 years.

Toastmasters International, founded by Ralph C. Smedley in the basement of the YMCA in Santa Ana, California, is that group. This self-help organization for people who feel nervous about speaking in public has 8,100 chapters around the world. In recent years, Toastmasters, with about 170,000 worldwide members, has helped many technically oriented people feel at ease in front of a crowd by using its positive, peer-counseling approach.

Well-known companies, including Bergen Brunswig, Fluor Corp., and Rockwell International, host Toastmaster meetings in their offices to make it easy for managers to attend. Joining Toastmasters is easy and affordable. Most chapters are listed in the telephone book. Annual dues are $36; chapters usually charge another $16 for materials.

If you can't get to Toastmasters or afford to hire a speaking coach, there are some excellent books on the topic.

Effective Presentation Skills, by Steve Mandel (Crisp Publications; $10.95), features a simple workbook format. It begins with tips for reducing anxiety, including deep breathing and visualization techniques, and ends with a checklist to help you prepare for a presentation.

Managing Your Mouth: An Owner's Manual for Your Most Important Business Asset, by Robert L. Genua (American Management Assoc.; $17.95), is a lively, practical guide to becoming a good speaker and a good listener. Genua, vice president and general manager of a patent information service, provides great tips, including when saying nothing is better than saying the wrong thing.

If you find that you actually love speaking and want to pursue it as a career, buy a copy of *Speak and Grow Rich,* by Dottie and Lilly Walters (Simon and Schuster; $16.95). This 1989 book is a classic for professional speakers and wannabes. The Walters, a mother-daughter team who run a speakers bureau, explain in detail how to establish yourself as a professional speaker, including how to market your services and command big fees.

Find a Mentor

ALTHOUGH FINDING A MENTOR SEEMS LIKE A good idea, actually making the connection can be intimidating, especially for people who are reluctant to admit they need help.

But a mentor can steer you around the potholes and buoy you up when you are drowning in confusion. A series of mentors have played a significant role throughout my career as a journalist and entrepreneur. It's worth the effort to hook up with someone you admire—and someone who admires you.

My first mentor was Dr. James Julian, the journalism professor who taught media law at San Diego State University. He was tough, demanding, and terrifying. He peppered us with complicated legal concepts and rattled us with eye-crossing exams. One day he abruptly stopped his lecture to reprimand me for whispering to a friend. He ordered me to meet him in his office right after class. I was mortified.

Instead of yelling at me for disrupting the class, he handed me an application for a national student journalism contest and insisted I complete it. I did.

A few months later, when we were flying to Buffalo, New York, to accept the award, I realized that I had met my first mentor. For many years, he critiqued my work, pushed me to work harder, and praised my accomplishments. We kept in touch until he died.

Over the years, I've sought out a variety of mentors to help me overcome a number of professional and personal obstacles. I've looked for people who are much further down the path I want to travel. I seek out people whose accomplishments inspire me; people who lead lives of purpose and fulfillment.

A favorite mentor of mine is one of the smartest women I know. She runs a $65 million company with 800 employees. She's taught me tough negotiating skills and how to get what you want without crushing your adversaries. She's shown me how to gain leverage in a deal by being willing and able to pay cash. She's also proved that being slightly offbeat or eccentric can actually work to your advantage; people are so busy being surprised by the way you look or by the outrageous comments you make, that they forget just how smart you are.

I've learned how to manage difficult people from another mentor and friend in the entertainment business. She's an expert at dealing with the egocentric actors she works with—without sacrificing her integrity. She's skilled at negotiating the sensitive feelings of creative people and at pulling them back together when the pressure pulls them apart. She also puts her family first, which is essential to a happy and sane life.

Sometimes the best mentor you can find is in a totally different field from yours. One of my mentors, a successful business person, is involved in national politics.

Once, when I was embroiled in a sticky political battle surrounding a major project, I found that my mentor's view of the situation was far different from mine. He listened to my version of the facts, asked questions about all the key players involved, and explained how I could make some radical changes without further bruising the egos of the people I was brought in to help. His approach to crossing this political minefield was critical to the success of the project.

You're probably reading this and thinking, well, perhaps it's easy for Jane Applegate to find mentors—but what about me?

There are mentors to be found in every corner of America. No matter how small your town is, there is someone around whom you admire, someone who is living the kind of life you would like to lead.

Writing a simple note or making a telephone call is the first step. Tell the person that you admire what they're doing and say you would like to meet for a few minutes. Don't frighten them by saying, "I want you to be my mentor."

Busy, successful people won't always have time for a long lunch, but they might have time for a quick chat on the phone or a cup of coffee near their office. If the mentor you choose turns you down, try someone else. It's worth making the connection.

Organize a Company Retreat

AN ANNUAL OR SEMIANNUAL RETREAT IS AN excellent way to measure the pulse of your business and keep storm clouds from brewing.

You don't have to book a Caribbean cruise, rent a fancy hotel suite, or even get on a plane to host this event. You can use the back room of a local restaurant, sit around a picnic table in the park, or go to someone's home. Hire a temp to answer your phones for the day. Tell customers and clients about the retreat. Believe me, they'll be very impressed.

A few years ago, after we landed a major radio show contract, I flew the key members of my team—all three of them—to Tucson for the weekend. We held meetings at the spa, brainstormed at the pool, ate good food, and had some fun along the way.

It is best to bring in an outside facilitator, but if you can't afford it and have to act as discussion leader, that's okay, too.

The most important part of the retreat happens long before you leave the office. Sit down and decide exactly what you want to accomplish. You need to look back at what's been happening, evaluate current accounts and policies, do some troubleshooting, and specify future plans.

Be sure to create an agenda with space for notes.

Use flip charts or a write-on board to summarize the information and key points. Then open the meeting up to discussion. Go around in a circle to encourage participation.

After you discuss where you've been, tackle what's working and what's not. For example, my colleagues gently told me that my micromanaging was making them crazy. They couldn't do the work I asked of them because I was constantly inquiring as to their progress. This was important criticism and, once I realized what I was doing wrong, I forced myself to let go to become a better manager.

It's important to thrash out the little annoying things that get in the way of work and to set specific goals for the future.

It also helps to divide goals into short-term and long-term categories. Some things, like sending collection letters to clients, can be accomplished in a week; other jobs may take a month or even a year. The most important thing is to reach consensus. Make sure everyone agrees on reasonable deadlines. Give everyone a calendar and make sure it has room for notes as well as dates.

Spend time at the end of the day brainstorming and doing some free association. Remember to inject humor into the discussion, especially if you are dealing with serious issues.

Create a Smarter, Safer Workplace

BEING AWARE OF WAYS TO CREATE A SMARTER, safer workplace can improve health and morale, and enhance your bottom line. The Environmental Protection Agency estimates that, every year, indoor air pollution costs U.S. businesses about $1 billion in medical bills and $60 billion in lost productivity.

For ideas on a smarter workplace, I turned to Maryland-based researcher/writer Amy Townsend, author of *The Smart Office: Turning Your Company on Its Head.* She is director of Sustainable Development International Corp., in Olney, Maryland, which works with governments and organizations on sustainable development strategies. Her comprehensive book has hundreds of ideas and resources for business owners interested in cleaning up their act.

Here are some great ideas you can implement without spending a lot of time or money:

- **Design/landscaping.** If you are building a new office, make sure your architect orients the building to take advantage of natural light to reduce lighting bills. Try, too, to design a building that cuts down on unnecessary heating or cooling expenditures.

  Try to landscape with native plants that require less water and suit your climate. Try to avoid the use of chemical pesticides and fertilizers to protect the local water supply.
- **Building materials.** If you are building or retrofitting your office, avoid building materials that create indoor pollution. Avoid pressed wood products that are glued together or treated with formaldehyde or other toxins. Be sure your building is well insulated with recycled, nontoxic materials with a high R-value. Use double-pane windows with a high R-value to avoid air leakage.
- **Lighting.** Take advantage of sunlight whenever possible. Turn off the lights when they aren't being used and replace incandescent bulbs with compact fluorescent ones.

  Try to use local, "task" lights rather than general overhead lighting. Install light sensors that turn lights on when you enter a room and dimmers to allow lighting flexibility.

Contact your local utility company for help in creating better lighting at work. Be sure to ask about rebates and other financial incentives available to business owners. The EPA also has a "GreenLights" program that provides ways to improve your lighting efficiency.

Keep computers out of direct sunlight to avoid glare and tilt monitors away from the window. Buy blinds with silver on one side to reflect sunlight. Whenever possible, install glass along the tops of office partitions to allow light to filter through the office.

- **Equipment.** Be sure to purchase "Energy Star-rated" copiers, computers, and other equipment that "power down" when you aren't using them. Use laptop computers rather than desktop models to allow more flexibility.

  Try to use both sides of copier paper for documents. Buy a plain paper fax, because thermal paper is expensive and can't be recycled. To save money, time, and paper, use e-mail whenever possible.

  If you are buying a refrigerator for your office, check out the Energy Efficiency Rating (EER) and operating costs. Purchase a model that doesn't rely on chlorofluorocarbons (CFCs) to operate, because these chemicals deplete the ozone layer.
- **Office supplies.** Whenever possible, buy nontoxic highlighters, correction fluid, and dry-wipe markers. Buy recycled paper folders, notebooks, pencils, and pens.

  Consider using 100 percent recycled paper for everything from your printing to restroom needs. Reuse office paper for scratch paper and eliminate fax cover sheets whenever possible. Recycle all the paper you can: white paper, newsprint, and cardboard. Townsend says it takes one-third less gross energy to make one sheet of recycled paper compared to virgin paper.
- **Recycling programs.** Paper is not the only office supply that can be easily recycled. Recycle everything you can. One company's waste is another company's treasure. You can recycle carpets, CD-ROMs, computer batteries, computers, printer cartridges, construction-site waste, floppy disks, glass, lightbulbs, holiday cards, light ballasts, and packing materials.

The Association of Foam Packaging Recyclers operates more than 45 recycling centers around the United States. Check the phone book for the center closest to your office.

- **Telecommuting/transportation.** Encourage your workers to carpool, bike, or use public transportation. Try telecommuting at least one day a week to save time and fuel.

Townsend's book is available from Gila Press: P.O. Box 623, Olney, MD 20830; (800) 959-0917.

Think Ergonomically

INVEST IN GOOD OFFICE FURNITURE

I'M USUALLY THE LAST ONE TO URGE ANY entrepreneur to spend money on office trappings. In my previous life as a white-collar crime reporter, I quickly learned the glitzier the office, the worse the criminal who worked there *(see Great Idea 69)*.

But with repetitive-motion injuries costing U.S. business owners an estimated $100 million in lost productivity and millions more in workers' comp each year, it's important to make sure you and your employees are sitting on the right kind of chairs behind the right desks.

If you work in California, you have to comply with a variety of ergonomic regulations. As onerous as it sounds, providing a comfortable workplace is becoming mandatory, no matter where you live and work. In 1995, federal statistics showed there were 300,000 cases of repeated trauma disorders affecting workers from white-collar executives to meatpackers.

"The most important investment you can make is in a chair with adjustable lumbar support and height features," said Mark Dutka, founder of In House in San Francisco, a design firm specializing in home office furniture.

His personal favorite is the Herman Miller "Aeron" chair, which retails for about $1,150.

Rebecca Boenigk, chief executive officer and chairman of Neutral Posture Inc. in Bryan, Texas, is very familiar with good office chairs. Her father, Dr. Jerome Congleton, is a national expert on ergonomics and designer of the company's adjustable chairs.

"If you don't have proper support, you'll go home hurting every day," said Boenigk. "We want you to change the position of your chair all day long and make it easy to do so."

Recognizing that too many expensive chairs are not properly used, her company sends out a videotape and instruction booklet with every chair. They also have an animated computer software program that explains how to operate Neutral Posture chairs.

"Some people think a $200 chair is expensive," she said. "But the chair is the most important part of the workstation."

Boenigk said a minor carpal tunnel injury, caused by too much typing or repetitive wrist movement, can cost a company $12,000 in medical treatment and physical therapy. A serious injury can run into hundreds of thousands of dollars.

The market for comfortable office chairs is fueling the industry. There are about 100 ergonomic chair makers, with big companies like Steelcase selling $400 million worth of equipment a year.

How to gear up ergonomically

- Hire an ergonomics consultant to review your office.
- Determine what equipment you need to reduce back and wrist problems.
- Start by buying the low-budget items: back support pillows, wrist rests for keyboards, foot stools, copy holders, and good lighting.
- Work your way up to complete workstations and expensive chairs.

For a serious look at how ergonomics affects your bottom line, read *The Right Fit*, by Dr. Clifford Gross, director of the Center for Product Ergonomics at the University of South Florida in Tampa. The book is published by Productivity Press: P.O. Box 13390, Portland, OR 97213-0390; (503) 235-0600; $24.00

Neutral Posture, with its $14 million in sales, is a small player, but it's working closely with good distributors around the United States. Neutral Posture's 75 employees make more than chairs. They also make a portable workstation for laptop computers which lets the user stand or sit.

Preventing repetitive stress injuries by providing good office furniture makes economic (and ergonomic) sense.

Make Your Meetings More Productive

IN THIS HIGH-TECH ERA, IT'S A BIT SURPRISING to learn that face-to-face meetings are still the most popular form of business communication. In fact, 44 percent of executives surveyed by Office Team, an office staffing service, said they preferred to meet with people in person. E-mail ranked second, with 34 percent; paper memos, 12 percent; and voice mail, 7 percent.

Still, so many meetings drag on and accomplish very little.

"In these days of rapid change, time is precious, and you can't afford to waste it in meetings," said Dr. Mark Goulston, a Santa Monica psychiatrist who works with both big and small companies to solve all sorts of people problems.

He's also vice president of RecoveryNet Interactive LLC, the online division of the Recovery Network, which broadcasts a variety of self-help programs to millions of cable subscribers.

One of Goulston's most effective tips is to plan a quiz for the end of a meeting.

"We ask whether everyone really understands what was discussed," said Goulston, and also "what are you going to do differently and why."

This system, he says, avoids "collusion" between meeting leaders and participants who sometimes just pretend to be listening or interested—or, worse yet, agree with their bosses just to gain favored-employee status. There are no right or wrong answers to the "quiz." Sometimes the person won't suggest any changes but will be asked to justify his or her position to colleagues.

He said his method works especially well for new companies where people are more open to this unconventional meeting structure. But you can certainly try this to revitalize the meetings that put you to sleep.

Goulston says that "The purpose of the quiz is not to shame or embarrass anyone, but to make sure everyone is on the same page," he said.

Here are some of his other tips to make your meetings more productive:

- Schedule meetings just before lunch so people will act quickly.
- Send out an agenda before the meeting.
- Invite the fewest number of people necessary.
- Only meet when absolutely necessary.

Never Work with Anyone Who Gives You a Headache or a Stomachache

IF I HAD A MOTTO, THIS WOULD BE IT.

Life is *too short* to work with people who make you miserable. This isn't emotional hogwash. You can't do your best work when you hate the person managing you or the project.

I know. I've tried. Without naming names, I'll share a quick story. A very big company interested in selling its services to entrepreneurs asked me to come up with some good ideas to get them started.

I came up with a concept the company believed was a winner. My former partner and I wrote a formal proposal for funding. After months of "yes, it's happening," then, "no, it isn't," we were awarded a six-figure contract.

But it wasn't time for champagne. During the rocky negotiations, I realized that while my idea was embraced by the top brass, his second in command hated it. Why? Because it was "not invented here" *(see Great Idea 1)*. The guy felt obligated to manage my project because his boss told him to, but he hated it from day one and began to sabotage it.

He hired another consultant to manage *my* consulting contract. He added layers of bureaucracy and B.S. He second- and third-guessed everything we did. In short, he made it nearly impossible for us to function. I had a headache and a stomachache every day for nearly two years!

Despite all the roadblocks, we pulled it together and were ready to launch the new service. But then the marketing campaign went south. They wrote a few lines about it in a company newsletter and dropped the ball there. Instead of printing up a full-color brochure as promised, they told me to create something on my PC and "take it to Kinko's." This was a company with a $100 million advertising budget! That's when I pulled the plug.

When it was finally over, I felt as if I had been run over by a truck. Not only was I losing my mind, but I had lost thousands of dollars of my own money providing products and services to my client.

I swore I would never work with people like that again, and I haven't. I admit, I've had some unpleasant encounters with clients since then, but I always move quickly to resolve the difficulties and clear the air.

No amount of money is worth the pain. Success will evade you if you are working in a poisoned atmosphere. I walked away from a $10,000-a-month job because the person I had to deal with made me sick.

So think about the people you are dealing with today, this month, and this week. Do they make you ill? If they do, fire them. Or quit.

Do it. You'll be glad you did!

Meet Clients in Public Places

THE GREATEST THING ABOUT WORKING AT HOME is that by keeping your expenses low, you can spend more money on high-tech, high-productivity office equipment, travel, and entertainment. But of course there are some drawbacks to this arrangement.

Most home offices lack an appropriate space or place to meet with a client, vendor, or business colleague. If kids, dogs, and relatives preclude you from inviting a business associate to your home, and you can't meet in their office, don't panic: Make reservations.

No matter where you live, you can find an elegant restaurant or hotel lobby to host a meeting. Be sure to check out the location before you schedule the appointment. Make sure it's easy to park, or better yet, look for a place with valet parking.

Reserve a quiet table far from the kitchen. Make it very clear to the maitre d' that your meeting is very important to your professional life. When you arrive and are shown to your table, be sure to give the maitre d' a generous tip ($10 to $20).

If there isn't time to share a meal, invite your client to high tea at a luxury hotel. Late afternoon is an excellent time for a leisurely business meeting because it doesn't interfere with lunch or dinner plans.

If you or your client prefers to skip the food and drinks, meet in a secluded section of a fine hotel lobby. I have had many productive meetings in a quiet corner of a lobby.

Meeting important customers or clients in a public place is a wonderful solution for home-based entrepreneurs. Just be sure you pick the right place.

Do Something about Your Stress Level

THE ENTREPRENEURIAL LIFESTYLE IS *STRESSFUL*. And, just as you manage your time, you need to learn how to manage stress. It's important to your personal health, and to the health of your business, to maintain high energy and high spirits.

Dr. Mark Goulston, one of my favorite psychiatrists, sent along this stress quiz to help you gauge your stress level.

Circle all the items that apply to you. Add up the number of items circled and check your score at the end.

1 I find myself less eager to go back to work after a weekend.
2 I feel less and less patient and/or sympathetic listening to other people's problems.
3 I ask more "closed" questions to discourage dialogue with co-workers than "open" questions to encourage it.
4 I try to get people out of my office as rapidly as possible.
5 I don't think other people take enough personal responsibility

for their problems.

6 I am getting tired of taking responsibility for other people's problems.

7 My work ethic is getting worse.

8 I am falling further behind in many of the responsibilities in my life.

9 I am losing my sense of humor.

10 I find it more and more difficult to see people socially.

11 I feel tired most of the time.

12 I don't seem to have much fun at work anymore.

13 I don't seem to have much fun outside of work, either.

14 I feel trapped.

15 I know what will make me feel better, but I just can't push myself to do it.

16 Even if what you have to tell me makes sense, I'll still probably say, "Yes, but."

Total items marked:

SCORING:

0–4 More exhaustion than stressed out
5–8 Beginning to stress out
9–12 Possibly stressed out
13–16 Probably stressed out

ONE OF THE GOOD THINGS ABOUT STRESS IS THAT YOU HAVE the power to deal with it. The bad thing is, if you don't get rid of it, it can do serious harm.

Take it from me: Not dealing with stress can ruin your health. In the spring of 1997, I caught a flu bug but just kept going. Work was stressful, and I was deep into writing this book. It was also March, the month in which our eldest daughter, Julie, had died after open-heart surgery in 1986. She was 4½ and loved life.

Every March is rough, no matter how many Marches we've been through since her death. Anyone reading this who has lost a child knows you never get over it, no matter how wonderful your life turns out to be after your loss.

Although I knew March is a killer month, I refused to get into bed and rest. I kept going until I collapsed. Apparently, the virus moved into my central nervous system and did everything it could to shut me down. I had terrible headaches. Light hurt my eyes. I couldn't eat. I was so weak I could barely get out of bed. I was tested for pneumonia, meningitis, and bronchitis. All negative. I had blood tests, X-rays, and electrocardiograms. Nothing. My doctor was relieved, but it didn't help me get well any sooner.

I was done in by a combination of flu and stress, and it took more than two months to get my strength back.

So here's my sage advice: Devote at least one hour a day to yourself. It doesn't have to be a full hour. For instance, read the newspaper over a cup of tea in the morning and take a nap in the afternoon.

Or meditate in the morning and run a few miles after work. It doesn't matter what you do as long as it makes you happy. Talking on the phone to a good friend always cheers me up. So does a chocolate bar with raisins and almonds, a brisk walk, or petting my cats. Watching cartoons with my son, Evan, or chatting with my daughter, Jeanne, also blots out all business problems—at least temporarily. And just being around my husband, Joe, is relaxing because he's usually so calm and centered.

No matter how busy and important you are, take one hour a day for yourself. It will be the best investment you'll make today and going forward.

And if you still feel seriously stressed out much of the time, speak with your physician and decide how you can make a change for the better.

Work the Phones or Walk the Floor

ELAINE PETROCELLI, CO-OWNER OF BOOK Passage in Corte Madera, California, was named bookseller of the year in 1997 by *Publishers Weekly*.

She's done many things to deserve the honor, including battling nearby chain stores head-on and continually emphasizing customer service. Book Passage hosts hundreds of classes, author events, and workshops every year. They keep in close touch with 40,000 active customers via newsletters and many more via their Web site: **www.bookpassage.com**.

Petrocelli shared one great idea that anyone who owns a retail store or small business should try: Work on the floor. "The company execs are scheduled like everyone else to get out and sell books," said Petrocelli. "*Everyone* here has been on the floor as a bookseller."

Covering the lunch hour while your employees take a break is a great way to stay in touch with the front line of your business. Sit in for the receptionist and answer the phone.

Don't make a big deal out of it. Just roll up your sleeves and be the best employee you can be.

"We had a marketing meeting, and so much of the information came from people saying, 'when I was on the floor yesterday . . . '" said Petrocelli.

You'll be surprised how much valuable insight can be gained by working directly with your consumers. It might even provide you with the ideas and ammunition you've been searching for to put you ahead of your competition.

Join a Business Owners' Support Group—There's Strength in Numbers

ENTREPRENEURS HAVE A VERY TOUGH TIME admitting they need help. But the smartest entrepreneurs I know aren't too proud to seek outside counsel and objective perspective.

There are many groups set up to function as self-help or peer counseling groups for troubled business owners. San Diego–based The Executive Committee or TEC, as it is known, has been around since 1975. Until recently, it focused mainly on big business, but now the group has a program for smaller companies—organizations that have been in business for three years or more with at least $3 million in revenues and 25 employees.

The by-invitation-only organization created the "TEC for Emerging Entrepreneurs" program with more than 200 members in 13 states. There is a one-time enrollment fee of

$400 and dues of $450 a month, billed quarterly.

Each group includes no more than 14 CEOs from noncompeting industries who can afford to spent $5,400 a year on peer support. For more information on TEC, phone (800) 274-2367.

Ray Silverstein, a Chicago-based management consultant and former business owner, runs an affordable alternative to TEC called the President's Resource Organization, or PRO.

He manages and counsels nine groups around the region. Ten to 15 business owners each pay a one-time initiation fee of $750, plus $3,000 a year to meet for one morning a month with Silverstein and each other.

Subjects range from sex discrimination to cash bonuses and incentives. They also share their current problems and solicit suggestions from each other. These entrepreneurial groups are comprised of an amazing cross section of Midwestern small businesses.

For example, PRO 1997 members included a real estate attorney who owns a bathroom accessories business, a general contractor, a tee-shirt silkscreener, an auto body shop owner, a printer, and a man who audits the cleanliness of restrooms at franchises.

They're all doing something completely different, but face the same challenges—managing people, products, marketing, and money. Silverstein said their revenues average between $2 million and $5 million a year.

"The biggest concern of our members is managing time," said Silverstein, who owned two companies before selling them and devoting himself to helping others succeed.

Beyond time management looms the issue of managing business growth.

For more information on joining PRO, call (773) 244-1585.

Create a "Roundtable" Editorial for a Trade Publication

VETERAN PUBLIC RELATIONS COUNSEL HARRIETT Ruderman dreamed up this great idea for her clients: "You get companies together in a group to discuss a key issue in a specific industry," she explained. Then you submit the story to a trade publication.

Ruderman, based in Port Washington, New York, said hosting the roundtable is a "very good method of gaining respect and visibility within your industry. It's good for an up-and-coming organization or small company that wants to put itself on the map."

She suggests scheduling the discussion during a trade show or conference where all the players and the press are in attendance. Rent a quiet conference room and serve refreshments to keep everyone happy and full of energy. Make sure the conversation covers several key, even controversial, issues and tape-record it with good equipment for easy transcription.

"The roundtable discussion becomes the story," said Ruderman, adding that six to eight participants is the ideal number. "If it's done well, it always turns out to be a great story, and it will cement your relationship with the publication."

What better way to get your name in print, brand yourself as an industry leader and, at the same time, network with other companies in your field?

Get Help from a Restaurant Consultant

ISIDORE KHARASCH IS A SKILLED CHEF, BUT most of his clients don't even know he can cook. "I'm more comfortable managing the business end of a restaurant," said Kharasch, president of Hospitality Works, a Chicago restaurant consulting and turnaround company.

He's a very busy guy. About 27 percent of all restaurants fail after the first year, and 60 percent close down after five years, according to researchers at Cornell and Michigan State University.

About half of his clients own struggling restaurants. The other half are thinking of going into the restaurant business and need expert help.

"Our goal is to either have you committed to doing it or abandoning it," said Kharasch, who charges about $175 an hour. "I teach people how to take general costs, like rent, and then figure out gross sales."

He once helped a couple that was ready to invest $1 million in a pastry shop in downtown Chicago.

"By the end of the evening, I showed them that they would need to have 600 people spending $7 per person, seven days a week, for them to make any money," said Kharasch. "They were ready to sign a lease, but they spent $800 for one night with me and walked away with their $1 million."

He said there are many reasons a restaurant fails. Leading the list are poor design, poor location, overstaffing, and no cost controls.

Kharasch *does* enjoy many successes, too. When we

Kharasch's tips for restaurant owners

- Reduce the number of managers you hire by reorganizing your schedule.
- Make sure the kitchen is designed to let the chef easily supervise cooking and to get the food out to customers fast.
- Make sure your menu is easy to understand, and promote high-margin items like appetizers and desserts.
- Insist bartenders measure the alcohol they pour. Bartenders who pour using guesswork "drain a restaurant of profit."
- Be sure your staff is well trained and motivated to provide good, friendly service.

spoke, he was on a two-month contract at $2,500 a month to help a troubled restaurateur.

"We found $300 a week in misspent dollars right away, which pretty much paid our entire tab for the consulting," he said.

In fact, he said his clients usually save between 10 and 20 times the amount of money they spend with his firm. He now has three full-time and 12 part-time restaurant experts on his team and is working in 23 states and abroad.

"Izzy conducted a search for us and hired our chef and general manager," said Dave O'Grady, manager of O'Grady's in Arlington Heights, Illinois. "He also made drastic revisions to our kitchen design."

Kharasch's reputation for improving customer service is spreading beyond the hospitality business. In 1997, he began offering training and seminars for banks, law firms, and hospitals.

"They are learning about hospitality as a way to beat competition, and it has nothing to do with food," he said.

Listen to the Telephone Doctor

NANCY FRIEDMAN, KNOWN AS THE "TELEPHONE Doctor," is one of my favorite customer service experts. She's an energetic, intelligent woman who teaches people how to make the most of their most valuable business tool—the phone—via seminars, books, and tapes.

Unfortunately, many people take their telephone for granted. They answer it without enthusiasm, half-listen to what's being said, and take poor, incomplete messages. We may carry cellular phones around and worry about missing calls, but Friedman's contention is that we don't appreciate or make use of the telephone's real power.

If you teach your employees to answer the phone properly and place calls in a professional manner, it will boost sales as well as morale.

She was gracious enough to contribute a few great ideas for this book:

- **Teach your employees to smile before they answer the phone.** Even if it's forced, smiling brightens your voice and boosts your energy.
- **Keep important numbers handy.** In all print correspondence, type the addressee's phone number directly under the city and state in the opening part of a letter. This makes it easy for you to call the person to follow up.
- **When you are out of the office, call your staff at a specified time.** When you check in, ask them to tell you exactly what's been going on that day. No business owner or boss ever wants to hear "nothing's going on" at the office.
- **Learn to love voice mail.** No matter how annoying you might think it is, voice mail is here to stay. Learn to swear by it, not at it. If you don't want to hear that robotic, annoying "thank you for calling . . . ," hit the "0" and most of the time you'll reach a live operator. If you don't want to go into someone's voice mail, return to the operator and ask if you can leave a personal message.

To find out more about improving telephone skills, check out Friedman's Web site: **www.teldoc.com**. Or contact Nancy Friedman: Telephone Doctor, 30 Hollenberg Ct., St. Louis, MO 63044; (314) 291-1021.

Create a Disaster-Recovery Plan

NOBODY LIKES TO TALK ABOUT THE POSSIBILITY of disaster, but that doesn't mean you shouldn't have a comprehensive disaster-recovery plan for your business. You may not be hit with a hurricane, tornado, or earthquake, but even a broken pipe or minor fire can temporarily wipe out your business.

Big companies have committees and consultants to deal with recovery planning. Smaller businesses are finally recognizing the need for similar plans, according to Judy Bell, a recovery consultant in Port Hueneme, California.

"We see chief financial officers and company auditors wanting to do plans," said Bell. "People who lease space are also asking their building managers how they can prepare jointly."

Bell, who helped develop disaster-recovery plans for Pacific Bell, said insurance companies are also urging clients to plan for disaster recovery.

You might want to check out her do-it-yourself recovery planning manuals and software available through Disaster Survival Planning Inc., 669 Pacific Cover Dr., Port Hueneme, CA 93041; (800) 601-4899.

Meanwhile, here's a list of questions to answer to get you started on developing a plan:

- Where would you work if you couldn't work in the office?
- Can you arrange to share office space with another business?
- How would you reach your clients and customers?
- Do you have a list of every employee's name, address, and home phone number?
- Do you have copies of your client or customer list at someone's home?
- Do you have copies of your invoices and accounts receivable somewhere other than at the office?
- Are all your important business records backed up and stored offsite?

AS PART OF YOUR PLAN, YOU SHOULD KEEP IMPORTANT records at your home or in another safe place. This includes tax records, returns, patents, training materials, policy manuals, personnel records, and payroll checks. Put all the pertinent information in a special binder or notebook and give a copy to one or two trusted employees. Be sure to include current phone numbers for your insurance agent, plus policy numbers and copies of your insurance policies.

A list of computer equipment serial numbers is also helpful. Keep an inventory of all your office equipment so it can be replaced in case it's damaged or stolen.

Before a disaster strikes, develop a plan for exiting your building safely. Install fire extinguishers and schedule a fire drill. Assign people to act as safety monitors.

When the 1994 Northridge earthquake knocked out power and jolted Los Angeles, my husband, Joe, a copy editor, raced to the *Los Angeles Times* to cover the disaster. He drove through darkened streets to reach the stricken office.

There he found chaos. Electric generators failed, and it took hours for power to be restored.

Although they had lists of people who volunteered to implement the *Times'* disaster plan, most of the emergency team leaders had retired and had not been replaced. It was pretty scary, but they did manage to get the paper out that night.

Speak to your insurance agent about buying business interruption insurance. There are all kinds of insurance policies available to keep your business going even if you experience a major problem.

To find a disaster-recovery consultant in your area, call the Los Angeles chapter of the Association of Contingency Planners at (213) 243-8950.

Work Hard and Play Harder

THE MOST SUCCESSFUL ENTREPRENEURS I KNOW work hard and play even harder. One friend, who built a $60 million company by working seven days a week for nine years, now frequently jets around the world to fabulous places for long weekends to meet her boyfriend. He's a top executive in the entertainment business who stays only in the best hotels, so she's happy to meet him anywhere from London to Beijing.

She called me the other day, fresh from playing golf in Stratford-on-Avon. "Imagine playing golf in Shakespeare's backyard!" she enthused.

Another friend in the health care business thinks nothing of flying to France to do some "serious eating and drinking" for a few days. "I've worked hard to build up my company for 18 years, and I deserve to play," she said, looking sated and blissed-out hours after she landed back in Washington, D.C.

This work hard/play hard strategy fits the entrepreneurial lifestyle perfectly. In the start-up years, as most entrepreneurs know, you rarely get a day or weekend off—and a vacation is totally unthinkable. There are so many personal sacrifices involved in running a small business. So, when things finally do take off, it's time for you to take off.

Getting away, even for a few days, is incredibly rejuvenating. New sights, a comfortable bed, a zippy convertible, or a sizzling beach to stretch out on can recharge your batteries when they are low.

And remember, it's only money. Cash in your frequent flyer miles for free tickets. Or buy coach and upgrade to first class. Bring plenty of mad money and stay in a great hotel. Check into the spa and get a massage. Soak your troubles away. Think of your playtime as an investment in your mental health. It sure beats going to a psychiatrist.

And if you're thinking that only the really well-off can afford to play hard, forget it. Anyone can sneak off to the golf course or bowling alley for an afternoon. Or check into a day spa for a few hours of pampering. Rent a Harley-Davidson soft tail and leathers and play bad-boy biker for a day. (Look for EagleRider rental agencies near airports in major cities.)

So set your guilt aside and get into the habit of rewarding yourself for all you've accomplished.

Know When to Reach Out for Help

EVERY BUSINESS HITS A ROCKY PATCH ONCE IN A while; it's nothing to be ashamed of. You have to reach out for help and work with whomever you can to solve your problems. If you don't, you are jeopardizing your business, your family, and your reputation.

Read through this quick checklist to monitor your current business health:

		YES	NO
1	Are vendors or suppliers calling you and demanding to be paid immediately?		
2	Has your banker reduced your credit line or demanded full payment of a loan?		
3	Are you having trouble meeting your payroll?		
4	Are you dipping into personal savings to pay your bills?		
5	Are customer complaints increasing?		
6	Do you have trouble sleeping and feel out of control?		

If you checked more than one "Yes," face it: You need help ASAP. First, decide whether any of your current advisers can help you sort things out. Your accountant may be able to figure out ways to boost your cash flow. Your attorney can draft stern collection letters which might help you get paid faster. A freelance marketing consultant can help create a low-cost, short-term promotion aimed at bringing in new sales.

If you feel your business is in serious jeopardy, you might consider hiring a professional turnaround consultant. These highly skilled and experienced experts step into your shoes and take charge. They work quickly to negotiate deals with creditors and vendors to keep them at bay. They often deal with your banker, your suppliers, and your landlord, convincing them to give you more time to sort things out.

Bringing in an outsider to rescue your company is a dramatic measure, but it tells the world that you care enough about your business to step aside—at least temporarily. Turnaround consultants do not work cheaply. A good one may cost thousands of dollars that you probably don't have, but it's worth borrowing the money from friends or relatives if it's necessary to save your business.

Here's the rub: If you do hire a turnaround consultant, you must step out of the management picture, relinquishing the day-to-day responsibility of running the business. You can't disappear, though. You have to be available to answer questions and provide information.

One turnaround consultant I know actually found $60,000 worth of uncashed checks in the drawer of a panicked controller.

For less severe problems, schedule some affordable counseling at a Small Business Development Center. There are nearly 1,000 centers around the country, jointly funded by the U.S. Small Business Administration and private organizations, usually colleges or universities. You can find the closest SBDC by calling the SBA office listed under federal government in the white pages.

Ignoring your problems is a sure way to kill your business. No one likes to admit they're stressing, but sending up a flare is the only way to be rescued before it's too late.

Know the Dos and DON'Ts of Buying a Franchise

FRANCHISING IN THE UNITED STATES IS AN $800 billion-a-year concept. Some 600,000 franchised small-business owners provide jobs for more than eight million American workers. There is virtually no product or service that can't be bought through a franchised business. But it's not for everyone, and it is not a get-rich-quick scheme.

Here are some tips from the International Franchise Association in Washington, D.C.:

DO:

- Talk to as many franchisees as possible.
- Talk to the franchiser; get to know key players.
- Consult any and all advisers you feel can help you.
- Ask all the questions you can. No question is too trivial.
- Compare other franchise systems in the same field.
- Evaluate yourself. Make sure you'll be comfortable doing what the business requires.
- Read and understand the Uniform Franchise Offering Circular, and know all the terms of your contract.
- Check the history and experience of the franchise's officers and managers.
- Research, research, research. The more you know, the better your decision is likely to be. Remember, only you can determine if owning a particular franchise is right for you.

DON'T:

- Hurry. Short-cutting your research will increase your likelihood of failing.
- Overextend your finances. Always plan for more expenses than you think you'll have.
- Skip consulting the professionals. Skimping on fees will deprive you of critical information.
- Take anyone's word. It's your risk and opportunity.
- Settle. Get the business you want, not the first one that comes along.

Contact the International Franchise Association at 1350 New York Ave., NW, #900, Washington, D.C. 20005-4709; (202) 628-8000; e-mail: ifa@franchise.org. The Web site is **www.franchise.org**.

Consider Joining the Family Business

JOINING THE FAMILY BUSINESS IS NO PICNIC. But with more people spurning the corporate world for entrepreneurship, taking over the family enterprise has become an attractive option for many.

"I felt like there was a real need for me to get out of the corporate world," said Susan Chicone, who left a job in corporate communications about two years ago to join the family's Orlando real estate and citrus company.

Since then, she's been busy not only learning the business, but also figuring out where she fits into the big picture. The job skills she acquired in New York were helpful, but she didn't know the nuts and bolts of growing oranges and developing land.

She's had a good teacher: Her father, Jerry Chicone, was given his first orange grove when he was seven years old. His father founded the business in 1919, and there was no question Jerry would join the company.

Susan admits she was a little nervous about the move because her brother had worked in the business and found that there was a good deal of friction involved when working with family members. But she decided it was worth a try.

One of the first things her father did was suggest Susan take some accounting classes to hone her financial skills.

"I want her to be sharper than me about planning and zoning and the ability to put together partnerships with adjoining landowners," said Jerry Chicone. "I have a good network, and it's important that she develops a good network as well."

While Dad meant improving her network of people, Susan was thinking more about computer networks. One of her first moves was to install computers in the office.

"Nothing was computerized when I started here," she said.

"Things here had been done the same way for 50 or 60 years. I like to get things done and move on."

Although she owns a piece of the business with her siblings and a cousin, Susan Chicone is the only one involved on a day-to-day basis.

Susan said she expects that someday she'll take over her father's job, but they haven't discussed a time frame.

Halfway across the country, Barbara Gondela decided that buying her Chicago-based family business was the best strategy for her and her husband—but it wasn't easy. Her parents preferred to sell the Service Stamp Works, Inc., rather than letting the kids fight over who would inherit it.

"There was a lot of emotion involved," Gondela said of the stressful 18-month process. They finally turned to the family accountants to act as negotiators. When it was all over, Barbara and her husband basically bought the building and acquired the stamp company's assets.

Working out the terms of the purchase was tough, but the biggest sticking point had nothing to do with making rubber stamps. Frank Gondela, her father, didn't want to give up his season tickets to the Chicago Bears, although technically they belonged to the corporation.

They finally agreed that the tickets would still be delivered to the company, but Frank would be the one to use them. With that issue resolved, she took over as owner and manager of the company.

When choosing a successor for your family business, communicating your future hopes and goals is critical, not only on the management side but also on the financial side, according to family business financial experts.

"Waiting until you are terminally ill to think about succession is not a good idea," said Henry Ritter, chairman and chief executive officer of Trust Company of America in Chevy Chase, Maryland. "Analyze the business now and look at the real cost of estate taxes."

Ritter said too many family-owned businesses end up on the block to pay estate taxes, which can be close to 55 or 60 percent of the company's value.

"Sit down and talk about the future of the company with

your kids," advises Ritter.

Be sure to figure out ahead of time who will own the business, who will manage it, and how outsiders fit into the picture.

Get Free Government Counseling

AFTER WORKING IN RETAIL FOR 22 YEARS, Barbara Galloway wanted to start her own business. One of her first stops was at the Jacksonville State University Small Business Development Center.

Counselors there provided her with help in finding a good location, setting a budget, record keeping, and product pricing. She opened the BG Boutique on the town square in Jacksonville, Alabama, in 1991. The business has been profitable from the start.

"It's really great to know I can call the SBDC and say, 'I need help,'" she said. The center also partnered Galloway with a mentor in 1994. They worked together for a year.

"My mentor is wonderful," said Galloway. "She helped me with problems such as how to deal with vendors and all the paperwork involved."

There are about 1,000 SBDCs around the country. You can find one by contacting your local SBA office.

Another helpful government program is SCORE. The SCORE program provided assistance to one million businesses in 1996 and more in 1997. The nonprofit association matches veteran business people with entrepreneurs. There are 12,000 SCORE volunteers with years of experience in financing, business planning, and every aspect of running a business.

Like the partnership between the SBA and SCORE, the Business Information Centers are a joint venture between the SBA and the private sector. They offer computers, software, reference libraries, videos, and seminars.

The SBA publishes numerous booklets on a variety of topics from business planning to boosting cash flow. Most are free or at a very low cost.

If it applies to you, check out the Minority Business Development Centers. They provide counseling and technical assistance around the country. The SBA's Office of Women's Business Ownership and the Office of Veterans Affairs also provide special assistance.

Several Women's Business Centers have opened around the country to assist women. "Many of the success stories born in these centers result in true economic development," said Sherrye Henry, who runs the women's office of the SBA. She said more than 47,000 women have participated in the various programs.

Contact your local Small Business Administration to learn more about the variety of assistance programs near you.

Move Your Business into a Main Street Revitalization Zone

WHEN PAUL CURTAIN, OWNER OF RAYMOND'S Jewellers in downtown Sioux Falls, South Dakota, needed a loan to remodel his store, he borrowed money, below prime rate, from a revolving fund set up especially for downtown merchants.

"As a small retailer, I couldn't have afforded to do what I've done in a mall location," said Curtain.

Moving merchants from malls to Main Street is a trend sweeping America. Small-business owners looking for a fresh start are taking advantage of a variety of state, local, and federal Main Street revitalization programs.

"There is a new breed of merchants, and they live in Downtown, USA," said Kennedy Smith, director of the National Historic Trust's Main Street Center program. Thousands of deteriorating and abandoned communities have been revitalized by funds and technical assistance provided by the program, which started in 1976. About 1,300 communities in the United States and Puerto Rico have received help. The Main Street program takes credit for creating 33,000 new businesses and 115,000 new jobs.

"Every dollar a community spends on downtown revitalization brings in $30 in new investment," said Smith.

Communities across the country are revitalizing their

downtown areas in a variety of ways. Peekskill, New York, for example, is working hard to create a downtown area filled with art galleries and art schools. Affordable rent and remodeled lofts are luring many artists from Manhattan, city officials said. Venice Beach, California, has also created a mecca for art lovers along Abbott Kinney Boulevard to revitalize the business district.

For small retailers, moving downtown has many advantages. You can set your own hours and operate your store without being restricted by mall regulations. Rents are usually cheaper in downtown business districts.

"If we didn't have retailing, we wouldn't have downtown as we know it," said Susan Scott, owner of Scott's Ltd., a women's clothing store in downtown Sioux Falls, Idaho. "Anytime you can be a part of a district that's doing well, your business is bound to benefit."

If you are interested in starting a Main Street program or improving your downtown area, here are some tips from the National Trust's Smith:

- Schedule a meeting to introduce the idea to merchants, civic leaders, lenders, and restoration-minded citizens.
- Meet with public officials and city planners to gauge their interest in redevelopment efforts.
- Meet with a cross section of community groups to enlist their support.
- Organize a downtown festival to focus attention on your downtown area.
- Visit another Main Street program to see how it works.
- Create a task force of business owners, property owners, and government officials to set priorities and make plans.

For technical assistance, contact the Main Street Center program: 1785 Massachusetts Ave., NW, Washington, D.C., 20036-2117. Or visit their Web site: **www.nthp.org**.

Keep the Office Fridge Stocked Up!

I ASKED RICHARD FUNESS, MANAGING DIRECTOR of Ruder-Finn Americas, for his greatest business idea. He came up with an interesting one I hadn't heard yet: Put a small refrigerator in your office, he said.

A refrigerator? That's it? I asked.

Yes. Fill a small refrigerator with cold drinks to offer people when they come into your office for a meeting. You'll see that it really perks them up.

Here is what you'll find in Richard's refrigerator: Evian water, root beer, Diet Coke, a pint of vodka, and horseradish.

Horseradish? The horseradish is for the roast beef sandwiches he eats at his desk.

Now, having a refrigerator in your office is not revolutionary, but it is a great idea for busy people nonetheless. It saves time because you or your assistant won't have to run out to buy cold drinks. People will look forward to a meeting in your office because they know you'll offer them something refreshing, even if they aren't thrilled about the topic of discussion.

Free food and drinks have always been a powerful management tool. Many companies offer free caffeine and snacks to keep employees buzzing, but Mike Bloomberg has taken free refreshments to the max. At Bloomberg L.P.'s Park Avenue headquarters, the kitchen in the lobby is always busier than Grand Central Station at rush hour.

Bloomberg loves to provide free snacks and drinks to guests and employees. He often hangs out in the kitchen, chatting with people. Guests appreciate his generosity, but busy employees rely on the available sustenance to keep going. At Bloomberg, leaving the building for lunch is frowned upon. It's just not part of the corporate culture.

No matter how small your business may be, it makes sense to provide free drinks and snacks. Stocking up at the local warehouse store quickly builds morale and productivity. Just be sure to watch your waistline.

Take This Self-Help Quiz for Managers

SELF-HELP QUIZZES AND DO-IT-YOURSELF diagnostics are popular features in women's magazines, but rarely appear in business books. Yet it's worth taking a few minutes to think about how you are coping with the toughest job in America—running a small business.

Being an entrepreneur is incredibly stressful. Despite computers, cellular phones, pagers, scanners, and e-mail, an entrepreneur's life is not simple. For most of us, it's a chaotic juggling act.

So spend a few minutes with this quiz. There are no right or wrong answers. It's meant to provoke thought—and action.

There are three sections: Management and Personnel, Money, and Time.

Management and Personnel

1 Do you dread it when someone walks into your office to speak to you privately?

2 When was the last time you had breakfast or lunch with your key employees?

3 When was the last time you hosted an offsite staff meeting?

4 Have you implemented any new ideas proposed by your staff since the beginning of the year?

5 If you had a magic wand and could vaporize aggravating employees, who would be on your list?

6 Do you spend an inordinate amount of time each day handling personnel conflicts?

7 When was the last time you hired someone?

8 Fired someone?

9 Do you offer onsite training or tuition reimbursement?

10 Do you have a mentor or colleague to call when things aren't going well?

Based on your answers, you might want to make some

personnel changes. Life is too short to work with anyone who gives you a headache or a stomachache. In a small business, every person counts. And, since you're the boss, you can choose who you work with every day. If there is a "storm cloud" on your staff, think seriously about replacing that person. Why pay someone money to make your life miserable? On the positive side, take advantage of your staff's bright ideas. You are paying them to be smart and creative. Let them do their job.

Money

1 When was the last time you spoke with your banker?
2 Have you thought about next year's tax return?
3 Without opening your business checkbook, how much money is in your account?
4 How many of your accounts are past due?
5 How much money do you owe to vendors?
6 Are sales higher or lower than last year's at this point?
7 Do you have enough money to buy the new equipment you need to boost productivity?
8 Is your accountant doing everything legally possible to minimize your taxes?
9 Is he or she up-to-date on the new tax laws and provisions?
10 How many new clients or customers have you gained since January? How many have you lost?

Too many business owners play ostrich when it comes to facing financial issues. You need to monitor your cash flow every day, every week, and every month. Slow-paying or no-paying customers are not worth having, and it may be time to fire them. Be sure to communicate openly with your banker—bankers hate surprises.

Time

1 How much time do you take for yourself every day?
2 Do you feel exhausted before going to work?
3 Are you working longer hours, but not accomplishing much?
4 Is your to-do list longer than your shopping list?
5 Do you have trouble keeping track of phone numbers and

important notes and papers?

6 Is your desk a mess and your to-read pile sky-high? *(See Great Idea 158.)*
7 Do your family and friends say you look tired?
8 When was the last time you took two weeks off?
9 How many times a day do you laugh? (It's important!)
10 Is your Day Runner or Day Timer so thick you can't close it anymore?

No one is busier than a business owner. But being busy does not necessarily mean being productive. If you find you have little or no time for yourself every day, make some. Try taking a short walk or afternoon nap rather than gulping coffee. Ask a staffer to clip interesting newspaper and magazine articles and put them in a file. Then tote them along to read while you are waiting in line for appointments. Bring your calendar home at the beginning of the month and ask your family to book some time with you. Put those dates in ink and don't change them. Taking care of yourself should be your first priority, because so many people depend on you.

Understand What Success Means to You

WHEN ASKED FOR THREE WORDS THAT DEFINE success, entrepreneurs offer a variety of terms:

"Independence, control, security."

"Happiness, financial reward, recognition."

"Pride, acclaim, money."

"Friendship, practice, failure."

Success is tough to define, yet most entrepreneurs are obsessed by it. How do you define success when everyone's concept is different? The best approach is anecdotally, not scientifically. The initial responses to an extensive, ongoing national questionnaire are worth sharing. Common themes emerge: Successful people work hard to balance their work and family life. Successful people rely on a mentor or series of mentors as their business grows. Successful people also surround themselves with other successful people and set limits on how much time they devote to their business.

"I drop work the minute I leave the office," said Marcy Carsey, a successful television producer who participated in the survey. Carsey and her partner, Tom Werner, have brought an unending stream of hit sitcoms to the networks, including *Roseanne, Cybill, 3rd Rock from the Sun,* and the *Cosby Show.*

Although she does a few hours of paperwork at home in the evening, fighting workaholism has paid off for Carsey, whose firm, Carsey-Werner, is regarded as one of the world's most successful independent television production companies. The company is growing rapidly. It moved worldwide distribution of its popular shows in-house and added a feature film group.

Despite the pressures of managing a high-profile, high-profit business, Carsey puts her family first, frequently speaking to her husband and kids from the office.

"I very much needed the ability to balance my life," said Carsey, who has a daughter and son in college. "I believe in a team approach to doing everything—and I believe wholeheartedly in delegating."

Carsey, who vows to spend more time out of the office, "living and meeting people," defines success this way: "courage, perspective, clear-headedness."

They may not be as well known as Carsey, but about 100 business owners attending a recent San Francisco Chamber of Commerce breakfast offered their own definitions of success.

Mary Ann Maggiore, a consultant in Tiburon, California, has two mentors, "a spiritual director and a business coach." She speaks to both once a week. She said she will consider herself successful when she is less than $5,000 in debt, is recognized as an authority in her field, and "my children are on their own and doing well."

Regina Phelps, founder of Health Plus, defines success as: "freedom, happiness, making a difference."

Suzanne Tucker, owner of One Stop Graphics in San Francisco, strives for "consistent profitability, less stress, recognition/reputation."

Tucker said she can say she's successful when she is able to take more time off and when she has finally hired a strong general manager to free up more of her time.

Terry O'Sullivan, with CAL Insurance in San Francisco, said a successful person is happy, free, and focused.

"I try to prioritize obligations, bearing in mind that special life events take priority over business activities," he said.

John Quezada, founder of Quezada Staffing Inc. in San Francisco, had an interesting definition of success: posterity, historical perspective, relationships. When asked when he could consider himself successful, he responded quickly: "Just after birth."

As an entrepreneur, it's important for you to know what it will take for you to consider yourself a success. Think about what it means to you—and then achieve it.

CHAPTER 2

Money Matters

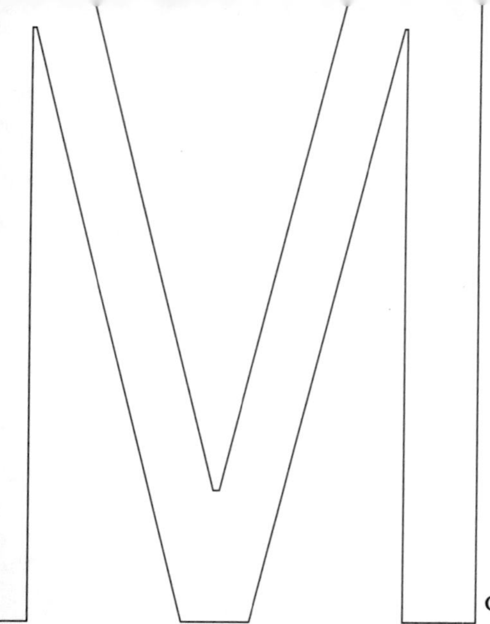

ONEY FUELS YOUR DREAMS. Without enough of it, your business will shrivel up and die. Entrepreneurs are obsessed with money. We fret about raising it, saving it, borrowing it, and spending it.

This section covers a wide range of great money ideas. Some I've learned through experience, from managing The Applegate Group. For instance, I know that most projects will cost three times as much as projected and will take twice as long to complete.

Too many entrepreneurs forget that they still have to cover their living expenses while waiting to draw a salary from their new business. They assume they will be able to earn a real profit within a few months. Ha, Ha, Ha. It always takes much longer than you think to make any money, especially enough to pay yourself a living wage.

Having someone else pay your family living expenses for the first year or so is ideal—even critical. I'll always be grateful to my husband, Joe, for paying the bills while I maxed out all our credit cards and gambled everything we had on our business.

Our first two years in business were very tough. After a short time, I started asking myself why I had quit my prestigious, well-paying reporting job (with benefits) at *The Los Angeles Times*.

Joe often wondered why my first assistant, Josette, was making more money than I was. He wondered why we spent $10,000 of our own money to promote my first book. Did we really need to buy another computer? A printer and a fax?

All the doubts and anxiety nearly wore us down, but eventually things picked up, and we began to make a profit. My *Succeeding in Small Business*®

book took off after I was profiled in *USA Today*. The next year, I was retained by American Express to write and produce my own small-business radio report. That radio report, combined with my column, served as a magnet for business, and from that time forward we never looked back.

To be as helpful as possible, this chapter covers a wide spectrum of topics.

You'll find really great ideas about how to attract angel investors, how to sell stock in yourself and to your customers, how to collect debts, and how to save on your taxes without raising an eyebrow from Uncle Sam.

Check out the section on leasing space and look into renting a financial expert to help you sort through your money problems. You'll learn how to work with a debt arbitrator, how to shop for long-distance service, and how to take advantage of a special tax provision for couples who work together.

The section begins with one of my favorite ideas: becoming a "profit enhancement officer," or PEO, for your business.

If you've had it with your current business, there are also some good ideas about selling out and moving on.

Become a Profit Enhancement Officer

WE'RE ALL FAMILIAR WITH CEOS, BUT EVER HEAR of a "PEO"? A PEO is a "profit enhancement officer," and that's what every business owner should be, according to Barry Schimel, a Maryland CPA who quit doing tax returns to devote his life to boosting business owners' profits.

"If you ask employees what their responsibilities are, the word 'profit' rarely comes out of their mouths," said Schimel, co-founder of The Profit Advisors in Rockville, Maryland. "People do work, but there's no relationship between what they do and how it affects the bottom line."

Beefing up the bottom line is the goal of Schimel's rigorous analysis and intense brainstorming sessions. Although he charges clients five-figure consulting fees, Schimel claims he's helped them reap more than $200 million in additional profits over the past few years.

"Because he was a complete outsider, he gave us new ways of looking at things," said Debbie Hastings, vice president of East End Moving and Storage Inc. in Rochester, New York. After hearing him speak at a moving-industry conference, Hastings hired Schimel to turn 20 of her 60 employees into "profit champions." Everyone from packers to salespeople was taught how to dig up new profits.

Schimel was quick to implement money-making strategies. His first focus was clerical. East End employees pledged to vigilantly complete all the move-related paperwork, because when packers and movers didn't keep track of all the materials used or hours spent on a job, the customer couldn't be billed—and profits were lost. Hastings said that simple tactic added about $1,000 a week to the company's bottom line.

After receiving Hastings' permission to tape-record his calls to East End's sales department, Schimel played the tapes at the brainstorming session.

"That was a real eye-opener," said Hastings. "One salesperson was essentially giving away out-of-state business by referring customers to other movers." The employee was counseled and sales policies were changed.

Some profit-boosting suggestions were small, such as putting supervisors in charge of distributing office supplies to cut costs. "It's hard to keep track of specific savings, but based on our financial statement, we're doing better," said Hastings.

Schimel, who hands out $2 bills to reward good ideas during his brainstorming sessions, said another company was able to save the $300,000 it was about to spend on gas cylinders. The client, which rents tanks to hospitals, was ready to order 2,100 new cylinders until Schimel found a much better solution. It turned out that the company's delivery drivers were paid a 60-cent bonus for delivering cylinders—but weren't rewarded for picking up empties.

"We suggested they pay $1.20 to drivers for every cylinder they picked up in excess of what they dropped off," said Schimel. "Within 60 days, they increased the number of cylinders collected and didn't have to buy new ones."

With Schimel's help, Washington Express Service Inc., based in Beltsville, Maryland, found that it could reap a windfall just by reviewing customer accounts. The company, with annual revenues of $7.5 million, serves mostly white-collar clients such as law and accounting firms.

"We found a lot of customers with special discounts that no one had reviewed for years," said Gil Carpel, president and CEO. He immediately updated the old rates. Then they began charging extra for mileage, round-trips, and waiting time. Very few customers complained about these minor adjustments, which brought in an extra $100,000 a year.

"It was really manna from heaven," said Carpel. He also "fired" some customers to eliminate the expense of servicing companies that rarely called with business. Based on Schimel's brainstorming sessions, they also installed a toll-free 800 number for drivers who had been calling dispatchers collect, consolidated vendors, and installed an e-mail system to improve internal communications.

After working with Schimel for a while, Carpel also fired his chief financial officer, "because he never came up with any profit-making ideas."

Now, Carpel said, he has a company full of PEOs who search for ways to boost his profits every day. For more information, contact The Profit Advisors at (301) 921-4755.

Look for "Smart Money"

BYRON ROTH, PRESIDENT OF CRUTTENDEN ROTH in Irvine, California, has watched his small investment banking firm grow to $60 million in annual revenues with 225 employees. His job is helping entrepreneurs finance their dreams. Based on years of dealing with thousands of entrepreneurs, he said small-business owners make two major mistakes while hunting for financing:

1 They often give up too much equity too fast, instead of thinking long term.
2 They take money from anyone with a checkbook, rather than

holding out for "smart money" from investors who know their industry and can help grow the business.

"WHEN WE PUT MONEY INTO A DEAL, ONE OF THE MOST important things to me is, who else can I get to invest, and what do they bring to the party?" said Roth.

Finding investors who can help your business flourish by making high-level connections and serving on your board is critical to success.

"Some people say 'all money is as green as the rest,' but I don't agree with that," said Roth. For example, Roth helped finance a small apparel company that was lucky enough to attract a major investor in the industry.

The investor, who owns about 10 percent of the company's stock, also serves on their board, and his presence has helped attract other prestigious investors. It's a situation that's truly benefited both parties.

Too many entrepreneurs make capricious financial decisions "in order to get to the next step, without thinking two or three steps beyond," said Roth.

For example, two partners in a popular 25-location restaurant chain wanted to raise some quick cash by selling Bay area and other U.S. rights to their concept. "I discouraged them because it seemed like they were selling their soul for too little money," Roth said.

He recommends that entrepreneurs consider giving up a bit more equity to investors who have the knowledge and contacts to help grow your business. "If you want to raise $2 million, an investor may require 20 percent of your company, but you might want to instead give up 25 percent to attract smarter money," he explained.

He said that smart money investors are usually looking for a long-term relationship, and they may be turned off if your focus is on increasing sales at the expense of other goals.

Still, money does fuel growth. "When a company gets big, with smart money behind it, it's scary how quickly they can move and grow," he said.

Cruttenden Roth has offices in Irvine, Los Angeles, Seattle, San Francisco, and Denver.

Write a Killer Business Plan

IF TWO DOWN-ON-THEIR-LUCK BEGGARS approach you on the street asking for money, are you more likely to give money to the dirty, dangerous-looking guy or the sincere, clean guy who asks politely for spare change?

I'm not saying you are a panhandler, but too many entrepreneurs send out bum business plans and wonder why they never get funding.

Remember this: Your business plan has less than a minute to catch the eye of a serious investor. Messy, typo-filled, poorly written plans end up in the trash, according to the private investors and busy venture capitalists I've interviewed. They receive thousands of business plans a year and don't have time to waste on second-rate pitches.

My sister Dr. Andrea Weisman Tobias, a venture capitalist and consultant specializing in biotechnology deals, has some good advice to offer. An expert in the area, she says that a well-written business plan will stand out from the pack. She looks for succinctly written plans printed in an easy-to-read type font.

Tobias, who reads hundreds of business plans each year, said: "The lighter weight, the better. I always leave the weighty, two-pound ones until last."

Tobias said that although you'll need a detailed company history, marketing summary, and management biographies, the most important element is the executive summary. It should be clear and concise, yet comprehensive, she advised. If snappy writing isn't your strong suit, hire a business-plan consultant or freelance business journalist to help.

"Of course, the content is very important, especially in a technical area like biotechnology," she said.

If you are in any sort of engineering or technical field, always include the most compelling research results and data. Your plan should also explain the benefits of investing in your company rather than competing firms. Consider the investor's perspective and include all the perks beyond making money. For instance, if your product is really popular, your investors will benefit from the press coverage it generates. Some investors like to be invited to glitzy parties and industry trade shows when they have money in a high-profile deal. List all specifics that will make your company more attractive to investors.

Good products and great writing aside, luck and personal contacts play a significant role in raising capital. Although U.S. venture capitalists invested more than $10 billion in 1997, thousands of great companies never attract a dime. Timing is essential. Your company has to be poised for growth to appeal to venture capitalists.

Because people lend money to *people,* not companies, picky investors put a lot of weight on where the deal came from.

"The source of the deal is very important to a venture capitalist," said Tobias. "If we like the source, we'll pay attention to the deal."

So if you want your business plan to land on the right desks, take advantage of every possible contact. Attorneys, accountants, and successful business people can often help you get your business plan to the appropriate investor.

Then it's up to your plan to act like a magnet for money.

Learn from David Bowie

DAVID BOWIE MAY NOT AT FIRST BE YOUR IDEA OF a savvy businessman, but in 1997 he did a bond deal that pulled in $55 million—and attracted a lot of attention. Instead of waiting for future royalties, Bowie went to Prudential Insurance Company and offered to assign future earnings from 25 albums to the insurance giant. He had, in effect, "securitized" his royalty income.

The Bowie bonds, which are expected to yield about 7.9 percent over 10 years, will pay more than a 10-year Treasury bond. John Wilson, a manager with Prudential Securities, said the idea came up when Bowie and his manager mentioned to an investment banker that the performer wanted to get his hands on more liquid cash.

If you are a Bowie fan and want to invest, you're probably

out of luck. The bonds are not sold to individuals, only to institutional investors who spread their risk among different kinds of investments. Why would Prudential do such an unusual deal?

"We had a very major, very high-quality record company essentially guaranteeing the royalties," Wilson told a radio interviewer. "Their knowledge of the industry, which is far beyond anything that I have, gave us a lot of comfort that these bonds were quite safe."

The deal works well because Bowie owns his own music catalog, and he continues to be a popular and visible recording artist.

"It's a very conservative investment," said Tim Biggs, a Prudential spokesman. "It's an investment-grade bond with a financial guaranty provided by EMI records."

Biggs said Prudential is talking with other artists about similar royalty-based bond deals. "It could be a pool of artists with a collective royalty stream," said Biggs. But he said Prudential remains focused on more conservative investments. "It's still a very new type of deal."

On a much smaller scale, aspiring actress Caroline Ilana sold shares to pay for her drama school tuition. In 1995, with help from her father, who is a solicitor, she created Caroline Ilana Ltd. and launched a public offering, selling 100 shares at $160 each. Within a year, her investors included actors Emma Thompson and Bob Hoskins. "She obviously has what it takes to survive in a very tough business," actor Hayley Mills told *People* magazine after buying a share.

Locate a Good Accountant

NO MATTER WHAT STAGE OF LIFE YOUR BUSINESS is in, you'll need an experienced accountant not just to prepare your taxes, but also to help you plan your long-term financial goals.

A good small-business accountant understands and keeps up with state and federal tax laws, but should know enough about your business to become a vital member of your advisory team. Your accountant should be consulted before you buy any equipment, sign a major deal, or sell or relocate your business.

But how do you find the right accountant for your small business? If possible, look for someone with experience in your specific industry. If you are in the apparel business, you want someone who knows fashion. If you are in the construction industry, you want someone who knows the ins and outs of leasing heavy equipment and dealing with subcontractors.

The best way to find a good accountant is via word-of-mouth; start by asking your friends, neighbors, and business associates for recommendations.

Remember, in order to do a good job your accountant has to know nearly everything about you, your family, and your business. This is why it's essential to find someone you feel comfortable talking with. They should not only be competent, but also have good chemistry with you and your staff.

Once you assemble a list of potential candidates, call their offices and ask someone there to send you a company profile, brochure, or other written material. When the package arrives, study it. Is the material clear and well presented? Is the cover letter neatly typed? You want to make sure the firm makes a positive first impression, because they are representing you and your company to the Internal Revenue Service and to the rest of the business world.

If the package looks good, call and make an appointment to meet with someone at the firm. Many entrepreneurs prefer to work with small accounting firms because they are more likely to work directly with a partner or principal. But if your business requires a big company with international offices, don't be afraid to go with a Big Six firm. Schedule at least an hour for an initial visit. If the person says they plan to charge you for the get-acquainted meeting, cancel it. A reputable accountant will meet with prospective clients at no charge.

Make a list of questions you want to ask during your interview. Sit back and listen to what they say. Ask yourself if you feel comfortable talking with the person. Remember, you will be sharing very personal financial information.

If the chemistry and credentials are right, ask for a short list of other clients you can call for references. If the person is reluctant to provide such a list, this is a major red flag.

You should ask whether or not they are up-to-date with the professional courses they are required to take by their accrediting organizations. You also want to know if they are a certified public accountant. If their references check out, be sure to discuss these specific issues:

1 What is the charge for specific projects and services?
2 Who, specifically, at the firm will do the hands-on accounting and tax preparation? Can an introduction with that person be arranged?
3 How does the firm expect information to be provided to them? By fax? On disk? In person? Via e-mail?
4 When, specifically, does the firm need the information?
5 Can the firm represent my company in a dispute with the IRS?
6 How does the firm expect to be paid?

Remember, if things don't work out, don't be afraid to change accountants. There are thousands out there who would be happy to have your business.

Find Yourself an Angel

IF YOUR COMPANY IS TOO YOUNG, TOO RISKY, OR too offbeat to qualify for traditional bank financing, you might want to look for an angel. An angel is a private investor, often a successful entrepreneur, who invests in small businesses close to home.

Angels prefer to invest in companies they are familiar with. They usually seek out small and growing companies in their own industry. Although the figures vary widely, angels are believed to provide billions of dollars in capital to entrepreneurs every year.

How do you find an angel for your business, besides praying for help? Here are some tips:

1 Prepare a well-researched, detailed business plan that emphasizes why you need additional financing and exactly what you

plan to do with the new money.

2 Write an executive summary for the plan that spells out in one page *why* someone should invest money in your business. Explain, too, how you plan to repay the money and when.
3 Join a professional association or trade group for your industry. Begin attending meetings on a regular basis. This is the best way to get acquainted with successful business owners in your field.
4 Discreetly inquire about the people who appear to be the most successful members of the group. You might ask the executive who runs the professional group whether or not those people invest in small businesses.
5 Once you find a prospect, send a letter requesting a short meeting to discuss your proposal. A letter is better than a phone call. If the answer is "no," it's less awkward to find out via the mail, rather than on the telephone.
6 If you are fortunate enough to schedule a meeting, bring along copies of your business plan and executive summary.
7 Practice your presentation before the meeting. You want to be as confident and relaxed as possible.
8 If the investor is interested, bring in your accountants and attorneys to draft an agreement.

ANGELS MAY PREFER TO MAKE STRAIGHT LOANS AT RATES comparable to banks or at a slightly higher rate. Others may want to be repaid in stock if your company eventually goes public. Be sure to tailor the financial arrangements to fit your angel's needs.

If possible, encourage your angel to become a member of your informal advisory board. Many angels like to keep a close eye on their money; plus, they can offer you invaluable advice. If your angel is well connected in the local business community, he or she may help you find additional investors, introduce you to a banker or an attorney, or bring in new customers. An angel may also help you gain membership in a club or professional society that will benefit your business.

Remember, every relationship is different. The key to success is doing everything you can to increase your angel's comfort level so the person's investment and relationship with you and your business will be longstanding and profitable.

When you find an angel:

- If your angel happens to be a friend or relative, be sure you treat him or her the same way you would treat a stranger.
- Draft the appropriate legal documents and make your payments in full and on time.
- Be sure to give your angel frequent status reports. If business falls off or problems arise, keep your angel informed. You don't want your angel to hear any bad news via the grapevine.

To learn more about angel investors, read *Finding Your Wings*, by Gerald Benjamin and Joel Margulis (John Wiley and Sons; $34.95).

Choose the Right Bank

ONE OF THE BIGGEST CHALLENGES A SMALL-business owner faces is establishing a good relationship with the right bank. The problem is, bankers are often cast as villains by the small-business community.

While the myth is that bankers just don't like entrepreneurs, the reality is that bankers have nothing against entrepreneurs personally. The problem is simple: Bankers are by nature conservative and risk-adverse. Entrepreneurs, on the other hand, are risk-takers and thrive on uncertainty.

If you look at the problem as a communication gap, not a personality clash, you'll be on your way to building a tremendous relationship with your banker.

But how do you find the right bank for your company?

Step One: Determine exactly what services you need a bank to provide. Your needs will depend on where you are in the business life cycle. In the first year or two, you'll probably need a business checking account, a savings account and, if you process credit card orders, you'll need merchant card services.

Other services you might require:

- Letters of credit (domestic and international)
- Notary service
- Travelers checks
- Commercial line of credit
- Small Business Administration–guaranteed loans
- Wire transfers
- Direct deposit of payroll checks for employees
- Payroll tax deposits

Step Two: Your goal is to match your needs with the right bank in your community. Many entrepreneurs prefer to open their business account at a small community lender. The advantage to being at a small bank is that you will probably get to know the people better. And, if you are lucky, you'll receive better day-to-day service.

The downside to dealing with a smaller bank is that it may be limited when it comes to the amount of money the bank can lend. A smaller bank may not be as financially sophisticated as you would like it to be if you are dealing globally.

After my company completed extensive market research for a major bank, I was surprised to find that the most important thing small-business owners wanted from their bank was a personal banker—a banker who is responsive to their specific needs and knows their business and their accounts.

Unfortunately, most banks, big and small, are moving toward centralized processing for just about everything. The branch-banking system is shrinking as many people prefer to use ATMs, bank by mail, and move money via electronic-funds transfer.

Despite these drawbacks, it's still possible to create and maintain a good relationship with a banker. Choosing a banker is like choosing a good doctor. You want someone who is competent, personable, and a good listener. Your banker, if he or she is dedicated, will become an integral part of your strategic planning or management team.

Here's how to find a good banker:

1 Ask friends and colleagues to recommend their favorite bankers. Many bankers move around, so if you find someone

you like, you may be forced to follow them from one financial institution to another.

2 Set up interviews with a few potential bankers. Meeting face to face is critical to making an informed decision. You should ask for references and call other business owners who are bank clients. Because changing banks is such a hassle, you want to invest time up-front and make a decision based on research, as well as on gut feeling.
3 When you have selected a banker, schedule a time to open all your accounts at once, if possible. Be sure to link your accounts together if you plan to move money back and forth between them. If your deposit is large enough, you'll probably qualify for a free safe-deposit box and other perks.
4 Once your money is safely tucked away, a good banker will spend time getting to know as much as they can about you and your business.

Your responsibility is to provide your banker with current and continuous information so there will be no surprises. Invite your banker to visit your office or factory. Send them copies of new catalogs, press releases, annual reports, and so on.

Find a Niche Bank

DEPENDING UPON WHAT INDUSTRY YOU ARE IN, you might want to consider finding a niche bank. When Karl Karlsson, founder and CEO of Scoop Inc., is in Monte Carlo entertaining potential investors on his 70-foot yacht "Mirabelle," he faxes or e-mails his banker at Silicon Valley Bank in Santa Ana, California, if he needs to move money around.

"They'll stay up till midnight to speak with me if they have to," said Karlsson, whose Santa Ana, California–based Internet company went public in 1997, raising about $7 million in an initial public offering. The company's 40 employees provide a variety of customized news and information products for clients.

Karlsson, 33, spends a lot of time on his yacht and in

Europe expanding his company's operations. He switched to Silicon Valley Bank at the suggestion of his investment bankers.

One reason he likes the bank is that it lets him use shares of the company's stock as collateral for loans.

"We can borrow money favorably against our stock, much more liberally than most commercial banks would allow . . . and the interest is low," said Karlsson.

The bank's executive banking group also handles "a reasonable amount" of his personal money, which simplifies things.

Silicon Valley Bank, founded in 1983, focuses its efforts on serving high-tech and biotech businesses. It also makes a fair amount of real estate and commercial loans and caters to religious organizations.

"Through the niche approach, we bring value-added knowledge of the industries," said John Dean, president and chief executive officer. "We are known as the bank that lends to emerging growth companies."

The bank—which has offices in Atlanta; Wellesley, Massachusetts; Austin; Boulder; Rockville, Maryland; and the Seattle area, as well as in California—works closely with venture capital firms, both as clients and as a source of referrals.

Once wooed to the bank, most entrepreneurs deal with Jean Blomberg, senior vice president and manager of the executive banking division. Her view of private banking is a bit different from that of most commercial banks.

"We don't require a minimum net worth, and we are anxious to work with entrepreneurs," said Blomberg. "Some of our products and services are more creative."

For example, customers sometimes act impetuously and need cash fast. One client called from his jet to say he had just flown over a beautiful piece of land in Montana and needed cash to buy it—that day. Another customer called from London requiring immediate funds to buy a new jet. A third client, who owns three homes, buys a new one every year. He keeps Blomberg and her associates busy because he likes to set up a homeowner's equity line for each home.

"The big-ticket item in the Silicon Valley is housing," she explained. "There are bidding wars with homes selling $100,000 over the asking price. It's unbelievable. Then the buyers often bulldoze the homes and start all over again."

The first thing most male entrepreneurs do when their company goes public is buy a very fast, very expensive toy. "We have our fair share of yacht loans, Ferrari loans, and airplane loans," she said.

Because most of their busy clients are in their boats, planes, or cars, Silicon Valley bankers communicate via phone, e-mail, and fax. The bank is looking into other high-tech modes of keeping in touch with its busy customers.

Sell Stock in Yourself

GREAT 42 IDEA

DO YOUR CUSTOMERS LOVE YOUR PRODUCTS? Then maybe they love your company enough to invest in it. Small companies with loyal customers and growing potential are likely candidates for an alternative form of financing called the direct public offering, or DPO.

"Ninety-five percent of the people who invest in a DPO don't have a broker and have never bought shares directly in a company," says Drew Field, a San Francisco securities lawyer and certified public accountant who has helped clients raise more than $100 million since 1976. Through the years, he's worked with a variety of companies from banks to a clothing manufacturer, pasta maker, and a homeopathic pharmacy.

Field, who charges a fee for his services rather than taking a piece of the deal, cautions that DPOs are not for start-ups; they work best for successful companies with devoted customers or "affinity groups," as he calls them. Successful DPOs take about a year to complete and require an investment of time and money. Company owners and managers usually offer shares directly to customers, generally via direct mail.

Many successful DPOs are launched by companies involved in selling alternative products, such as natural foods and energy conservation products.

For example, a DPO launched by Annie's Homegrown, a natural pasta maker based in Chelsea, Massachusetts, raised more than $1 million in 1996. The average stock purchase was about $580, said Field, who helped manage the deal. The company let its customers know about the stock offering by putting a coupon in the macaroni box.

This down-home approach works very well for companies with a strong commitment to customer service.

"You can't have a better customer than someone who owns the company," says John Schaeffer, president and chief executive officer of Real Goods Trading Corp.

If you are considering a direct public offering

SAN FRANCISCO ATTORNEY and DPO expert Drew Field has these tips for entrepreneurs considering selling stock directly to their customers. Ask yourself these questions:

- Is my business profitable, and would it interest prospective investors?
- Can my business be understood by people who may have no experience buying stock?
- Does my company have affinity groups who would recognize our name and products?
- Can we obtain names, addresses, and phone numbers of people in our affinity groups?
- Can our management team devote time to the offering?
- Do we have audited financial reports for at least two fiscal years?

If the answer to most of these questions is yes, look further into DPOs. Also, read Field's book, *Direct Public Offerings: The New Method for Taking Your Company Public* (Sourcebooks; $19.95).

The *SCOR Report* is available for $280 a year from Tom Stewart-Gordon. Write to P.O. Box 781992, Dallas, TX 75378.

Schaeffer, who hired Field to help raise nearly $4 million via two DPOs in the 1990s, is a true believer in the process. The 12-year-old Ukiah, California–based company sells energy and conservation products through catalogs and at a handful of retail stores. In 1996 the company, which employs about 100 people, opened a 12-acre Solar Living Center in Hopland, California, to demonstrate its products in action. The center has since become a major tourist attraction.

In July 1996, Real Goods began selling its shares on the NASDAQ Small-Cap Market—good news for investors seeking more liquidity for the stock.

Despite a few solid DPO successes, like Annie's Homegrown and Real Goods, the market for DPOs remains limited. "DPOs haven't reached critical mass yet, because not enough people know about them to make a market," said Tom Stewart-Gordon, publisher of the *SCOR Report,* a Dallas-based newsletter that tracks small corporate offerings.

Still, he said, in 1995 40 companies raised the funds they set out to raise, compared with 28 in 1994.

Figuring out exactly how much money is raised through these small offerings is tough, he said, because although companies file a form with the Securities and Exchange Commission, there is no agency or person tracking completed DPOs.

In 1996, Stewart-Gordon expects 300 companies to launch small stock offerings.

One of the smallest DPOs in history raised $470,000 for Hahnemann Laboratories Inc., a homeopathic pharmacy in Albany, California.

Founder and president Michael Quinn said he turned to his customers for help because he didn't have the money needed to build an FDA-licensed laboratory. The company produces natural homeopathic remedies, which are considered an alternative to synthetic prescription drugs.

Quinn, a former hospital pharmacist, sent 30,000 letters to people on his mailing list. He followed up with a prospectus to 2,100 people who asked for more information. A total of 242 investors ended up investing just under $2,000 each.

The company, which has 14 employees, reported revenues of $673,000 for the year ending in June 1996, compared with $580,000 in 1995.

The new lab in San Rafael cost about $250,000—money raised by the DPO. Quinn said legal, accounting, printing, and postage costs for the offering were about $103,000, but said it was money well spent.

"It's worth the time and money it takes if you are totally committed to the work you're doing," said Quinn.

Rent a Financial Genius

WARD WIEMAN, FOUNDER OF MANAGEMENT Overload in Santa Monica, California, helps small, fast-growing companies manage rapid growth. To manage his own cash flow, he says, "I rent a financial genius once a month."

Relying on this kind of outside expertise helps him keep track of his big financial picture.

"These temps have proven to be exceptional," said Wieman, who pays about $250 to $300 an hour for savvy financial advice. "For many business owners, these finance managers do a good job at managing the resources the company already has. Sometimes they will tackle or identify a potential problem, like when a business owner doesn't know whether he's making or losing money."

Many businesses can't afford, or don't need, a full-time chief financial officer. If that's the case, you can "rent" a very competent one. "A finance pro can highlight the problems and the strong points of your business," Wieman said.

He also reminds business owners that no matter what happens in the business world, "cash is king."

"The only true growth is in profits," Wieman said. "If profits are not growing faster than revenues, something's wrong."

In addition to renting a financial expert, you can rent a credit manager. Eric Shaw, founder and president of New York Credit in Marina del Rey, California, handles accounts receivable for many small- and medium-sized companies.

You can hire a financial genius to handle numerous tasks—in-firm accounting, accounts payable, long-term financial planning, fiscal year-end bookkeeping, valuing your business, and any number of other figure-crunching feats.

But remember that discretion is often of the essence here. Shaw, for instance, prefers that his clients be unaware that the person calling them for payment is a "hired gun."

For your business purposes, however, it doesn't really matter whether your financial genius is on-staff or rented—as long as he or she can keep an eye on the finances.

Sell at the Right Time and Price

BUSINESS BROKER COLIN GABRIEL HAS SOME simple advice for entrepreneurs: Keep your financial statements audited and buff up your business plan. Why? Because you never know when a buyer will show up.

"The best buyers are the ones who come knocking on your door, because they have an interest in your company," said Gabriel, author of *How to Sell Your Business* and founder of Gwent Inc. in Westport, Connecticut.

Gabriel specializes in selling manufacturing companies with annual sales in excess of $3 million. With a sizzling economy, sales of small businesses are soaring. Plus, in today's global economy, there are no limits on where your buyer comes from. For example, Gabriel recently brokered the sale of a New Jersey firm to a company in France that he found on the Internet. It gets even better: It didn't matter to the French buyer that the New Jersey company's electronic products were made in a Taiwanese-owned Chinese factory.

Savvy sellers know they will be put under a microscope during a transaction, but they turn the tables on the buyer by learning as much as they can about them. Doing your homework may reveal what Gabriel calls "nasty surprises." But it's better to know of problems in advance, in case you need to call off the deal.

Don't be afraid to ask the prospective buyer for a current balance sheet and details about the financing. Gabriel said many deals are highly leveraged, and the new owner may be planning to saddle your company with debt the minute the deal closes.

"With a leveraged buyout, someone will borrow 70 to 80 percent of the purchase price and laden the company with debt. The astute seller has to decide in advance whether to engage in a deal like that," said Gabriel.

Borrowing money to buy a small business is common, he said, because it's much easier to finance a $100 million deal than a $3 million deal. Your buyer may also ask you to provide some of the financing by taking back a promissory note. If you don't want to end up owning the company again, don't get involved in financing the deal.

Gabriel has this advice for the timing of your deal: "Go slowly before shaking hands on the price; after shaking hands, go as quickly as possible." Moving quickly will help your employees and vendors accept and adjust to the changes.

Even when they are approached by an eager buyer, sellers

Gabriel's best tips for sellers

- Don't be unrealistic about the value you place on your firm.
- Be patient. Art is auctioned; houses are sold slowly. Most businesses are like houses.
- Sell future profits and document these expectations.
- Invest in audited financial statements that permit you to close the deal faster and demand more cash at closing.
- Understand the financing, and know what the balance sheet will look like after the closing.
- Disclose everything; problems can threaten the price and the deal.
- Remain on guard until the deal is signed.
- Take charge, listen to your advisers, but don't give up the helm.
- Sell the assets or sell the shares. It's usually better to sell shares rather than assets. If you sell the assets, you may face double taxation.

often face a rude awakening when it comes to setting a value for their firm. Most entrepreneurs set the price for their business too high because they have worked so hard to make it flourish.

"They are successful people, making lots of money, beating their competitors. They think this will be similar to other negotiations they have had," said Gabriel. "It is not."

He said many business buyers are practiced "and know the subtleties concerning taxes and other issues."

Before considering any deal, make sure you get solid legal and accounting advice. You have to determine whether to sell the assets of the business or the shares. Both have tax advantages and disadvantages.

Gabriel's parting words surprised me: "Finding the buyer is not difficult; buyers are abundant. Good sellers are the ones in short supply."

Think about it!

You can reach Colin Gabriel at P.O. Box 5026, Westport, CT 06881; (800) 462-9183. The e-mail address is cgabriel@compuserve.com.

Be Prepared for the Sale

GREAT IDEA 45

THOUSANDS OF SMALL BUSINESSES CHANGE hands every year, but often not enough money is left in the hands of the seller.

I asked David Troob, chairman of the Geneva Companies, an Irvine, California–based mergers and acquisitions firm, to share some advice about preparing your business for sale. Here are his tips:

- Have an exit plan. "Most entrepreneurs have start-up plans and growth plans," he said. "But too many fail to prepare for the time when they want to sell the business or reduce their day-to-day involvement."
- Know the market value of your business. Know the value in the world marketplace. "Simple formulas are often misleading and inaccurate measures of the value of a private business."
- Explore ways to increase value. "A business could be made

more attractive to prospective buyers if changes are made in the organization, key personnel, or marketing strategies."

- Understand when the market is ready. "Be ready when buyers are active, money is plentiful, and interest rates are low."
- Don't assume the best buyer is local.
- Document the growth potential of your business.
- Consider which perks you'll miss after selling your business. "Usually the transaction can be structured to retain those executive perks which you enjoy while meeting the buyer's needs."

In addition to implementing Troob's tips, be sure to work with a competent attorney and accountant. This is not a time to scrimp on professional help.

Utilize a Savvy Real-Estate Broker

IF IT'S TIME TO MOVE OUT OF THE BACK bedroom or garage, it means your business is doing well enough to pay rent. But moving into commercial space is a serious financial commitment. In many cases, rent is the second-highest expense after payroll.

It's also something that takes time and energy away from managing your business. So if you're feeling cramped now, get going, because depending on the market, a relocation can take six months or more to execute.

If you and a couple of staffers are looking to rent basic office space, you can probably do it on your own. But if you have more than five employees and need more than 1,500 square feet, working with a savvy broker is a good idea. Plus, in many cases, landlords pay the broker's commission.

Leasing space is a complicated business deal, so relying on professional help is smart.

"You as a small-business owner are not in the real-estate market day in and day out," said Steven Swerdlow, executive vice president at CB Commercial in Manhattan. "It's very important for you to organize a team that's expert and that you can trust."

Swerdlow recommends working with both a broker and a

real-estate attorney because few business owners are familiar with real-estate law or jargon. "A lease is a specialized document," he said. "There are people who work with leases and know how the game is played."

Being able to get out of your lease by subletting the space is very important, he said.

"Keep your flexibility," advises Swerdlow. "I can't tell you how many lease transactions we've been involved in where we did all kinds of planning for long-term leases and, invariably, the world changes, and you're either too small or too big for the space."

Sit down with your employees and decide exactly how much space you need. Brokers say figure on renting about 250 square feet of rentable space per employee as a rule of thumb. Write down what you need in terms of private offices, conference rooms, a reception area, storage space, kitchen, parking, and security.

Be sure to factor in growth.The worst thing is moving in and realizing that you will soon outgrow your new digs. If you end up with an extra office or two, you might consider subleasing to another small-business owner. But be sure your lease allows you to sublease.

Feeling good about where you work is essential. It's well worth your effort to find the right broker to help you locate space and sign a lease that suits your needs.

For tips on choosing office space that fits your specific business, see Great Idea 71.

Shop Carefully for Long-Distance Service

EVERY DAY, ENTREPRENEURS ARE BOMBARDED with offers by long-distance companies. Deregulation has created absolute chaos and confusion in the marketplace. But you can sort it out if you know the right questions to ask.

Gerald Dunne Jr., president and chief executive officer of Group Long Distance Inc. in Fort Lauderdale, Florida, put together this list of questions to ask. Before you make comparisons, get the answers from your current carrier.

1. Does your company bill in six-second increments, or will I be charged for a full minute no matter how brief the call?
2. Will I be billed at the same rate for calls made during the day, evening, or night? How will interstate, intrastate, and international calls be billed?
3. Do you bill me directly, or will I have to resolve any billing disputes through my local phone service provider?
4. What other services do you provide? Conference calling? Calling cards? Debit cards? Internet access service?
5. Does your company own its own switches, or will my calls be subjected to multiple rerouting?
6. Who is your underlying carrier? Is it AT&T or a smaller, less-known carrier?
7. How long has your company been in business?
8. Are you privately or publicly owned?
9. In how many states are you licensed to operate? Licensing by the public service commission in all 50 states indicates a strong, established company.
10. Are you a member of the Telecommunications Resellers Association? Membership in this trade group is important to reputable companies.

After getting answers to these questions, you should be better able to make an informed decision. Periodically check your bills to make sure you are being served by the company of your choice. "Slamming"—illegally switching customers—is a nasty and prevalent tactic. You shouldn't be switched unless you personally sign an authorization form.

If you receive bills from an unknown company, call your local phone company and demand to be switched back.

Lock Your Supply Cabinet

PROFIT-MEISTER BARRY SCHIMEL SHARED THIS idea. If your office supply bill is skyrocketing, and the supply closet shelves are always empty, try locking the closet. Hand the key to one responsible person, the office manager, or if that's not feasible, to a couple of managers or supervisors on different shifts. This way, no one can just root around for an armload of supplies. Add a sign-out sheet, too, to monitor who is taking what.

If this sounds too draconian, take a lighter approach. At the end of a staff meeting, ask everyone to go back to their desks and rescue all the pencils, pens, and markers hidden under piles of paper or tucked into the backs of drawers.

Look in your briefcase or purse, too—you'll be surprised by how many writing implements you will find there.

Set Up a SIMPLE Retirement Plan

UNTIL RECENTLY, A BUSINESS AS SMALL AS Grassland Media in Madison, Wisconsin, had few pension plan options for its owners and three employees. The nearly 20-year-old company, founded by Stu Stroup, makes industrial videos for a variety of clients.

"We had been interested in establishing some kind of retirement benefits," said Stroup. "But a 401(k) plan seemed intimidating with all the paperwork."

Paperwork and complex tax filings discourage many smaller companies from offering any sort of retirement benefits for workers. However, with a push from former Senator Bob Dole, Congress did entrepreneurs a favor in 1996, when it established the Savings Incentive Match Plan for Employees of Small Employers, better known as SIMPLE.

"There was a gap for companies with five to 50 employees, so that's where SIMPLE meets a need," said Jeanette LeBlanc, marketing manager for T. Rowe Price in Baltimore. "The plan allows employers to share the cost of funding, and it's really easy. There are no IRS filings to be made, no testing for discrimination, and minimal paperwork."

In fact, T. Rowe Price and other major financial firms make it very easy to set up a SIMPLE plan. They'll happily send you a kit that includes forms for the employer and employees to fill out and return. The employer fills out a 5305 form for the IRS that allows the brokerage to establish the plan and give it a number.

The employee completes some paperwork establishing an Individual Retirement Account (IRA) and makes a deposit.

"The employees select all the funds their money goes into," said LeBlanc. "Employers like it because it's very hands-off."

Employees can contribute up to $6,000 a year on a tax-deferred basis. Employers match their contribution with 1 to 3 percent of annual compensation.

Saving a few thousand dollars a year may not sound too impressive, but consider this scenario offered by LeBlanc: Your employee earns a salary of $50,000 a year and contributes $6,000 a year to his or her own retirement account; you kick in $1,500 a year. At the end of 20 years, the employee would have just under $400,000 if the investments selected generated a fair 9 percent rate of return.

Meanwhile, Stu Stroup's employees are happy about having the SIMPLE plan in place.

"We're matching the first 3 percent of the employee's contribution, dollar for dollar," said Stroup. "Getting started was pretty straightforward. It didn't take more than three or four hours to do. Much of that time was spent just talking with our employees about the plan. Basically, we just had to fill out a few forms, and we were done."

Create an Employee Stock-Ownership Plan

WHEN A SMALL-BUSINESS OWNER WANTS TO CASH out or pull some equity out of his or her business, there are several options. One of the best options for both employers and employees is an employee stock-ownership plan, or ESOP.

ESOPs allow business owners to sell company shares to

employees at a fair price. ESOPs also provide significant tax benefits for owners while providing retirement benefits for workers. Workers who own shares usually feel more loyal and driven to perform, so productivity increases and, as a result, their stock increases in value. An ESOP can also help finance the expansion of the business, so everyone benefits. ESOPs work especially well for small, stable companies with fewer than 100 loyal, long-time employees. "The employees get all the economic benefits of being a shareholder without the liabilities," said Steve Bohn, senior vice president of business advisory services for Merrill Lynch. Merrill Lynch helps finance ESOPs for companies around the country.

Bohn, who had 21 ESOPs in progress when we spoke, said there are about 200 to 400 ESOPs set up every year. They work well for a variety of companies in a wide cross section of industries.

America has about 10,000 employee stock-ownership plans, according to the ESOP Association in Washington, D.C. In a 1995 study by the ESOP Association, 60 percent of member companies said productivity increased after the ESOP was put into place. Eighty-six percent of those surveyed said creating the ESOP was a "good decision"; only 2 percent said it was a "bad decision."

One huge perk for business owners is the ability to deduct both the principal and interest on any loan used to finance an ESOP.

"In essence, you are sheltering a bunch of income that you used to pay taxes on," said Bohn. "You can use the entire distribution tax-free."

If you are thinking of creating an ESOP, you'll need a team made up of an attorney, an accountant, and a banker or brokerage to provide the cash to buy the shares. You'll also need a skilled administrator to keep track of the paperwork and distribute shares when employees quit or retire. Most employees are vested in the plan after five to seven years.

"We were the ideal company for an ESOP," said Skip Musgraves, chief financial officer for Tesco Williamsen in Salt Lake City, Utah. "It doesn't work for everybody, but in our case it was a perfect fit."

The company, which began making covered wagons in the 1890s and now makes truck-mounted heavy equipment, had merged with another equipment maker in the 1980s and soon after hit a sales slump. “Two struggling companies came together, and it was a rough road,” said Musgraves.

In 1994 the company president wanted to liquify some of his investment and was looking for tax benefits, Musgraves said. Tesco Williamsen did a leveraged ESOP, borrowing under $5 million from its local commercial bank to set up the plan.

Every dollar spent paying off the loan is tax deductible, “dollar for dollar,” said Musgraves.

The 85 loyal employees each received stock in the company and are fully vested seven years from October 1, 1994, when the plan was created. “They not only have the money they make in salary but a piece of the action,” said Musgraves.

He said it is important to explain the ESOP process to employees to make sure they fully understand the benefits. They also need to know it doesn’t cost them anything, because only the company invests in the plan. “Make sure your employees understand what a wonderful, rich benefit it is,” said Musgraves.

If you are interested in finding out more about ESOPs, contact Merrill Lynch or any other major brokerage for information. Contact the ESOP Association at 1726 M St., NW, Washington, D.C. 20036; (202) 293-2971; via e-mail: esop@the-esop-emplowner.org; or at their Web site: **www.the-esop-emplowner.org**.

Join a Captive Insurance Company to Cut Costs

SIGN MAINTENANCE WORKERS PERCHED IN “cherry-pickers” 300 feet above Times Square would make most insurance brokers sweat. But not Richard Butwin, who has been the Artkraft Strauss Sign Co.’s broker for the past seven years.

Two years ago, Butwin, a principal in the Nathan Butwin agency in Great Neck, New York, encouraged Artkraft to join what is known as a "captive" insurance company.

Captives are a form of self-insurance designed to serve small manufacturing companies seeking to reduce their workers' compensation and liability insurance premiums. There are about 3,200 captive insurance companies in existence.

"The primary reason to join a captive is to gain long-term control over your insurance costs and make them level and predictable," said Butwin.

Captives are best suited for companies with good safety records, especially ones that are willing to implement worker safety programs aimed at keeping claims at a minimum. Members of the captive hire an outside firm to process claims and purchase extra insurance to pay off major claims. They share overhead expenses and investment income, if any remains after paying all necessary expenses and claims.

To take advantage of favorable tax benefits, most captives are based in Bermuda or the Cayman Islands, Butwin said.

He said the annual premium is based on each company's five-year claims history. "Companies pay about 20 percent less going into the program and over time can save 40 to 60 percent on their insurance premiums," he said.

Butwin encouraged Artkraft to join a captive insurance company about three years ago, when its workers' compensation and liability insurance premiums approached $500,000.

Insurance is a major expense for the 100-year-old sign maker. The company's 85 employees design and build neon and electronic signs in a 40,000-square-foot building overlooking the Hudson River. Published reports estimate the privately held company's annual sales at about $15 million.

Like many successful entrepreneurs, president Tama Starr said she is too busy running the company to fret about insurance. "Workers' comp is a big issue, and it's always been a headache," said Starr. "This [the captive] has offered some relief."

Neil von Knoblauch, Artkraft's chief financial officer, said the captive has reduced the company's overall insurance bill by about 20 percent.

Knoblauch, who serves on the captive insurance company's board of directors, says he receives detailed monthly reports of all claims and activities. He also casts a vote on whether to admit new members to the group. In the past two years, he's watched their captive's membership grow from 16 to 25 members. The member companies are involved in a variety of industries located across the United States, he said.

As for the investment income shared by members, von Knoblauch says "It's really a little bit of icing on the cake." Kept in an offshore bank account, the money earns about 5 percent on a tax-deferred basis. "The money that's down there is really to pay claims—you don't want to put it in risky investments," said von Knoblauch.

For more information on captives, contact your insurance broker.

Be Ready to Deal with the "Euro"

GREAT 52 IDEA

WHILE MOST BIG AND SMALL BUSINESSES ARE busy at work solving the "Year 2000" computer challenge, many are ignoring another serious change looming on the international horizon: the Euro. The new currency will affect every company that does business abroad.

"Failure to grasp the importance of the European monetary changeover will have disastrous implications for the North American economy," warns Carlton Showe, president of IMI Systems, a division of Olsten Corp., the temporary-help giant. IMI consultants help companies solve all sorts of major management and technology problems.

Showe said every U.S. company doing business abroad must research how the Euro conversion will affect them because "in today's global environment, the economies of both continents are joined at the hip."

The politics surrounding the creation of a single currency are highly charged and seem to change by the minute. However, plans call for the new monetary unit to go into effect on January 1, 1999, when all aspects of the European financial system, except currency, will convert to the Euro, Showe explained. Three years later, Europe's 13 billion notes and 76 billion coins will be replaced by Euro money. Rather than marks, francs, and lira, you'll be dealing with Euros if you have any foreign customers, employ any workers in foreign countries, or buy advertising abroad.

Once you figure out how the Euro may affect your financial and accounting systems, don't forget there will be an impact on your computer systems. Nick Jones, research director for the respected Gartner Group, predicts it may cost more than $100 billion to reprogram the world's PCs to deal with Euros. Yet a recent survey of 300 senior U.S. executives revealed that only 47 percent were in the planning stages of coping with the Euro conversion or had even heard of the problem.

If you already have foreign subsidiaries or trading partners, ask them for help with the Euro conversion. You need to be prepared for the change.

Collect the Money People Owe You

WHEN PEOPLE OWE YOU MONEY, IT HURTS YOU and your business. No matter how careful your credit-granting policy may be, someday, sometime, someone will fall behind on their bills and owe you money.

The key to collecting money from customers is to do it in a way that won't ruin the business relationship. First, you have to determine whether the person or company has *temporarily* fallen on hard times, or if it is going under and has no ability or intention to pay up.

If a good customer is experiencing a short-term cash flow crunch, you might want to be patient. But speak directly with the business owner and tell him or her that while you are prepared to wait a few weeks longer for payment, you expect to be paid what is owed on their account. You should also ask for a partial payment as a sign of their good faith.

If you find out a customer is going out of business, move quickly to try to collect something before all the assets vanish. Ask your lawyer to write a strong collections letter.

If there is no immediate response, you might look into filing what is called a "writ of attachment" in court. This puts the matter before a judge, who can call a hearing to determine whether there are any assets to attach. You may not end up being paid in cash, but if the business is liquidated you could end up with office furniture, a truck, or some other equipment. However, try a firm collections letter before going to court.

When you write a collections letter, be sure to:

- Clearly tell the customer what he owes.
- State your demand; spell out exactly what you want him to do.
- Explain your next course of action if he doesn't pay right away.

IF YOU DON'T HAVE THE TIME, PATIENCE, OR STAFF TO DEAL with deadbeat customers, it might be better to turn matters over to a collection agency. Collection agencies work on a contingency basis, usually keeping about 35 percent of what they collect as payment for their services.

For more tips on collecting money that is owed to you, read *The Check Is Not in the Mail* by Leonard Sklar. It is available for $19.95 from Baroque Publishing, 783 Mediterranean Lane, Redwood City, CA 94065; (650) 654-9038.

Tips for finding the right collection agency

- Ask for a client list; call other clients for references.
- Visit the company offices to check out the operation firsthand.
- Try to meet with the owner or manager.
- Don't base your decision primarily on price, because paying an agency a higher percentage to work harder on your behalf may actually bring in more cash.

Hire a Debt Arbitrator

AT 10, ROBERT "BOBBY" BLUMENFELD WAS already working the sales floor of his parents' retail stores in the Catskill Mountains. At 12, he was selling men's suits. So Blumenfeld isn't bragging when he says he knows every aspect of the retail business. He's worked both inside and outside of companies as an investor, owner, and consultant. Through the years, he's seen too many companies drown in debts when they could have been saved.

He said many creditors misinterpret a company's failure to pay as a lack of desire to pay. These misunderstandings lead to costly litigation and aggravation. That's when he steps in to help.

"I always enjoy trying to save a business, versus shutting the door on them," said Blumenfeld, who now works as a debt arbitrator, negotiating settlements to help both sides resolve their financial distress.

As a debt arbitrator, Blumenfeld sorts through the situation to negotiate a settlement. He works on a contingency basis for debtors, earning a percentage of the savings he creates. For example, if you owed a creditor $100,000 and Blumenfeld settles the debt for $30,000, you would pay him about 35 percent of the $70,000 you saved.

"A settlement provides creditors with immediate cash and avoids the enormous financial and human costs of litigation," said Blumenfeld. "Debtors have the opportunity to reduce their debt burden, improve their balance sheet, and increase cash flow."

Arbitration can often save a small, struggling business from disaster. Blumenfeld can also help clients locate financing and sort out other financial problems as part of the process.

"Large companies can turn to an army of internal specialists who can often negotiate highly favorable terms with creditors," he said. "That leaves small- to medium-sized businesses without the resources to assist them in debt negotiation."

Blumenfeld said American business owners are often in a cash crunch because they aren't paid for 30 to 60—or even 90—days after they deliver the goods. In Europe, terms call for payment in 15 days, which really keeps the cash flowing.

Blumenfeld has been very busy lately because the apparel industry is in tough shape. On a recent visit to the children's apparel building in New York City's garment district, he was sad to see the showroom floors half empty.

"There is massive consolidation and a whole new set of rules in retailing," he said.

Debt arbitration, he said, is very common in Europe and slowly catching on in this country. You can find a good arbitrator by contacting the International Association of Business Mediation Consultants at (800) 549-2128.

Fight Unnecessary Chargebacks

EVERY YEAR, HUNDREDS OF SMALL APPAREL manufacturers are charged millions of dollars for failing to ship clothing to stores in "floor ready" condition. Retailers, contending that without specifications there would be chaos in their stores, deduct funds for items that are not packed in the right kind of box, hung on the right hangers, or properly tagged.

Smaller manufacturers have the most trouble meeting these demands, and while they can protest these deductions or chargebacks, it's a long and tedious process. Major retailers publish telephone book–sized packing and shipping guides for vendors who want to do business with them. There is little consistency; every retailer has a different set of specifications.

Bill Chapman, accounting manager for Seattle Pacific Industries Inc., offered a recent example: "We were charged $150 for putting a piece of tissue paper in a carton."

Seattle Pacific, which sells trendy casual wear to Sears, Mervyn's, and Federated, among others, is trying to reduce its chargebacks from about $10 million a year to $2 million. Company executives have made reducing chargebacks a top priority, and the company's 250 employees are working hard to reduce problems caused at their end.

John Metzger, founder and chief executive officer of Creditek, a financial services outsourcing company based in Parsippany, New Jersey, said U.S. retailers have grown so huge through consolidation that it's difficult for a $10 million clothing company to do business with an $8 billion retailer.

"I fear that in five to 10 years, the innovative, small fashion houses are going to go out of business," said Metzger. "It's a scary scenario for the apparel industry."

Metzger said small companies find that dealing with chargebacks "is gruesomely technical, detailed, and labor-intensive work."

Sandi Wolf, chargeback manager for Gabar Inc., a Farmingdale, New York, maker of resort and swimwear, agrees. Plus, she said, the penalties have become "beyond outrageous." On the day we spoke, Wolf was dealing with a $2,000 penalty for shipping too many swimsuits to a store. She said chargebacks can equal 2 to 5 percent of total annual sales, which is significant for smaller companies like Gabar, with sales of under $50 million.

Ken Green, president of the Internal Audit Bureau in Hamlin, Pennsylvania, helps companies like Gabar recover chargebacks and provides other accounting support services. IAB is paid a percentage of the funds collected, usually less than 50 percent.

Green said the big guys win most battles in the chargeback war. "It used to be a 65/35 percent split in favor of the retailers," said Green. "Now, it's 75/25 percent in favor of retailers."

To their credit, several major retailers, including Federated, are involved in an industrywide effort to make life easier for small manufacturers.

"The wave of the future is the Web site, where, with the proper security codes, manufacturers could find out what's wrong and correct the problems in advance," said Kim Zablocky, president of the New York Credit and Financial Management Association (NYCFMA), which represents credit managers in many industries.

Henry Gerstman, a NYCFMA member and treasurer of

Century Business Credit Corp. in Manhattan, which finances apparel transactions, agrees that better computer systems can simplify the complex relationships between manufacturers and retailers.

He serves on a high-level industry committee revising the standardized computer codes used in the apparel industry. Gerstman said small companies who want to sell to major retailers have to become computer literate. Sears, Penney's, Dillard's, and Wal-Mart already require vendors to use electronic data interchange, or EDI, to transmit purchase orders and/or invoices and payments.

"We are also in the process of developing a prototype Internet facility for retailers," said Gerstman. "We recognize the tremendous value of this Internet idea." He cautioned that it could take five to 10 years for electronic commerce to solve the problems.

Meanwhile, back in Seattle, Seattle Pacific's Chapman said the company is taking a new approach to the chargeback dilemma. "We are going after the specialty stores," which have much friendlier shipping and receiving policies, he said. "With smaller retailers you [the manufacturer] are in the driver's seat."

Buy Disability Insurance

A BUSY ENTREPRENEUR RISKS LOSING EVERYthing if he or she is temporarily or permanently unable to work and is not properly insured. Yet insurance executives estimate that only 30 to 40 percent of the nation's small-business owners have disability insurance. This is a chilling statistic, especially when you consider that at age 37—the prime age for an entrepreneur—the probability of becoming disabled is three and a half times higher than the probability of death.

Virtually all personal disability policies offer the same kinds of benefits. They generally pay a monthly benefit that is slightly less than what you would earn if you were healthy and working. This gap is intentional: Insurers want you to have an incentive to get well and return to work.

The kind of policy you qualify for depends on what you do for a living. Professionals, such as attorneys and architects, usually have the easiest time buying disability insurance. Automobile and real-estate salespeople, subject to the ups and downs of the economy, have a tougher time. People in risky professions—such as private detectives, construction workers, and actors—may have to look a long time for a policy. Insurance companies tend to distrust home-based entrepreneurs, thinking they are less stable and more likely to fake accidents. When my firm was home-based, I managed to buy disability insurance only because my insurance agent visited my office several times and convinced his bosses that I was running a legitimate communications business.

Insurance underwriters look at the probability and length of possible disabilities when determining the type of policy you might require. They also consider the number of employees, the length of time you have been in business, and your industry's disability claim history.

One way to save money on insurance premiums is by choosing a 60-to-90-day elimination period. This means you will have to wait a while before your payments begin. Insurance companies think if you are willing to wait for benefits to

How to find the right disability insurance

- Figure out how much you need to cover all your personal monthly expenses.
- Obtain estimates from several insurance carriers.
- Check the financial stability of the company you buy a policy from.
- Although it costs more, try to buy a policy with lifetime benefits.
- Consider buying business interruption insurance to further protect your business from closing if something happens to you.

kick in, you might be less likely to claim a disability.

Normally, disability benefits are tax-free. Always pay with a personal check. If your company pays for the premium and takes a tax deduction, your benefits will be taxed.

Make sure your policy covers your specific occupation, not just any occupation. If you have a stroke and can't do your old job, you can collect your benefits even if you take up a less taxing, lower-paying occupation.

Although it's cheaper to buy a policy that provides benefits to age 65, many agents recommend paying a bit extra for a policy with lifetime benefits.

Expand Your Vendor Network

IS YOUR BUSINESS OVERLY DEPENDENT UPON ONE or two suppliers for the things you need on a regular basis? What would happen if your primary supplier called today and said he or she unexpectedly ran out of the materials you need?

What would your employees do if the delivery truck broke down in Ohio, and your raw materials were sitting on the side of the highway for three days?

Although most small-business owners prefer to establish stable, long-term relationships with vendors and suppliers, savvy entrepreneurs always find alternative sources for key products. Being loyal to vendors is important, especially if what you need is in short supply. But things change. You have to protect yourself and your workers by having alternative sources.

No matter what business you're in, begin looking around for new places to buy materials:

- Order catalogs from competing companies.
- Send away for brochures.
- Collect current price lists.
- Put all the information you receive in a file, with the hope that you'll never need it.

When you begin looking around for new or alternative suppliers, you might be surprised to find that you are paying too much for essential products or services. If you do find a better deal, there's nothing wrong with going back to your primary suppliers and asking them to meet or beat the new prices you found. Your current suppliers probably won't want to lose your business. They will often propose a discount or new payment terms to maintain the business relationship.

If it's been so long that you don't know where to look for new suppliers, browse through an industry trade magazine or newsletter. Trade magazines are a terrific source of new ideas and products. Check out all the advertisements placed by companies that serve your industry.

Another great way to expand your business horizons is to attend a trade show or professional meeting. You'll be able to find new products, services, supplies, and customers—all in one place.

Ask for a Deposit

FOR MANY ENTREPRENEURS, MAKING A SALE IS easy. The tough part is getting paid. But without steady cash flow, even the strongest business will starve.

In the 1980s, small businesses buffeted by the recession began asking customers for deposits before they started the work or filled an order. Asking for a deposit is a great way to boost your cash flow. If handled fairly and properly, it won't alienate good customers.

Professional consultants often require 50 percent of the first month's fee when they are retained. Payments are made along the way, and the balance is due when the project or report is completed.

If you haven't required deposits before, draft a short letter of explanation and send it out to all your customers or clients. Make sure you are clear about your new policy and don't play favorites. If you begin asking for deposits, you have to make sure every customer or client is required to comply with the policy.

You don't have to be a painter or carpenter to ask for a

deposit. Your customers shouldn't object to paying 20, 30, or even 50 percent down when they place an order or sign a contract. So ask for a deposit to secure your products and services. It makes good business sense.

Discount Accounts Receivable

HERE'S ANOTHER CASH-FLOW BOOSTING IDEA. If people owe you money, consider offering them a discount on the balance—if and only if they pay up immediately. Try this only after you've called and asked why they haven't paid up on time. This incentive often does the trick if the person actually has the cash but is just holding back.

For this to work, you need to offer a significant discount—at least 20 percent—because most people need a real incentive to send the check immediately. Set a tight deadline for them to respond. To sweeten the offer, include a self-addressed, stamped envelope. Even if just a handful of customers respond, it may bring in needed cash. Be clear that if they don't respond by your deadline, the discount expires.

If you want to avoid the hassle of deadbeat customers in the first place, be very picky when it comes to granting credit. Require every new customer to fill out a detailed credit application. Check their business references, call their bank, and ask Dun & Bradstreet to send you any information they have on the company. When you grant credit to a customer, you become their banker, so *think* like a banker before you lend out a single dollar.

Be Talked Out of a Bad Idea

BRUCE TYSON MANAGES MONEY FOR A LIVING. Big money. As president of Weston Capital Management Inc., in Los Angeles, California, he manages about $150 million for wealthy entertainment-industry clients.

Tyson is extremely bright, fiscally conservative, and a careful listener. He serves as a sort of financial adviser/shrink for his clients. Tyson's favorite great idea? "Be willing to be talked out of something," he said.

It turns out that he spends quite a bit of time talking clients out of investing in harebrained schemes. For example, a young client wanted to lend her boyfriend $50,000 of her inheritance to buy out his partner in a Santa Monica restaurant. Tyson diplomatically pointed out to her that this was a bad idea for several reasons.

First of all, the loan would have been collateralized by an expensive car, which is known as "moving collateral" and often disappears without a trace. Tyson also knew the restaurant didn't have a liquor license, and the chances of getting one were slim. It was located in a very popular area of the beachfront city, and local officials had been opposing new liquor licenses in order to cut down on crime and congestion.

Of course, his client was not happy with his advice, but she listened. Good thing, too. A few months later, the restaurant went under—and so did the romance.

Another client called Tyson requesting a check to buy her boyfriend a sailboat so they could sail around the world. "Do you sail?" Tyson asked her.

Silence. "No."

"So I said to her, 'Why don't you go sailing for a week with him and see how you like it?'" She did. She didn't like it. She didn't buy him the boat, and the wind went right out of the relationship's sails.

I guess that you could say that the real moral of Tyson's great idea is "don't mix romance and money."

But seriously, willingness to step back and think through a serious financial decision takes maturity. Listen to your advisers. You pay them well to be financially smarter and more prudent than you are.

Hire an Enrolled Agent to Do Your Taxes

NOBODY LIKES TO PAY TAXES. IT'S EVEN WORSE IF you're unhappy with your current tax preparer. If you are thinking about a change, you might consider hiring an enrolled agent.

Although they've been around since 1884, and prepare millions of tax returns a year, enrolled agents, or EAs as they are known, are a well-kept secret.

While certified public accountants (CPAs) and public accountants (PAs) are licensed by the state, enrolled agents are licensed by the federal government. Enrolled agents specialize in preparing tax returns and can represent taxpayers before the Internal Revenue Service, just like CPAs and tax attorneys.

They have to renew their license every three years after completing 72 hours of education in taxation. Despite their background and education, EAs tend to charge lower fees than CPAs or PAs.

EAs are definitely outnumbered: There are only about 35,000 enrolled agents in the United States, compared with 500,000 certified public accountants and public accountants.

There are probably so few because it's tough to become one. There are only two ways: pass a tough, two-day exam given once a year by the IRS (only about 30 percent of those who take it pass it), or work for the IRS for five years.

Through the years, EAs have had to battle CPAs who have pushed legislation aimed at limiting an EA's ability to prepare balance sheets and financial statements for business clients. CPAs contend EAs should only do tax returns. EAs insist they can't do a good tax return without an accurate financial statement.

"CPAs treat us as a subspecies," said Sid Norton, president of the California Society of Enrolled Agents, based in Sacramento, California. Norton said that in 1986 California CPAs launched a major political battle to keep enrolled agents from preparing financial reports for business owners. The EAs fought back and prevailed, but similar battles have been waged in other states.

"CPAs are very upset when we use the word 'accounting,'" said Sharon Flynn, who has been an EA since 1969. "But the state Supreme Court said we can use the word."

Flynn said about 300 of her 650 clients are small-business owners filing Schedule C tax forms. For example, one of her newest clients operates a driving school; another just opened a bakery.

David Costello, president of the National Association of State Boards of Accountancy in Nashville, Tennessee, said his group, which deals with state licensing matters, considers "EAs very beneficial" and "serve a useful purpose in the scheme of things."

"I wouldn't have a problem taking my tax return to an enrolled agent if I didn't do it myself," said Costello, who is a CPA.

The National Association of Enrolled Agents is working with legislatures in South Carolina, Indiana, Florida, and Georgia to clarify the services EAs are permitted to perform, according to Janet Bray, executive vice president of the Gaithersburg, Maryland–based group.

If all this has inspired you to find an EA, try not to call them in March or April, when they're working on tax returns. "Trying to interview a tax pro during the peak of tax preparation season can be like chatting with a doctor during brain surgery," said Sid Norton.

For information on EAs, send a self-addressed, stamped business envelope to NAEA, 200 Orchard Ridge Dr., Suite 302, Gaithersburg, MD 20878.

The NAEA also operates a free referral service. For information, call (800) 424-4339, 24 hours a day.

I recommend buying a couple of good books and surfing the Net for help with your taxes. *Tax Savvy for Small Business* (Nolo Press; $26.95), by Frederick Daily, is filled with practical tips and suggestions. Nolo Press, which publishes a wide variety of self-help law books, has a Web site at **www.nolo.com**.

Intuit, publisher of Quicken and TurboTax software, offers help via its Tax Center. The online service offers a variety of personal and business tax information. Check it out at **www.qfn.com/taxcenter**.

Take Advantage of a Tax Break

THE OLD CLICHÉ, "IF SOMETHING SOUNDS TOO good to be true, it probably is" applies to many schemes and scams offered to small-business owners. However, an obscure provision of the federal tax code actually gives mom-and-pop businesses a real break.

Although it sounds too good to be true, Section 105 allows very small, family-owned businesses to reimburse themselves for 100 percent of their uninsured medical, dental, and vision-care expenses. The regulation has been on the books since 1954, but few business people seem to know anything about it.

Those who do take advantage of Section 105 have to meet strict requirements set up by the Department of Labor and the Employee Retirement Income Security Act, known as ERISA. You also have to file the appropriate forms with your tax returns and keep careful payroll records, according to Juda Kallus, a Manhattan accountant who is familiar with Section 105. "First of all, you have to have a bona fide working relationship with your spouse, " said Kallus. "Then, the record-keeping requirements are very severe."

Kallus says Section 105 may work for you, if:

1 You operate a husband-and-wife sole proprietorship or partnership.

2 One spouse works for the other.

3 You pay your spouse a reasonable salary.

4 You withhold payroll taxes and keep careful time sheets.

5 You keep a separate business banking account for reimbursements.

6 The spouse on the payroll incurs the expenses and requests reimbursement from you, the business owner.

7 You are willing to file the necessary paperwork with the federal government.

Kallus, who has about 15 clients using Section 105, said he advised Patricia Buckley to look into Section 105 when she lost her job and began managing her husband's photography studio about three years ago.

Buckley and her husband, Ned Matura, are typical of those who take advantage of Section 105. "I'm a full-time employee of our business," said Buckley. "I invoice clients, write up estimates, and run the office."

Before they heard about Section 105, Buckley said they were spending about $9,000 a year for a health insurance policy through a federal plan which allows people who have lost their jobs to pay insurance premiums on their own. It's generally more expensive than group coverage, but better than nothing.

By switching to a cheaper, catastrophic medical insurance with a high deductible, Buckley said they save about $4,000 a year. Under Section 105, she's now reimbursed by the business for all out-of-pocket family medical expenses.

Although any accountant can learn how to fill out all the forms, many refer clients to a company set up exclusively to administer Section 105 reimbursements for business owners. "I would not set up a plan for my clients on my own—it's too complicated," said Don Yoder, founder of Yoder's Tax and Accounting Service in Kalona, Iowa.

Yoder, who prepares tax returns for scores of farmers and small-business owners, lets AgriPlan/BizPlan, based in Adel, Iowa, handle all the Section 105 paperwork.

In 1995, AgriPlan/BizPlan had 40,000 clients taking advantage of Section 105; in 1997, the number grew to 50,000, says president Phil Harrington.

Harrington, who joined the company in 1989, said it was founded in 1986 by Don Rashke, a Wisconsin insurance agent. Rashke, now retired, wondered why big corporations could legally deduct 100 percent of the cost of providing medical benefits, but small businesses couldn't. He found Section 105 when he was digging around for answers. "Our clients have an average tax saving of $1,800 a year," said Harrington. BizPlan, which relies on computers to keep the administrative costs down, charges clients a flat fee of $175 a year to handle all the necessary paperwork.

Their client base is growing, even though small-business owners can now deduct 40 percent of their health care costs under the Health Coverage Availability and Affordability Act. By the year 2007, the deduction increases to 100 percent.

BizPlan markets its services to accountants and pays them a modest referral fee of about $50 per client.

There is one big catch to Section 105: If you have employees, you must provide similar health care benefits to the ones you provide for your family. "You can't discriminate; you have to offer it to everyone," he said.

For more information, contact your accountant or BizPlan at (800) 422-4661.

Know about Economic Development Incentives and Agencies

IF YOU ARE THINKING OF RELOCATING OR expanding your business, be sure to investigate the wide variety of economic incentives and tax breaks. Hundreds of local, state, federal, and private agencies offer scores of programs designed to entice business owners to move into economically disadvantaged areas.

President Bill Clinton created federal empowerment zones across the country as a way to revitalize the economy. For example, New York City received $300 million for its empowerment zone when the state and city matched a $100 million federal commitment in 1994. The program encompasses a wide range of tax credits and direct investment—all designed to revitalize the business and cultural aspects of the historic but economically depressed Harlem area.

In upper Manhattan, $1.2 million was earmarked to stimulate tourist spending by developing a tour package and gift shop for the Apollo Theater. Another $600,000 was spent on training new dental assistants and bakers.

Businesses located in the empowerment zone also receive a variety of tax credits and incentives. Employers can earn up to $3,000 in tax credits for hiring a resident of the upper Manhattan empowerment zone. The credit will be reduced by 5 percent each year, beginning in 2002, according to Rodney Lopez, spokesman for the Upper Manhattan Federal Empowerment Zone Development Corporation.

Every year, business owners in an empowerment zone can also deduct $37,500 worth of business equipment and supplies, about $20,000 more than business owners located outside an empowerment zone. Businesses can also apply for tax-exempt bonds to help build new facilities.

Most empowerment zones operate an information center to help business owners learn more about the various programs that are available. Upper Manhattan's Business Resource Investment Service Center, or BRISC, helps business owners apply for services and programs, including SBA-guaranteed loans. The phone number at BRISC is (212) 866-5640.

Richmond, Virginia's public/private economic development group, the Greater Richmond Partnership Inc., was formed in 1994 after government efforts failed to bring in enough new business. The group is composed of 300 private investors and four counties surrounding Richmond. In 1997, the group worked with 35 companies to create 2,068 jobs and invest $1.1 billion in the local economy.

They have several success stories to brag about. "We selected Richmond because of its growth and potential as a business center, because of its excellent infrastructure and interstate access, and because it's a good central location for our business," said Keith Dobson, president and chief executive officer of VehiCare Corp., a truck fleet contract maintenance firm.

Dobson said VehiCare's new headquarters will employ about 25 and involve a capital investment of $300,000.

Another growing firm also moved to Richmond in 1997. "By the end of 1998, we estimate employing 200 to 250 people in Richmond," said Tim Grider, general manager of Barber & Ross Millwork, a Leesburg-based maker of exterior windows and doors. "We saw a lot of other major companies coming into the Richmond area, like Motorola," said Grider. "We knew there was going to be growth."

Grider, who started looking for a new site in 1995, said Richmond officials were "extremely helpful" in getting them up and running.

"The state also conducted a series of four seminars exclusively for our management staff," said Grider. Virginia offers low taxes and some of the lowest workers' compensation insurance rates in the country, according to Greg Wingfield, president of the Richmond partnership.

New or expanding companies can qualify for programs where the state helps pay part of the cost of training workers. There is also a variety of tax credits and incentives available for employers, Wingfield said. To contact the Greater Richmond Partnership, call (804) 643-3227. Contact your local SBA chapter for information on federal empowerment zones in your area.

Use Frequent Flier Miles for Meetings

FUTURIST DAVID SNYDER FLIES MORE THAN 150,000 miles a year, giving speeches and consulting for private and government clients. To build up frequent flier miles, he flies first class and books his own tickets, although his clients reimburse him for travel expenses. Every few years, he cashes in all those free miles to hold retreats for The Snyder Family Enterprise.

"We prefer United for its service and because it covers most national routes," says Sue Snyder, David's wife and managing director of the company. "If he can't fly United, we charge the tickets on his American Express card and transfer the miles to other airlines."

So if you are always on the road and in the air, bank those miles and cash them in for a business-related retreat.

Finance Your Independent Film

POWERED BY BLACK COFFEE, PETER HALL RACED downtown in New York City to pick up 10,000 slick postcards promoting *Delinquent,* his independent film which opened in September 1997 in Los Angeles and New York. Rushing back uptown, he double-parked in Columbus Circle, risking a ticket to FedEx 5,000 cards to Los Angeles.

"I have to pour it on the opening weekend, then go back into battle," said Hall, a former financial journalist turned entrepreneurial filmmaker. While major studios spend an average of $19.8 million marketing their films, Hall spent about $5,000 on postcards, stickers, buttons, and tee-shirts to promote the film that has been his life for the past five years. After two years on the international film festival circuit, he finally found a distributor willing to give it a shot in America.

Like hundreds of other independent filmmakers, Hall personally raised the $300,000 he needed to write, produce, and direct *Delinquent*. He maxed out a collection of high-limit credit cards, directed karaoke videos, ghost-wrote articles, and cashed-in on a few high-flying biotech stocks.

He had to do it all himself because, "This is a movie full of people with no connections," he said.

As tough as it is to make your own movies, getting them seen is becoming a bit easier. In 1997 actor and director Robert Redford teamed up with Newton, Massachusetts–based General Cinemas to open a chain of Sundance Cinemas to show independent films. Redford's Sundance Channel also is cablecasting independent films 24 hours a day in selected markets around the United States, and the Independent Film Channel has been showcasing entrepreneurial films since 1994. "Filmgoers are starved for new ideas, voices, and visions," said Redford, who founded the Sundance Film Festival in Utah 18 years ago.

Although the number of art movie houses is dwindling, the success of many bigger-budget independent films, including *Like Water for Chocolate, The Brothers McMullen,* and *Sling Blade,* inspires novice filmmakers to raise money any way they can. "It's hard [to make a movie] even with $1 million," said Caroline Kaplan, director of programming and production for the Independent Film Channel.

Across the country, Cedar Creek Productions, based in San Clemente, California, recently finished shooting its second independent feature film, *Time Shifters*.

In 1995 Michelle and Michael Wehling set up a limited liability corporation to raise about $180,000 from friends and family members to produce their first film, *Out of the Darkness*. The R-rated psychological thriller stars Michelle, who plays a sweet but dangerous pregnant robber. "Our investors made a 55 percent return on their money on our first film," said Wehling. They made money by selling distribution rights to about a dozen foreign countries, although the movie was not widely seen in the United States.

Cedar Creek's investors stayed around for *Time Shifters*, which cost about $350,000 to produce. The film is a futuristic drama featuring television star Corbin Bernsen and his mother, soap-opera star Jeanne Cooper.

The Wehlings decided to make their own films after struggling to find work as actors for 10 years. "We had to treat it like a business to make it work," said Michelle Wehling. But she admits making a movie is not the way to get rich quick. In fact, they had to sell one of their cars to pay a sound editing bill. "Still, nothing else is as fulfilling as this," said Wehling, who is confident that with two well-known actors, they'll sell *Time Shifters* to a big cable channel.

Despite the expense and anxiety, independent filmmakers continue to thrive. Last year, Redford's Sundance Institute received 650 feature-length films, 200 documentaries, and 1,200 short films, according to John Cooper, associate director of the respected festival. About 40 feature films are screened at the high-profile festival, but about 80 percent of those eventually end up in a theater somewhere, even if for just a few days.

"It gets harder every year to make a film, but at the same time, more get made every year," said Cooper. "People used to put together grants to make these films; now private investors are big."

That may give some hope to Peter Hall, who is still paying off the bills for *Delinquent* while raising money for a new film.

Take Advantage of Special Lending Programs for Women

ALTHOUGH THERE ARE EIGHT MILLION WOMEN business owners in America, employing roughly 18.5 million people, women still have a tough time securing bank loans.

But there is help: SBA chief Aida Alvarez said the women's prequalification program, which was launched as an experiment in 1994, handled about 700 loans totaling $70 million by 1997.

The program works like this: The SBA directs women business owners to a nonprofit group that helps them write or polish up their business plan and fill out a loan application. The completed application package is then presented to the SBA. If it looks good, the SBA issues a letter stating that the applicant qualifies for a government loan guaranty. Letter in hand, the business owner goes to a commercial lender to apply for a loan of up to $250,000.

"The SBA's stamp of approval helps women get what they need," said Alvarez. She said initiatives like the prequalification program not only fuel business growth, but also "help change lives and keep families secure."

To its credit, with President Clinton's support the SBA has worked hard in the past four years to put more bank loans in women's hands. In fiscal 1992, the SBA guaranteed 3,377 loans to women-owned businesses; in fiscal 1996, the number increased to 10,459. But, day to day, many women around the country are still having a difficult time getting bank financing.

Fortunately, two of the nation's largest banks are embracing women business owners by aligning with major women's business organizations.

San Francisco–based Wells Fargo Bank has teamed up with the National Association of Women Business Owners, a Washington, D.C.–based group with 60 chapters, while Bank of America recently linked up with Women Inc., a Los Angeles–based trade association.

Both giants have committed billions to the women's market. "The success of our efforts has exceeded our expectations," said Terri Dial, vice chairman responsible for small business and consumer lending at Wells. "What's really exciting about reaching this goal is that we accomplished it by making lots of small loans. In fact, most of the small businesses seeking loans want $25,000 or less."

Wells' loans are unsecured and require a one-page application form with no tax returns or financial statements. The minimum loan amount is $5,000. To qualify for a loan, women must have good personal and business credit, be in business for two years, and be profitable.

Bank of America (BofA), in conjunction with Women Inc., has jumped into the market with its own lending program targeted at women.

"We are excited to be working with an organization that shares our goal of financially empowering women business owners," said Kathleen Brown, executive vice president of BofA. She said the bank committed to lend $10.6 billion to small-business owners over a three-year period.

"We expect about 30 to 40 percent of that will finance women-owned business, based on the makeup of the small-business segment, but there is no upper limit."

Women Inc.'s members benefit from a discount on setup fees for new Advantage Business Credit loans of up to $100,000. The bank also offers a one-page loan application. For information, call Women Inc. at (800) 930-3993.

Before you apply for a bank loan, make sure your financial records are in good order. *Minding Her Own Business: The Self-Employed Woman's Guide to Taxes and Bookkeeping*, by Jan Zobel (Easthill Press; $17.00), is a great addition to a woman's business library.

Get Free Financing Help

USE A SCORE COUNSELOR

IN 1997 COUNSELORS FROM THE SERVICE Corps of Retired Executives counseled more than 250,000 entrepreneurs. Since its founding in 1964, more than 3.5 million business owners have participated in SCORE's extensive counseling and seminar programs.

No matter where you live, free and low-cost help is provided by more than 12,000 counselors working through 389 chapters across the United States.

"Probably the most frequently asked question is how to find money and manage finances," said Ken Yancey, SCORE's executive director. To provide high-quality help, SCORE partners with major corporations like Visa to provide extra help to business owners. In 1997 Visa underwrote the cost of a two-part workbook series that focuses on financial issues.

In addition to bookshelves filled with books and helpful publications, SCORE offices sponsor all kinds of workshops ranging from starting a business to more advanced sessions on export financing. You can find your closest SCORE chapter by calling the local Small Business Administration office or by going online to **www.score.org**.

Get Some Help from Uncle Sam

GOOD OLD UNCLE SAM. HE STANDS THERE WITH his finger pointing at you, but most business owners think he should be portrayed with that same bony hand reaching deep into our pockets.

If you've ever spent an hour filling out a payroll tax form or dealing with a federal safety inspector, it's easy to think of the government as an evil entity. But there are many ways the government can actually help grow your small business.

The trick is to figure out what kind of help is available and how to get it. The truth is that the federal government is easier to access than ever. You don't even need to get in your car to get help from the U.S. Small Business Administration—you just need a computer and a modem. The SBA's Business Advisor Web site (**www.business.gov**) is a business owner's one-stop electronic link to government aid. It helps you identify and contact a variety of resources. Vikki Craven, founder of Fly By Night, a flight simulator software company in San Antonio, goes online when she needs help from Uncle Sam. "I spent hours—instead of days—figuring out what resources were available in my area," she said.

Although there is no such thing as "free money" for small-business owners, the SBA provides government guarantees for billions of dollars' worth of bank loans made to business owners every year.

If you need a government-guaranteed loan, check out the SBA's 7(a) Guaranty program. In 1996 the SBA guaranteed more than 65,000 loans worth $9.9 billion. Details about the loan program are available on the SBA's home page or by calling the Answer Desk at (800) U-ASK-SBA. The SBA's "Programs and Services" brochure is a good one to request for a basic overview.

Greg and Heather Green of Anchorage, Alaska, used an SBA loan to open a Play It Again sports-equipment franchise. The franchise sells used sporting goods at low prices. They started the business in 1992 and have grown to eight employees. In 1996 the Greens' store had the highest sales volume of 500 stores in the franchise.

There are other loan programs offered by the SBA. The Low Documentation (LowDoc) program relies on a one-page application for loans of $100,000 or less. The application process usually takes three days. There are also CAP Lines to finance short-term, working capital needs for cyclical businesses. Under this program, loan proceeds are usually advanced against a borrower's existing or anticipated inventory and/or accounts receivable. Some companies need a bridge loan, others just a small cash infusion.

For loans under $25,000, try the Microloan Program. Jim and Carla Italiano used this program for their J&C Coatings in Benson, Arizona. For 12 years, Jim had been working as a painter for other companies. He wanted to start his own business, but needed cash for supplies.

"So many times, when we ran out of funds, I thought about quitting," said his wife, Carla. "But we loved having our own business, and I knew there had to be something, somewhere to help us."

Fred Little at Western Bank in Lordsburg, New Mexico, was impressed with their determination. "I liked their conservative approach," said Little. After making a small loan and repaying it, the Italianos applied for $40,000. It was approved and guaranteed by the SBA.

Other SBA–financing programs include:

- The Certified Development Company Program (Section 504), which provides long-term, fixed-asset financing for up to $1 million.
- The Surety Bond Guarantee Program provides bid, performance, and payment bonds for contracts up to $1.2 million.
- The Defense Loan and Technical Assistance (DELTA) program offers financing and technical help to defense firms trying to diversify into peacetime products.
- ACE-NET is a nationwide Internet service that tries to match investors with entrepreneurs in need of capital. Companies pay a fee to register with the service.
- The Minority Prequalification Loan Program helps business owners prepare loan applications for under $250,000. The Women's Prequal program does the same for women.
- The Department of Transportation Bonding Assistance Program provides bonds for businesses working on transportation contracts or subcontracts worth less than $1 million. The DOT also offers short-term loans for minority businesses. For information, call (800) 532-1169, or check out the DOT home page at **osdbuweb.dot.gov**.
- The IRS offers more than 100 free publications to help you file your taxes. The three most popular are *Tax Guide for Small Businesses, Taxpayers Starting a Business,* and *Guide to Free Tax Services.* You can call (800) 829-1040 to order forms, but the lines are frequently busy. Don't call in March or April!
- If you need statistics, demographic, or economic data to write your business plan or to develop a marketing strategy,

it's available through the Economic Statistics Administration at the Department of Commerce. This group also releases Census Bureau data. You can go online to look for numbers at **www.stat-usa.gov**.

- The Bureau of Labor Statistics at the Department of Labor is a gold mine of information. Contact the BLS at labstat.helpdesk@bls.gov.
- If you are looking for information on publicly traded companies, the Securities and Exchange Commission provides the EDGAR database via the Internet. This allows access to corporate filings to the SEC. The SEC's home page also has information on what's needed to sell stock in your company.

So don't be afraid to turn to Uncle Sam for invaluable and affordable help. As Francis Bacon said long ago, "knowledge is power." And you might as well take advantage of programs paid for by your tax dollars.

Buy Used Office Furnishings

WHEN I WAS AN INVESTIGATIVE REPORTER, MY beat was white-collar crime. I chased after the slickest, sleaziest business criminals in the country as they defrauded investors out of millions with precious metals scams, stock frauds, and real-estate schemes.

The one thing they all had in common—other than a passion for stealing money—was a passion for glitzy, opulent offices. To impress prospective victims of their schemes, they always rented expensive space on the top floor of the nicest buildings, with a spectacular city or ocean view.

My favorite con man had a reception area the size of a small apartment, with plush gray carpeting and stained glass panels. His perfectly coiffed secretary sat behind a massive cherry wood desk. His private office was about 2,000 square feet with a panoramic view of the Pacific Ocean. It was no wonder that visitors were convinced he was a legitimate commodities dealer. Only a very successful businessman would have such a fabulous office!

He's why, to this day, I still equate fancy offices with criminal behavior. And that's one of the reasons I urge smart business owners to outfit their offices with as much used equipment and furniture as possible. Of course, there are economic benefits to this plan, too.

Unless you are running an advertising or modeling agency, which depends heavily on presenting a hip image, forget about buying expensive office furniture. In my view, the funkier the office, the smarter the business owner. Think of all the money you'll save if you rent space in a building a bit off the beaten track, or in a less than desirable area—as long as it's safe for you and your employees.

But before you spend a dime on furnishing your office, buy some graph paper and draw up a detailed floor plan. Then list everything you need. Make sure to take inventory of everything you have. We often hide old filing cabinets in a storage closet and forget about them.

Then, when it's time to buy, find the nearest used-office-furniture company. They are all over the country and offer tremendous bargains on barely used furniture. Companies going out of business are often forced to sell new or barely used desks, file cabinets, credenzas, and chairs.

You should also check the classified ads for private sales. I bought my big, white Formica desk for $150 at a garage sale in Los Angeles. I've moved it three times because it suits my needs perfectly.

Another option is refurbished office equipment, which is available at a fraction of the price, but make sure it comes with a solid warranty.

Here are some office furniture buying tips from Steelcase, a Grand Rapids, Michigan–based firm:

- Define your furniture requirements by what your employees need to work effectively, rather than by the features of a particular furniture line. Ask these questions: What kind of furniture do we need? Tables for meetings? Acoustical panels for privacy?
- Inventory all the furniture you have to avoid buying things you don't need.
- Buy furniture for its functionality, not for image. If furniture isn't appropriate for the way your people work, it becomes impractical.

- Consider leasing or renting furniture. This will increase your flexibility as your company grows or shrinks.
- Think about the health and safety of your employees—be sure to consider comfort and ergonomics *(see Great Ideas 13 and 14).*

For more information on buying office furniture, check out the Steelcase site on the Web at: **www.steelcase.com**.

Buy Prepaid Legal Insurance

DID YOU KNOW THAT 52 PERCENT OF ALL Americans have some sort of legal problem? And that one of every three people will need legal advice in the next 12 months? With attorneys charging an average of $175, legal bills can eat into your profits. Even a small legal problem can drag down your morale and your business. That's why many small-business owners are signing up for prepaid legal insurance.

One of the oldest providers of this benefit is Pre-Paid Legal Services® Inc. based in Ada, Oklahoma. The company sells coverage to both individuals and small businesses.

For $69 a month, businesses with fewer than 15 employees and $250,000 or less in net income can have access to experienced business attorneys. Their team of lawyers can review contracts, write debt collection letters, and deal with leases, partnerships, creditor harassment, and bankruptcy, among other problems. If you need additional services, you are given a 25 percent discount off their regular legal fees.

To get help, call the toll-free consultation line. A representative collects all the details and refers you to the right person in the firm. You'll usually get a call back by the end of the next business day, according to company officials.

Pre-Paid Legal Services, a publicly held company, was founded in 1992. It contracts with 2,700 law firms in 46 states. The company has paid $100 million to 100,000 attorneys on behalf of clients.

Shop around for the best deals, but consider this type of insurance as a way to sleep more soundly at night.

Locate the Right Space

ENTREPRENEURS CRINGE AT THE THOUGHT OF leasing office space. It's scary and expensive and takes time to do. That's why so many of us work at home until we get thrown out by our loving families.

The Applegate Group, founded in the cozy den of our home in Sun Valley, California, outgrew that space within a year. Taking a big risk, we invested $10,000 to remodel the garage. It was a great commute—down the driveway.

We stayed in the garage until we moved to New York. Our temporary quarters there were in a basement—it was either blasting hot or freezing cold. When my husband and I bought a spacious, three-bedroom apartment in a gorgeous pre-World War II building, it was evident that the company was going to be evicted.

So it was time to look for an office. We found a great, sunny space in the Pelham, New York, post office building in early 1997.

If, like me, you can no longer work at home, here are some options. First, look for a business incubator in your area *(see Great Idea 9)*. There are hundreds of private, university, and government-sponsored roosts for small companies. The rent is affordable, and there is great comfort to be found in the company of other crazy entrepreneurs.

Another great option is to share space with another small business. I once profiled two happy bakers in Orange County, California: a gourmet brownie baker and a cheesecake baker. They shared a commercial kitchen for years; the brownie guy worked days, and the cheesecake guy worked nights. They split the expenses and kept the ovens warm around the clock.

The owner of an upscale framing store in Hollywood rented out his extra space to an art dealer. They figured they would attract the same sorts of art-loving customers, and it worked out very well for a while.

I also profiled a nurse who became an expert witness. When she quit her hospital job, she moved into an empty office at a law firm that specialized in defending malpractice suits. They gave her a discount on her rent in exchange for a reduced fee when they needed her to testify!

If you must rent space on your own, prepare to do a lot of walking and talking. Many major cities have a glut of office space, so with some persistence, you can find affordable digs.

Here are some tips to help you find the right space:

- Drive around neighborhoods that appeal to you and look for "For Rent" signs.
- Check the neighboring buildings to see if they are well maintained. Take notes on the parking situation, proximity to mass transit, and street lighting.
- Check out the lobby. Is it well lit and clean? Remember that deodorant commercial that warned, "You never get a second chance to make a first impression"? Well, you don't want a building with a dreary lobby.
- Visit the restrooms and check the fire exits and hallways for cleanliness and accessibility for disabled workers and customers.
- Speak to other tenants before you meet the building manager. They will usually give you the scoop on life in the building.
- If you are renting retail space, find out whether the landlord expects a percentage of gross sales, as well as rent.
- Find out exactly what the landlord pays for and what you are financially responsible for.
- It may make sense to work with a commercial real-estate broker, especially if you are renting more than a small office.
- Ask a lawyer to review a lease before you sign it.

For more information on using a savvy real-estate broker, see Great Idea 46.

Build Up Your Credit Lines

HAVING A PERSONAL CREDIT LINE OR TWO IS A great cushion for the times when you are a little short on cash—if a client doesn't pay on time, or you decide at the last minute that you really must rent that exhibit space at an industry trade show.

This cool financial strategy was actually taught to me by a

banker. Ian Jack is a talented composer and musician who fell in love with my best friend, Francine, and went to work for her father's bank. He used credit lines to build an impressive real-estate portfolio and now owns his own mortgage banking firm in Los Angeles.

My credit helped our small company stay afloat until we landed our first big project. Through the years, we've relied on personal credit lines to fill in the gaps when our biggest client deliberately held their payments beyond 30 days to collect the interest on my money. We've never applied for a commercial credit line because, fortunately, our cash flow is steady enough to pay the bills.

Here's how you build up a personal credit line: First, consolidate all your accounts in one bank. Then introduce yourself to the branch manager and get to know the tellers. If you've held a well-paying job for at least a year, or your spouse has a good job, apply for a personal credit line of at least $5,000. A credit line is different from a credit card. It has a checkbook and operates like a checking account, but you're dealing with borrowed money and paying substantial interest.

After you obtain the credit line, it's time to use it. When you are absolutely sure you're going to receive a big payment, use the credit line checks to pay all your bills or to take a cash advance. A few days before the payment is due, pay off the entire amount and zero out your account.

If you do max out and pay off your account a couple of times, in most cases, the bank will automatically increase your credit line limit. Bankers like to see that you are using their money prudently and love to see a balance being paid off, even though they aren't making any money on interest.

If the bank doesn't automatically increase your limit after a few months of doing this, call the service center or ask your branch manager for an increase.

Once you've built up your borrowing power, you might want to apply for a couple of credit lines at different banks. It sounds crazy, but using credit wisely is the best way to create a positive credit history.

I have impeccable credit and never have problems obtaining new credit cards or credit lines, in part because I have zeroed out my balances over the course of our seven years in business.

So give this great idea a try. But remember, it only works if you have a good personal credit history and a steady income!

CHAPTER 3

Marketing Strategies

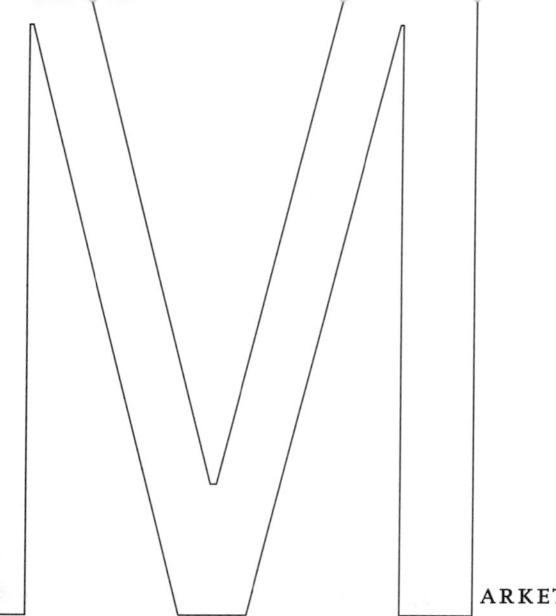

MARKETING IS CONSIDERED the "softer" side of any business plan. Yet without a well-executed marketing strategy, your business will never be as successful as it could be.

This is the chapter with the most great ideas for several reasons. I love writing about savvy marketing ideas—the nuttier the better. Marketing challenges your creativity. It's fun and compelling. For many entrepreneurs, it's the most confusing, expensive, and upsetting aspect of running their businesses.

It's not so squishy or confusing if you realize that the only way to judge whether something is working is to track, measure, and carefully monitor every marketing gimmick you try. If you spend money doing something zany without determining whether it's working, you might as well toss the money out the window.

Through the years, I've emphasized marketing strategies in my weekly *Succeeding in Small Business®* newspaper column and in my presentations. Why? Because I'm not great with numbers, and marketing is something I can wrap my arms around.

I love collecting and sharing great marketing ideas. I've met people doing wonderful things on a shoestring budget.

One of my favorite marketing ideas comes from a company called My Fortune, which makes acrylic fortune cookies filled with a customized message. I bought hundreds of fortune-cookie key chains and gave them away to promote my second book. They were a huge hit—I still meet people who remember those silly key chains.

Based on personal experience, I know the power of a clear marketing strategy. By carefully following the marketing plan developed in 1993 by marketing expert Brooke Halpin, of Halpin House West, I have watched our business flourish and my personal income soar.

Brooke, who lives and works in a Malibu canyon overlooking the Pacific Ocean, came to me with a simple premise.

"You could be the 'Dear Abby' for small-business owners," he told me over a cup of tea in a hotel restaurant. I remember staring at him and thinking to myself, "this guy is nuts." But I listened carefully to his plan. At the time, I was feeling increasingly frustrated. Although my small-business column was popular, I was broke. I was jealous of the wealthy entrepreneurs I was profiling every week—so many had no special education or talent, other than guts and a great idea.

The five-year marketing plan detailed how we would turn a popular newspaper column into a thriving multimedia communications company.

By connecting the dots, Brooke developed a unique way to fund my speaking tours by partnering with companies who want to reach my fans. Together we created and marketed a national small-business radio report, produced television shows, and developed all kinds of new features for Web sites. I've appeared at events all over the country sponsored by companies including IBM, AT&T, Ameritech, Pacific Bell, American Express, Microsoft, and Hewlett Packard. In 1998, GTE Communications is sponsoring a 26-city tour.

My secret of success is to know my market better than anyone else. I live and breathe the entrepreneurial life.

Your challenge is to figure out exactly who your clients or customers are *before* you spend a penny on marketing or advertising.

In this chapter, you'll find great ideas on how to create a cross-promotion, find a mascot, do co-op advertising and telemarketing. You'll learn how to put some pizzazz into your business cards and send pizza to potential clients, how to market to callers waiting on hold, and how to set up a network of dealers.

I explain what it takes to get your pet product on QVC, how to hold an off-season sale, how to take advantage of coupons, and why "free" is the most powerful word in the

English language. And if you've ever felt overwhelmed at a trade show, be sure to read about how to make the most of your time and money before you register for the next one.

This chapter also features some ideas for marketing your products to special-interest segments and using PR to boost your business.

Once you've read through the ideas in this section, your next course of action will be to implement some of your favorites and use the rest to fuel your creativity to construct a new and more creative marketing plan for your business.

Strike a Deal with a Giant

UNTIL 1997, ANYONE WANTING SANDRA Nunnerley's elegant, custom-designed furniture for their home or office had to have deep pockets as well as good taste.

Long accustomed to serving the upscale market, with a single chair tagged at up to $10,000, Nunnerley said she was pushed into the retail market by copycats.

"I started to notice that copies of my custom designs were appearing in retail outlets," said Nunnerley.

Skilled at managing a six-person boutique design firm, but unfamiliar with producing furniture for the masses, Nunnerley teamed up with furniture giant Lane Upholstery to manufacture her line. Her licensing deal for sofas, beds, chairs, and tables calls for Lane to pay Nunnerley a royalty on sales, as well as an advance against royalties to help cover her design and start-up costs. She declined to discuss the financial details of the deal, but said if the line is a hit, it would create double-digit sales increases.

Not every entrepreneur has the reputation, talent, and clout to strike a deal with a giant. Nunnerley was already established as a hot, young designer. Her furniture and interior designs, widely recognized by her peers and featured in *Architectural Digest,* among other publications, appealed to Lane Upholstery president Arthur Thompson.

"Sandra is a designer of remarkable talents, one who has consistently responded to a discerning international clientele," Thompson said when the line was launched. "Her simple, sophisticated designs fill a void in the marketplace for furniture that meets the demands of modern living without sacrificing elegance, style, and tradition."

In addition to designing the furniture and selecting fabrics, Nunnerley spends many hours on the Lane factory floor, teaching workers how to create her fashion-inspired upholstery details, like pleats and tucks.

Realizing that negotiating a licensing deal with a big company requires special contacts and skills, Nunnerley relied on Carl Levine, a veteran home-furnishings retailer and consultant to North Carolina–based Lane.

"I felt she had the talent and credentials," said Levine, a former top executive at Bloomingdale's. "I was familiar with some of her interior design work. I am very familiar with the mass market, and I know what the North Carolinians are looking for in furniture. I felt Sandra could bring a fresh angle."

Levine, who receives a percentage of her royalties for brokering the deal, said Lane benefits by its association with Nunnerley.

"Her name is like a brand," he said. "It's like putting Kellogg's on the A&P shelf rather than a generic brand. That's why many manufacturers want a designer name attached to their product. It gives them extra clout and prestige."

Levine not only brokered the deal, but helped Nunnerley decide what kind of pieces would appeal to middle America. Creating a win-win situation between designer and manufacturer is critical to doing a successful licensing deal, Levine said. He also recommends working with a skilled contract attorney to protect your interests.

If you have a concept or invention you hope to license to a manufacturer, check out *The Inventor's Notebook,* by Fred Grissom and David Pressman (Nolo Press; $19.95). The workbook helps you document your idea and covers the hows and whys of licensing.

Pitch Your Product on QVC

GREAT 74 IDEA

EVER WONDER HOW THOSE LUCKY PEOPLE GET their products on QVC or other home shopping channels?

Well, most manufacturers have to finagle an appointment with a buyer and wait their turn, but QVC is on the road looking for you. QVC reps travel around the country to 50 states searching for products at state-sponsored trade shows. You can get a jump on the competition now for the proposed 1999 shows.

The network's "The Quest for America's Best: QVC's 50 in 50 Tour" program has generated more than $100 million in sales since it started in 1995. About 1,000 businesses have pitched their products through the program.

"To anybody who has a product they believe is a local treasure, this is an opportunity to turn it into a national success," said Doug Briggs, QVC president. The first year, 16 small companies began significant businesses through QVC sales.

For instance, Marlene Wyatt, a homemaker from Yellville, Arkansas, watched her "No Mess Dough Disc" generate $4 million in sales.

Donald Hodgskin, from Orlando, sold 400,000 electronic pest repellers worth $17 million on his QVC appearances.

"I never dreamed what I thought was a simple solution for the bug problem in Florida would become a nationwide sensation," said Hodgskin. "I've gone from a weekend garage operation to a major Florida business that is still growing."

QVC executives say they like giving small businesses a real boost.

"One nationally televised appearance can jump-start any local business and help it become a national enterprise," said Bill Lane, QVC's vice president for new markets.

Here are the criteria for pitching your product to QVC:

- Your company must be a new supplier to QVC.
- It must be headquartered or the product made in the state QVC is visiting.
- The product must be made in America.

- It must have only local or regional distribution.
- The product must fit U.S. Postal Service or UPS shipping requirements.
- It must be in production (no prototypes).
- It should retail for no less than $12.95.
- The manufacturer must have rights to sell and distribute the product.
- All federal guidelines and requirements must be met.

To find out more about pitching your product on QVC, call (888) 5050-USA.

Take Advantage of Co-op Advertising

DO YOU EVER WONDER HOW LOCAL MERCHANTS get their name and address in the corner of glossy ads for a car, computer, or watch?

They do it through what's called "co-op advertising," and this form of cost-sharing has given small-business owners a marketing boost for years.

Ad agency executives say companies like Omega, the high-end watchmaker, "tag" 100 percent of their print ads with the names of local retail suppliers, because they don't have their own boutiques to sell watches.

"It's a kind of dual extortion," said Eric Dochtermann, chief executive of Katz, Dochtermann & Epstein, a Manhattan ad agency. "The retailer wants support, and the manufacturer wants the retailer to lay out money."

Dochtermann, who also works with Dress Barn and Barami Studio, said retailers typically spend 3 to 10 percent of the total sales of an item on co-op advertising. By hooking up with a big manufacturer, they can get more bang for their advertising bucks and significantly more exposure.

"For the manufacturer, it's the 80/20 rule—you spend more money on your big clients," Dochtermann explained.

To qualify for inclusion in a co-op program, retailers have to stock enough of the product to be considered a major player. In other words, if my slick ads are driving customers into your store, I expect you to stock enough of my products to meet the demand.

Many ads, especially those in magazines, are redesigned for specific regions, so local retailers benefit. A dealer in Denver wouldn't want to be listed in an ad appearing in an Atlanta newspaper.

One Omega retailer taking advantage of co-op ads is Refeal Solly, owner of Daniele Trissi Ltd. in Scarsdale, New York. Information about his store is featured in Omega posters prominently displayed on the Metro North railroad.

"The people who commute every day see these ads again and again," said Solly.

Solly, who opened his jewelry store in 1977, said Omega approached him about the co-op ads several years ago. He declined to discuss the financial details, but said he likes being part of the program.

"Ads in *The New York Times* are prohibitively expensive to a small business," he said. "This is the only way advertising can be affordable."

Meanwhile, Dochtermann said high technology may jeopardize the future of co-op ads. Why? So many big companies have their own Web sites that allow customers to collect product information and quickly access a list of local retailers.

"With so much retail happening on the phone, over the Internet, and by mail, tagging becomes less valuable as an advertising tool," said Dochtermann.

It's a good idea to check with all your major suppliers to see if they have a cooperative advertising policy. Most manufacturers have some kind of program to offer retailers.

Even the biggest companies in the world want to split the advertising costs. Hewlett-Packard, for example, relies on major co-op deals with Intel to promote the Pentium processors inside its computer equipment.

Market to Callers on Hold

"WE PUT OVER 100 CUSTOMERS ON HOLD EVERY day," said Elie Wade, president of Mortgage Makers in Oklahoma City, Oklahoma.

Wade turned that annoying waiting time into a marketing opportunity by signing up for a service that produces the messages callers hear while on hold.

"We make mortgage loans, so one of the things we put on the message is a list of things you need to bring to a [real-estate] closing," said Wade. "We also provide information about my radio show, and customers always say, 'Oh, you do a radio show!' and they don't mind holding anymore."

Wade worked with Tulsa-based Impressions on Hold, which has 10,000 clients and 70 franchises in 32 states around the United States, to set up and maintain her system.

"We gave them the information, and they wrote the script. They did everything," said Wade.

Wade, whose firm posted revenues of $3.5 million in 1997, said the messages-on-hold service is affordable and professional. "I've never had negative feedback," she said.

Not using your on-hold time to promote your business is like "having a blank billboard on your property. There's no return on the investment," said John Bersin, who founded Impressions on Hold in 1991 after working as a sales manager for a similar company.

"If you have 10 callers on hold every day, you're a candidate for this system," said Bersin. "Here's my logic—that's 220 to 300 people a month you can talk to about your business."

Bersin's firm offers one-, three-, and five-year contracts, which include the equipment and unlimited message changes. The one-year plan is $189 a month; a three-year plan costs $139 a month. The five-year package is $119 a month.

"We produce over 100 messages a month," said Bersin. "Small business is dynamic. Our packages offer unlimited changes."

He said too many small-business owners buy the wrong

kind of advertising for their business.

"You want to spend dollars impacting the right prospects," said Bersin. "We know we're dealing with a targeted audience because they wouldn't be on hold otherwise. They're at the point of purchase."

Set Up a Dealer Network

CONSUMERS ARE ACCUSTOMED TO BUYING CARS, tires, and computers through authorized dealers—and other businesses can benefit from a similar sales model.

David Usher, who died in a kayaking accident in March 1997, was a brilliant entrepreneur. A former paper salesman, he began selling artists' prints out of the trunk of his car 25 years ago. He traveled around the United States, establishing close relationships with galleries and framing shops, believing that direct distribution was the way to go.

Today Greenwich Workshop, founded by Usher, sells limited edition prints and porcelain collectibles through a network of 1,200 dealers across the country. Greenwich, which has four company-owned stores, posted about $30 million in 1997 sales. Usher said the secret of the company's success is to treat every dealer like part of the family.

"We're continually providing them with information, marketing, and resources, and helping them run their business," said Usher, who served as chairman and CEO until his death.

The company, which employs 75, provides dealers with affordable high-quality brochures and catalogs. It also organizes marketing seminars and sales contests and publishes a dealer newsletter filled with tested marketing tips. Every few years Usher and president Peter McEwen set out on a "Magic Bus" tour across the country, hosting workshops and sponsoring charitable events for dealers.

"It's a very close family," said Fred Turra, co-owner of Art Works, Etc. on Brookhurst Avenue in Fountain Valley, California. Turra, who's been a Greenwich dealer for 20 years, said the company helps attract customers to his gallery by sending noted artists to make personal appearances. One event, featuring a personal appearance by noted wildlife artist Bev Doolittle and two others, attracted nearly 1,000 people to his gallery.

"Greenwich provides us with turnkey materials so even the most untrained of art dealers can sound very professional when they approach the media," said Turra. Although he carries other lines of prints, about 90 percent of his inventory is provided by Greenwich. Total sales in 1997 were around $1 million.

Greenwich dealers buy the art outright at wholesale prices, but they can return unsold prints for credit. "Their art line seems to be at the core of what most Americans want," said Turra, who employs eight people. "We sell American illustrators, folklore, wildlife, western, aviation, and fantasy themes." Most of all, Turra said, he likes having a say in marketing the products.

Usher said that limiting the number of dealers and assigning them an exclusive territory has been an element in the company's success. In Southern California, for instance, there are dealers in West Covina, Sherman Oaks, Fountain Valley, and Corona del Mar. The dealers also keep in touch with each other, referring clients and sharing information and marketing hints.

The John Lane Gallery, located in Poughkeepsie, New York, was one of Usher's first dealers. "I remember when he drove up with the prints in the trunk of his car," said Erica Canevari, manager of the gallery owned by her family. "They are one of the best publishers to work with," said Canevari. "They are always asking what we think, asking for our opinions and suggestions."

The gallery, located across from Vassar College, relies on Greenwich for about 50 percent of its total inventory. Yet the Greenwich line represents about 60 percent of the gallery's total sales, she said. "They consider each one of their dealers to be part of their family," she said. "They make a point to make sure we are happy and understand what's going on."

The limited edition print market, with industry sales of between $300 and $400 million a year, is highly competitive. Greenwich, which also publishes art books, cards, calendars, and videos, recently expanded its line to include porcelain collectibles. Unframed prints start at about $75. A porcelain figurine by James Christensen runs up to $595.

Usher never wavered from his original plan of relying on dealers to sell his products. Based on his success in the art world, entrepreneurs should consider applying Usher's model to selling their particular products and services.

Create an Active Database

IF YOU LOOK AT THE PILES OF BUSINESS CARDS on your desk and just see a mess—look again. What you're really looking at is potential income.

No matter how small your business may be, you should be creating and updating a database. With simple software, a current database allows you to easily mail newsletters and sales information to customers. You can also target prospective customers by *renting* mailing lists. Add telephone numbers, and your database becomes the basis for a telemarketing initiative.

Collecting detailed information about people and their companies is easier than you think. Business cards, sales invoices, catalogs, directories, and magazine and newspaper articles all contain invaluable information and contacts. Small-business magazines such as *Nation's Business* usually include contact addresses and telephone numbers in their articles.

The easiest way to create and maintain a database is with a simple software program. There are many very affordable programs on the market that keep track of the information and allow you to cross-reference and access it in several ways.

More complex programs, such as Goldmine, Act!, and Sharkware, organize your daily appointments and remind you when to place important telephone calls. The biggest headache is entering the data into the program, but you can certainly assign this task to a staffer or hire a temporary worker or student to do it. Before you hand the material over to be entered, be sure to indicate exactly what information to include.

Once your database is up and running, you'll find that you'll be using it frequently to keep in touch with the world. Be sure to add new information on a weekly or monthly basis and delete outdated information at least twice a year.

Market to the Gay Consumer

ABOUT FIVE YEARS AGO, CUSH HONDA OF SAN Diego became one of the first automobile dealerships to aggressively pursue the gay and lesbian community.

"The first year we participated in the San Diego Gay Pride Parade was a little difficult," admitted Frank Lechner, spokesman for the dealership. "We received some negative feedback from anonymous callers."

But Cush didn't back down.

"Our involvement is another part of embracing the community in which we do business," he said. "Why wouldn't we want to support it?"

Savvy businesses in all industries are reaching out to serve America's gay consumers. According to *Advertising Age,* up to 10 percent of the population in urban markets is gay, and that translates into a large chunk of market share—gay men and women spend about $514 billion a year.

Victoria Garcia, a San Diego marketing consultant who specializes in this segment, said it makes economic sense to cater to gay consumers.

"Mainstream businesses have now recognized the power of the gay dollar," said Garcia. "The fact that more celebrities and athletes have come out of the closet has a definite impact on the acceptance of the new trend [in marketing to gay people]."

Garcia, principal of the Marketing Impressions Advertising Agency, helps non-gay businesses reach the gay market. But she cautions clients against launching a campaign without careful planning.

"An effective gay-targeted campaign requires more than just showing a room full of men using a certain product or flying a rainbow flag," she explained. "It means demonstrating a *sincere* understanding of their perspective. It's very important for consumers to walk into a business and feel accepted and comfortable," she said.

More tips from Garcia

- Gay and lesbian consumers are often very well informed and can be extremely loyal.
- Keep advertisements simple and avoid overstating your "plea" for their business.
- Humor is a great tool to break the ice.
- Understand your community and find out exactly what local gay consumers are looking for.

Cash In on Millennium Mania

IF YOU SELL FIREWORKS, TEE-SHIRTS, OR PARTY favors, you can skip this section. You are probably way ahead of the crowd when it comes to cashing in on Millennium Mania.

Party planners and hotels have already dreamed up cool ways for wealthy revelers to celebrate New Year's Eve 1999.

Room rates will triple or quadruple, and rooms with the best views in major cities have been booked for years. The Rainbow Room in Rockefeller Center is planning a $1,000-a-person bash, but restaurants ranging from local diners to five-star cafés are working on their Millennium Mania menus.

Smart entrepreneurs are trying to protect their great ideas. The U.S. Patent and Trademark office has been deluged with applications to trademark and copyright every possible slogan related to the Year 2000. By the fall of 1997, the office had awarded 117 trademarks including the word "millennium" and more than 1,500 containing "2000." Thousands of applications were pending at this writing.

Even if you haven't applied for a trademark, you can still cash in on the marketing frenzy.

John Locher's Everything 2000 Web site is trying to keep up with the buzz, serving as a clearinghouse for information and conducting market research. When he asked visitors to his site what events they would consider for New Year's Eve 1999, international travel topped the list, with dining out and dancing coming in second and third. So if you want to know how to find a time capsule or a party, check out his site: **www.everything2000.com**.

Travel agents are cashing in big time, too.

"The millennium is a huge event for the travel industry," said Christa Brantsch-Harness, director of public relations for Abercrombie and Kent in Oakbrook Terrace, Illinois.

"We've selected the most interesting sites in terms of beauty, serenity, and magnificence," she said. "This is a once-in-a-lifetime travel experience."

Boating on the Nile topped the list of New Year's Eve choices for many of her clients. Most trips are sold out based on deposits, as the company hasn't set final prices for their Millennium excursions, she said.

Now is the time to market any sort of gimmicky product. For example, Branco International is selling "The Count-down Watch." The watch, which retails for around $80, has a little countdown window. If you are already sick of the Year 2000 hype, it can be programmed to count down to other important dates and deadlines.

"The Year 2000 solution project managers are buying them for their sales force," said Janine Gabay, marketing manager for Branco. "They can actually countdown the hours, minutes, and seconds to when the problem will hit."

If a watch isn't enough, Branco is also selling a wall clock for your home or office. This is your chance to get in on the festivities. If you're interested in marketing your products as a millennium tie-in, 2000 is *probably* your first and last opportunity!

Use Coupons to Attract Customers

ON A BALMY SPRING EVENING, I TOOK MYSELF out to the local movie theater. Standing outside the door was a young man in a Häagen-Dazs apron. He was passing out coupons offering a "double feature"—a free scoop of ice cream when you bought one scoop at the regular price. I immediately knew where I was heading after the show.

Ticket stub in hand, I trotted down the block to be the first in line. (I didn't want to embarrass myself by running.)

For a mere $1.85, I savored my calorie-laden pralines-and-cream and coffee-chip double scoop. The kid even let me keep the coupon for a repeat performance. Talk about generating goodwill!

Giving away a free scoop of ice cream brought me into the store for the first time. And, of course, it won't be the last. It also proved to me that a coupon is a low-cost way to attract new and repeat customers.

Coupons are great because they are cheap to print and easy to distribute. You can print them yourself on your PC if you don't want to do anything fancy. Then you can pay to have them stuffed into the local Pennysaver or newspaper. You can also pay the post office to deliver them to local households.

Or you can send an associate to place them under the windshield wipers of parked cars. Although, admittedly, this method can be annoying and produces litter, it's good for a local promotion. You might also consider giving your coupons to local merchants—and offer to pass out their coupons in exchange.

When you print up your coupons, be sure to code them so you can track response. For example, put an "N" on them if they were placed in a newspaper or "M" if they were mailed to "resident" or "occupant."

But before you run to the printer, think about an appealing offer. Anything "free" works if you have some sort of retail operation. If you own a dry cleaner, you can offer discounts on large orders. Any sort of "gift with purchase" coupon will attract customers.

It doesn't matter what you offer as long as it has a high perceived value and will draw people to your door.

Do Good for Your Community

ONE OF THE EASIEST WAYS TO DRAW ATTENTION to your business is to do something good for your community. Small-business owners across the country are coming up with terrific ways to contribute and make a positive impression at the same time. You don't have to spend a lot of time or money on your project.

Here are some of my favorite ideas:

- If you have a store with foot traffic, collect food or clothing for the homeless or for your favorite charity.
- Ask your employees and their families if they will participate in a blood drive for the Red Cross or a local hospital.
- Donate your services—it's easy. A dry cleaner in Ohio, for example, offered free dry cleaning to unemployed customers who needed clean clothes for job interviews. When someone got a new job, of course they became a steady, loyal customer for life.
- Join together with other business owners in your neighborhood to sponsor a trash pickup day or graffiti cleanup campaign. Ask a local paint store to donate paint and brushes in exchange for the publicity. A True Value hardware store in Mississippi provided supplies for the senior class to repaint the high school gym; it made the papers and kept the kids out of trouble for weeks.
- Ask city officials if you can plant trees or start a community garden.
- Check with your accountant about the tax advantages of donating excess inventory to a charitable organization. You can get rid of what you don't need and take advantage of a tax break at the same time.
- If you own a restaurant and want to attract new patrons, host a fund-raising dinner for a local charity. A small Greek restaurant in Maryland hosted a dinner and gave away a free trip to Greece donated by a local travel agency. To liven

things up, collect door prizes from other merchants and raffle them off at the dinner.

- If you really want to make a difference, create an apprenticeship program and hire local high school students or welfare recipients to work part time at your company. Solid on-the-job training can mean the difference between success and failure for a young or underemployed person. While many big corporations are doing this, small companies can do the right thing just as easily.

Once you've chosen a project, be sure to write a lively press release and send it to your local newspapers, radio, and television stations. The media are always looking for upbeat local feature stories.

Use Food as a Selling Tool

GREAT 83 IDEA

FOOD IS A POWERFUL SALES TOOL. EVERYONE NEEDS to eat, so take advantage of tasty treats whenever you can. This is a simple idea that really works.

Bright Star Resorts, which rents vacation homes and condominiums in Central Florida, hosts a monthly barbecue for their vendor travel agents, owners, and employees. The barbecues not only give people a chance to socialize, but also help Bright Star's management keep up with what's going on in their offices.

Food is also the most appropriate gift for many business purposes. Holiday gift baskets filled with southern delicacies, including divinity, pecan rolls, and miniature pecan pies, are a huge hit among our clients and associates. So much so that I sent the same basket two years in a row, then switched back to Harry & David fruit baskets the following season. In 1997 we sent Godiva chocolates to some and the pecan treats to others.

One of the nicest presents we received from a client was an attractive wicker basket filled with wine, goblets, coffee, and gourmet snacks. We love to receive any sort of edible gifts.

Food has another advantage: It's very affordable and appreciated by people, no matter how affluent or important they are.

Set Up a Strong Referral Network

UNLIKE THE FOLKS AT BIG COMPANIES, SMALL-business owners are usually eager to help each other out by making referrals. Entrepreneurs really believe that "what goes around, comes around."

While many referrals are made informally by word-of-mouth, some entrepreneurs take it a step further.

Dana Adkinson, owner of Keepsake Floral Inc. in Orlando, Florida, runs a national floral preservation service. Because her service relies heavily on referrals from florists and wedding consultants, her challenge is getting these folks to recommend her services.

"We put together information so it looks like they're providing a very needed service for their clients, yet the end result is a valuable referral," said Adkinson. "We do all the work, then give them a 10 percent commission for each referral."

The beauty of this cash-incentive system is that Adkinson in effect expands her sales force "for the cost of postage, printing, and phone expenses."

You don't have to be in the floral preservation business to share customers. For instance, years ago I wrote about a group of Orange County, California, hardware and software companies that formed a marketing alliance to provide better service. If someone called one of the companies for help, they would inquire if they should also bring along someone from an associated company.

Business owners benefited from the extra service and usually appreciated a turnkey approach to solving their computer problems.

David McLean, with the Institute of Business Excellence in Orlando, suggests faxing a coupon to customers and clients offering them a discount on their next order if they provide three referrals.

Betsy Holtzapple, with Apple Irrigation Inc. in Orlando, also sends coupons to clients offering them a free sprinkler system inspection if they come up with three referrals.

Setting up a strong referral network is a great way to receive a constant stream of new customers.

Give It Away

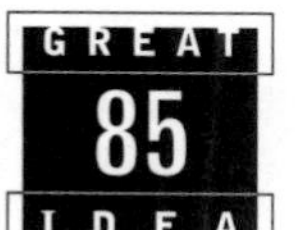

NO MATTER WHAT KIND OF BUSINESS YOU'RE IN, "free" is the most powerful word in your marketing vocabulary. Offering potential clients or customers a no-charge deal is an excellent way to gain new business. For example, Sprint has signed up thousands of new customers by offering small-business owners free phone calls on Fridays.

"I was given a Sprint deal which pays all my local telephone service for two years and provides free calling on Fridays until the year 2000, plus free 800-line pagers for my employees," said Bob Dudley, president of Amerisat, a San Diego commercial satellite-dish provider.

But you don't have to be as big as Sprint to offer customers something for free.

Consultants can host a free educational seminar to attract potential clients. The session is a perfect way to show off your expertise and prequalify clients without spending a lot of time or money. Breakfast meetings work best because people can stop by on their way to work—and breakfast is the cheapest meal of the day!

If you sell clothing, consider giving free fashion consultations, by appointment, to new customers. Of course, after the private consultation, encourage customers to buy the clothes and accessories that looked best on them.

If you are an image consultant, create free "dress for success" seminars for local businesses. Business owners welcome the program because the consultant's outside expertise helps them establish a more professional dress code for employees.

Offering a gift-with-purchase is another effective way to boost sales. Big cosmetic companies have done this for years, giving away tote bags, umbrellas, and sample-size goodies. You don't have to sell cosmetics to make this free promotion work.

Other industries such as food distributors also find this tactic particularly effective. Free samples are an inexpensive and effective way to get products into the mouths of consumers.

Food companies rely on in-store demonstrations quite frequently to test-market products.

Years ago, I was browsing through the aisles of a gourmet food store when a woman ran up and stuffed a bite of plum pudding in my mouth. I ended up buying some as a gift—and also interviewing her for my syndicated column.

So whatever you do, figure out a way to give it away for free.

Design a Great Sign for Your Business

WHEN YOU DON'T HAVE A LOT OF MONEY TO spend, your sign becomes a magnet for business. It's a perpetual advertisement.

Lloyd Miller, with Canterbury Travel Inc. in Winter Park, Florida, uses a clever sign to lure customers.

"I own a travel agency on a high-visibility corner," said Miller. "We put our cruise price specials on a dry-marker board labeled 'Cruise Catch of the Day.' The graphic is a cruise ship on a fish hook.

"The success has been phenomenal, with some people calling on their car phones looking at us through the window."

It doesn't take much time or money to design an eye-catching sign for your business. Many sign makers rely on computer technology to design a sign and then cut the letters out of durable vinyl sheeting.

The first step is coming up with a great name for your business. Then decide whether you need a logo or graphic element to go along with your name.

A street sign usually features just your business name and possibly the phone number. A window sign may include your hours of operation and other details.

I've always been partial to a good neon sign, but whatever type you choose, it should fit the style of your business and that of your community, and it has to be carefully maintained.

Produce an Infomercial

IF YOU THINK MARKETING YOUR PRODUCT VIA AN infomercial is a quick and easy way to make millions—think again. Industry experts say only one product in 20 actually hits the big time.

Although consumers bought more than $1 billion worth of products via infomercials in 1997, it remains an "imprecise science," according to Chris Ourand, spokesman for the National Infomercial Marketing Association, based in Washington, D.C.

Ourand said infomercials (which first hit the airwaves in 1984 when Congress deregulated the television industry) fall into a few broad categories: health and beauty products, exercise equipment, motivational programs, and household products.

One big success on the housewares front was the Smart Mop, designed and manufactured by Santa Monica–based Smart Inventions Inc. Cofounder and president Jon Nokes, a former biology teacher from England, began selling his super-absorbent rayon mop on the county fair and home-show circuit about seven years ago.

Although retailers expressed strong interest in the mop, Nokes decided to market it directly to the public. When three established infomercial producers turned him down, he and a team of out-of-work actors and models hit the home show circuit, selling enough $29 mops to raise the $65,000 needed to shoot their first infomercial.

In 1993 they bought about $15,000 worth of air time on a few stations to test consumer response. The mops took off, and in nine months they sold millions.

Nokes, who started the company in a tiny apartment and stored the mops in rented garages, said the secret of making money is to make something easy enough for an eight-year-old to use. It has to be cheap to make but have a high perceived value. In his case, the mops cost under $5 to manufacture, but they sold for six times that much (including refills) on the air.

Another surprising secret, he said, is that a truly successful infomercial sets the stage for dynamic retail sales.

"We went into retail stores in July 1994 and during the first three months we sold one million mops a month," he said. "In 1995 we sold almost four million units."

No longer using the 30-minute infomercial format, Smart Inventions now airs a two-minute version, which in 1996 tied for first place in the short-form category at the National Infomercial Marketing Association convention.

Nokes, whose company also sells the Smart Chopper and Quick Sand easy-cleaning cat box, said he believes infomercials are a great way for entrepreneurs to introduce new household products.

"It doesn't matter how good the product is if the public doesn't know about it," he said. "When you have a new product, you need to educate the public."

Nokes attributes much of his success to business associates and vendors who cut him some slack when times were tough. For instance, he said, when cash was tight his media buyer and fulfillment house waited a few extra days to be paid.

Moving mop production from Europe to Southern California also boosted profits. Smart Inventions initially made the mops in Holland, with special fabric made in Germany. But when sales skyrocketed, they couldn't get the mops over here fast enough to meet demand.

Moving their factory to Compton reduced costs and

Tips from the National Infomercial Marketing Association

- Do your homework. Find out what worked for successful infomercial producers.
- Pick the right stations, market, and time to air your infomercial.
- Offer strong money-back guarantees to boost consumer confidence.
- Believe in your product.

allowed the company to beat cheap, imported knock-offs to retail store shelves.

"One reason for our success is having a USA-made product," Nokes said.

He said that being persistent also helps. "Entrepreneurs who make it are people who don't listen to anyone who tells them that what they are doing is impossible," he said.

Put a Pig in Your Window

IRIS FULLER, FOUNDER AND PRESIDENT OF Fillamento in San Francisco, cried for two hours after attending a retailing seminar by Peter Glen. They were tears of joy and inspiration.

"He made such a difference in the way we do what we do," said Fuller, whose 10,000-square-foot, upscale home-accents store is a Pacific Heights landmark. The spacious store features dinnerware, lamps, pillows, candles, glassware, and unique gifts.

Fuller subsequently hired Glen, a former actor turned retail guru, to meet with her staff and push them to new heights in visual merchandising. Glen also inspired her to surprise her employees with an overnight trip to Las Vegas so they could collect ideas from Cirque du Soleil's magical performance.

The magic appears to be working: Fillamento is posting double-digit sales increases and expects sales to hit $5 million this year.

"For 16 years, I've kept a customer's point of view," said Fuller. "The store is crispy clean, we have fresh flowers—it feels good, and it smells good."

Fuller, who does all the buying for the store, is one of thousands of small retailers who rely on Glen's advice and zany ideas to get them out of a rut. Glen, who is a popular keynoter at retailing conferences, insists that smart retailers will not just survive, but flourish, if they set themselves apart from the competition.

Small retailers, Glen says, must create "cheap miracles" to attract shoppers. For example, Glen suggests spending $40 to tie a big ribbon around your store. Put a pig in the window, or a bull in your china shop—as one New Zealand shop owner did. Do whatever you can to create a stir.

"The retail business is routine and can kill you one day at a time," said Glen, author of *It's Not My Department* (Berkeley; $14.95).

"Retailers have to face the competition instead of whining about it," he said. "Most are waiting for Wal-Mart to kill them."

Surprisingly, he urges small retailers to sell merchandise at regular price.

"Don't discount it and don't give it away," he said. "You have the unique ability to provide real customer service and keep a customer for life."

Glen contends that retailing is splitting into two distinct camps: giants like Home Depot and small specialty shops where "it's clear what the store sells." He predicts department stores, going bankrupt and merging at record speed, will eventually disappear. He also predicts Americans will soon be buying groceries and other staples via the Internet, while shopping in small boutiques for luxury items like collectibles.

"We are becoming a nation of rich and poor," he said. "Wal-Mart and Tiffany's were the two most successful stores in 1996."

Small retailers also have to face the fact that people are spending less time shopping. A recent shopping-center industry survey revealed that five years ago Americans spent 142 hours a year out shopping; in 1997 it fell to about 40 hours, Glen said.

"And last Christmas, people bought entertainment and adventure, not things that came in boxes," said Glen.

He warns small retailers to pay attention to customers when they step into the store. "If you don't want someone to interrupt your discussion of who's in the hospital, why not just shut down?"

Glen urges retailers to "love your business again."

"Retailing is a terrible job—nobody is in it for the hours or the money," said Glen. "Concentrate on what you do best and go in that direction—furiously."

Put Your Company Name on Everything

WHEN THEY FIRST STARTED MAKING "RACK Sacks," plastic bag holders, Exhifix Inc. didn't have much money to spend on advertising. That's why they printed their company name and phone number on every product. As a result, it became very easy for people to order bag refills.

It sounds so simple, but too many small companies neglect to put their name and phone number on their products.

One small Arizona company that *didn't* forget benefited with a big reorder. After just one sniff, I fell in love with Tessita's Secret, a deliciously fragrant lotion made with cactus extracts and aloe vera. Before I used the last dab, I called the number on the bottom of the jar and ordered more—lots more.

It makes sense to use your product as its own billboard. If people liked it enough to buy it once, you want them to know how to buy it again.

Free Up Your Sales Force

"MOST SALESPEOPLE LOVE TO SELL BUT HATE TO generate their own leads," said the co-owner of a financial planning firm in Orlando. "So we invest a great deal of time and money for telemarketers to generate leads. This frees the salesmen to do what they love to do the most—sell."

Freeing people to do their best work is good not only for morale, but it's also good for your bottom line. For the aggressive salesperson who hates to dig up leads, a good telemarketer using a current database can provide dozens of leads in a few hours. They can eliminate the chilling aspect of cold calling. This two-pronged approach works best when you are selling a high-end product or service, like financial products.

Busy, well-to-do people don't like to be interrupted in the middle of dinner by an unsolicited phone call. But they will make an appointment to speak to someone if they are interested in what you are offering.

Supporting your sales force with telemarketers and appropriate communications technology makes good financial sense.

In many cases, top sellers not only hate to generate their own leads, but they also dislike and resist filling out the after-sale paperwork. And when they mess it up, it creates more problems down the line. So consider hiring an assistant to take care of the after-sale details. This expedites orders and frees the salesperson to move on to the next sale.

Smart managers know exactly what everyone's time is worth and provide all the necessary tools and support to maximize productivity.

Hire a Mascot or a Celebrity

GREAT 91 IDEA

BRENNY WATT DIDN'T SET OUT TO FIND A mascot for her small store, but she ended up with a famous cat.

"One day, a stray cat wandered in, and we started to feed her," said Watt. "Then one night, we accidentally locked her inside the store. The next morning, when we came in, she was asleep in the window. She became an instant celebrity."

People, especially kids, loved Lily the cat and came to visit her weekly. To raise money for a local school, Watt decided to host a "Tea with Lily." It was easy to promote the event, because by then most people knew who Lily was.

Today Watt works as a freelance writer, but she remembers her famous cat mascot. "She was wonderful PR for us and loved her unusual home."

But remember, if it's appropriate to have a pet in your business, make sure it's a people-loving one.

Some small businesses are fortunate enough to hook up with a celebrity spokesperson. David Blumenthal, president of Lion Brand Yarn Co. in Manhattan, learned that *Wheel of*

Fortune hostess Vanna White loved to crochet. He immediately contacted her agent to ask if she would be interested in becoming the spokesperson for their line of yarns and crochet patterns.

They made a deal that has endured through the years.

White worked with Lion on two illustrated pattern books on crocheting. She consistently wows customers when she appears at trade shows on behalf of Lion Brand Yarns, demonstrating her crocheting skills and emceeing a fashion show of crocheted creations.

It doesn't make sense in every single case, but many small businesses benefit enormously from a mascot or spokesperson. It's a component of your marketing plan that can help establish a brand identity for your product and stir up a good deal of excitement, too.

Publish a Newsletter

IN THIS AGE OF INSTANT INFORMATION ON THE Internet, it's comforting to know that there is still a vibrant market for old-fashioned printed newsletters. There are about 5,000 subscription newsletters and thousands more for free, according to industry experts. Newsletters cover everything from fly fishing and school violence to gluten-free baking.

With the right mailing list, exclusive or proprietary information, and a few thousand dollars, just about anyone who can write or hire writers can start one. But making money is another story.

"You have to pick a field as narrow as you can get it, but leave it wide enough so there's an audience to promote to," advises Howard Penn Hudson, president of the Newsletter Clearinghouse in Rhinebeck, New York. "Too often, people who start newsletters find they haven't narrowed the field enough."

Health care, technology, and celebrity newsletters are hot right now, according to Penn Hudson, who publishes the *Newsletter on Newsletters,* founded in 1964.

"Rush Limbaugh has a newsletter and attracts an audience with his name," said Penn Hudson, adding that "newsletters ride the trends."

"When we had an energy crisis in this country, there were two dozen newsletters about energy," he said. "When the crisis ended, so did those newsletters." Newsletter publishers charge whatever the market will bear, especially if they are offering specialized or competitive information. One of the most expensive newsletters, the *Daily Report for Executives,* costs $5,811 a year, according to Penn Hudson.

You might think that the Internet and all that free information is hurting newsletter sales. Not so, says Patty Wysocki, executive director of the Newsletter Publishers Association. She said newsletter publishers aren't too worried about competition from the Internet. Some even use it to market to potential subscribers.

Hundreds of kitchen-table publishers and major corporations belong to Wysocki's trade association, which offers several helpful publications.

Beverly Davis, editor and publisher of *Supermodel News,* started writing and publishing her newsletter after pursuing a modeling career.

"I started with $4 and a lot of faith," said Davis, who still works as a secretary to support herself. *Supermodel News* has grown from two to eight pages since she began publishing it in November 1995. Her 2,600 subscribers in 21 states are eager for her modeling tips, lists of model search contests, pageants, fashion events, fitness tips, and stories about top models.

Most of her subscribers are teenage girls, but one of her oldest subscribers is Mrs. Senior America 1995.

"Money from subscribers pays for postage and printing," said Davis. "I work on this about three hours a day, seven days a week."

Davis attributes much of her success to mentions of her newsletter in the press. "With no advertising budget, I rely totally on free publicity," said Davis.

Supermodel News, the Newsletter for Aspiring Models, costs $12 for an annual subscription.

Before you publish a newsletter, read *Starting and Run-*

ning a Successful Newsletter or Magazine, by Cheryl Woodard (Nolo Press; $24.95). Her book is a lively, easy-to-read bible for publishers. Meanwhile, here are Woodard's tips for first-time newsletter publishers:

- Concentrate on markets you know very well.
- Listen to your readers and advertisers and develop products responsive to their needs.
- Get help from experienced people.
- Adopt good ideas whenever you find them. Study what's already working for other publishers by collecting media kits or renewal promotion letters and use their best ideas.
- Befriend influential people and ask them to support your publication.
- Study your results and be prepared for change.
- Aim for readers who have continuing information needs.
- Look for ancillary profit opportunities. Many publications make most of their profits from special reports, books, and videos.
- Look hard before you leap into print. Don't go forward until you've got a long-term plan you can live with.

If you want to check out the competition before launching a newsletter, Penn Hudson publishes a newsletter directory and a variety of other relevant publications. For information, write to The Newsletter Clearinghouse, P.O. Box 311, Rhinebeck, NY 12572.

For additional information, write to Newsletter Publishers Association, 1401 Wilson Blvd., #207, Arlington, VA 22209.

Market Your Service-Based Business

SELLING YOUR EXPERTISE—AN INTANGIBLE product—requires a much different approach from selling a product that sits on the shelf.

Some professionals, like doctors and lawyers, are limited by professional ethics to marketing their services through specific channels. If you're a consultant, you have more options.

One of the best ways to market your services is to position

yourself as an expert in your field. This can be accomplished by writing articles for trade publications or general interest magazines. Or by being quoted in newspapers and making guest appearances on local or national television. You may think that you could never attract a reporter's attention, but it's easier than you think.

The first step is to find out who covers your particular industry at the local newspaper, radio, or television stations. Once you have a name, draft a short introductory letter. Explain that you are available to provide background information, resources, or a quote on a particular subject.

Attach your business card or company brochure. Wait about a week and then make a follow-up telephone call. Be sure to find out when that particular news organization is on deadline, and never call when the reporters and editors are closing an issue.

Reporters are continually looking for new sources. So be patient and continue to send along clippings and items of interest. You'll find that once you get quoted in one newspaper or magazine, other reporters will begin to call you and recognize your name.

Another good way to attract new clients is to offer them a sample of your expertise. Invite current and potential clients to a breakfast or seminar. Give a brief presentation to whet everyone's appetite and then take questions from the audience. Ask your existing clients to each invite one or two guests to expand your circle of contacts.

In fact, your current clients are always your best source of new business. You should be spending at least one hour a day soliciting referrals, sending out letters or brochures, or making cold calls. Ask your client if they can refer you to one or two potential leads. At first they may be reluctant, but if you give them time to think about it, they should be able to come up with at least one or two names for you.

Many consultants find that the cross-marketing approach is another effort that works very well. Team up with a consultant whose business compliments yours—but is not competitive. You might share mailing lists or produce a joint brochure.

Although the "Pig in the Window" approach is not the answer for most consultants *(see Great Idea 88)*, there are plenty of other similarly creative and effective ways to market your services.

Host an Open House

ONE OF THE BEST WAYS TO ACQUAINT CUSTOMERS and clients with your business is to arrange a visit. An open house combines a social event with the ability to do some serious one-to-one marketing. Of course, if you deal with toxic chemicals or dangerous machinery, you'll have to decide whether or not an open house is the best way to boost awareness of your business.

One of my strongest and fondest memories is touring the Pepperidge Farm bakery on a third-grade field trip. I'll never forget the sweet, yeasty smell of the bakery and the freshly baked loaf of white bread they gave each of us to take home. Since that tour, I've been a loyal Pepperidge Farm customer.

Hershey Foods is another big company that invites thousands of visitors into their factories each year. That open-door policy has turned Hershey, Pennsylvania, into a major American tourist mecca.

Even if you rarely have visitors, think of the things people would like to learn about your business. Few people ever have the opportunity to see how things are made and packaged.

You may not have a glitzy office, but even a small-scale open house can draw people to your door. Derek Selbo, program manager of The Knowledge Shop in Casselberry, Florida, decided to host just such an event to introduce people to the vast array of personal enrichment and professional classes they offered.

"We had a free 'Try the Internet Day,'" said Selbo.

Visitors were encouraged to ask questions and surf the Net. They sent electronic-mail messages to friends and learned how to find and navigate Web sites.

"This event brought us a surge of enrollment in our computer and social classes," said Selbo.

No matter how boring you think your business is, remember that people love to have a behind-the-scenes look at anything. Consider the incredible popularity of Universal Studios and the tours that visitors line up for.

Here are some tips for planning an open house:

- Create a small committee to make the preparations, but involve everyone you can in the planning process.
- Figure out whether you'll be giving organized tours or letting people wander around on their own.
- Plan a menu of easy-to-eat finger foods and beverages. Restrict eating to the lunchroom or other suitable areas.
- Pick a time of year when your business looks its best, and weather won't jeopardize attendance.
- Send out invitations at least a month in advance. Ask people to RSVP via telephone or fax. Schedule the event to last two or three hours—no more.
- Ask all your employees to tidy up their areas and find places to lock up any valuables about a week before the open house.
- Hand out a flyer with basic information about your company along with an event agenda.
- Assign plenty of staffers to act as hosts and guides.
- Buy flowers or plants to decorate the reception area.
- Rest up the night before so you are ready to meet and greet people.
- Try to have fun.

Promote with Prepaid Phone Cards

PHONE CARDS HAVE BEEN POPULAR IN EUROPE since the mid-1980s when British Telecom first issued them to make it easier for customers to call home from Germany and France.

But they took another 10 years to take hold in America.

"We in the United States are not used to prepaying for anything," said Aric March, president of MHA Communications in Highland Park, Illinois.

March, who previously worked in the telecommunications industry, decided to make his niche in phone cards. His company helps clients make a marketing splash with the popular plastic cards, which are now fast becoming collector's items. In addition to giving away free calls to clients as an incentive to use your services, you can also use the phone cards to take a market survey or to provide product information. For a survey, you send out the cards and ask recipients to call a toll-free 800 number. A menu-driven voice mail system asks a few short questions, and the answers are recorded. After completing the survey, customers can use the card to make free domestic or international telephone calls, depending on how you set it up.

A polling company provides help with the surveys, while MCI and Sprint provide the actual long-distance service, March said. The survey costs between $1,000 to $2,000 to conduct.

Even if a survey isn't for you, giving away phone cards as a promotion is very affordable. For example, a small company can buy 500 10-minute phone cards with their logo printed on the front and a recorded message for about $1,000, March said. You can send in your own artwork or pay his firm to design something appropriate.

"We can make a card with anything from five free minutes to three free hours," he said. Best of all, "there is a high perceived value of $5 to $10 for a 15-minute card, although it costs you much less."

March said the greatest thing about phone cards is that they are so easy to use.

He made me a terrific "Jane Applegate" calling card which people love.

For more information on marketing with phone cards, call MHA Communications at (847) 831-5091.

Generate Publicity in Your Community

MOST SMALL-BUSINESS OWNERS, AT LEAST AT first, can't afford to hire a professional public relations person. But you don't need expensive consultants to attract publicity. You can do it yourself if you do something noteworthy—and then focus on obtaining coverage by your hometown newspaper, radio, or television station.

One of the best ways to generate publicity for your company is to do something positive for the community.

Here are some suggestions:

- Sponsor a 5 or 10k run for your favorite charity. Print up tee-shirts for the runners. Put your company logo on everything from the paper cups to the signs along the route.
- Collect food or clothing for the homeless or a local shelter. Offer your customers a discount for participating in your charity campaign.
- Create a scholarship. Even $500 will make a big difference to a disadvantaged student.
- Create a photo opportunity by planting trees along a street, in front of your store, or in an unattractive part of town.
- Help organize a community flower or vegetable garden. If you have a parcel of land, offer it for public use.
- Organize a merchants' neighborhood crime-watch program. Hold the meeting in your store or office.
- Offer your conference room for community meetings. Then every time the paper lists the meeting schedule, your company is mentioned.
- Join with a local paint store to sponsor a graffiti paint-out campaign. Organize volunteers from several community groups to increase involvement.

Community service is perfect for local television news coverage, especially if you hold it on a slow weekend day. Community projects will merit at least a paragraph or two in your local newspaper. Local television stations are always looking for visual stories involving people doing something positive.

Once you decide on a project, draft a press release two weeks before the event. A couple of days before, send it on company letterhead to the editors of local newspapers and the assignment editors of the nearby television and radio stations.

Follow up a few days later with a brief phone call. Try not to call any news organization in the late afternoon. Most morning newspapers are edited and put together from 3 PM to 7 PM. Your best chance of reaching an editor is between

10:30 AM and noon. Take advantage of voice mail and leave a detailed message. You want to be persistent without being a pest. Television stations are more apt to assign stories on a daily basis.

But realize that if something more newsworthy happens, such as a crime, fire, or flood, your neighborhood cleanup story will never make it on the 11 o'clock news.

You might also invite your local station or paper to participate in your event as a media sponsor. This takes more time and effort, but it may be worth it. Be sure to involve all your employees and their families in your event.

Purge Your Database Regularly

CREATING A DATABASE IS A GREAT IDEA, BUT IF it's filled with out-of-date information it becomes a waste of time and money. Every year a certain percentage of people in your database will move or change jobs, so it's important to update the information at least once a year.

A simple, cost-effective way to clean up your database is to send out a perforated, two-part postcard with a simple offer or discount and a space for people to update their information. Be sure to print or stamp "address correction requested" on each card, so the post office will return the undeliverable cards. You'll pay the postage, but it's worth it.

Prepaying the postage on the return card will definitely increase your response rate. When the undelivered cards come back, spend time deleting the names. Then update the responses as they are returned.

Doing this kind of purge is important, particularly if you are planning to do a major mailing. A clean, accurate list will increase your chances of a strong response rate to any offer you send out.

Know the Difference between Marketing, Advertising, and PR

TOO MANY ENTREPRENEURS USE A SCATTERSHOT approach to marketing, advertising, and public relations, primarily because they don't understand the subtle differences between the three. But knowing which to use, and when, can save you time, aggravation, and money.

Marketing encompasses a broad range of tactics from calling customers on the telephone to attending a trade show and passing out hundreds of pens with your company name printed on them.

One of the most cost-effective ways to market your business is to put your name on something useful. Jack Nadel, a veteran marketing expert and author of *There's No Business Like Your Business,* specialized for several decades in developing promotion items for big and small companies.

Nadel says the key to putting your company name or logo on something is to make sure it's something people will keep around for a long time.

Nadel said tee-shirts, baseball caps, jackets, and fanny packs have been the most popular company giveaways in the 1990s.

Marketing involves a myriad of creative promotional campaigns—all designed specifically to push your products.

Advertising means paying for space in a newspaper or magazine, or buying time on a radio station, television station, or Web site.

But before you spend a dollar on advertising, figure out exactly what your competition is doing, establish specific goals, and set a budget, advises Andy Narraway, general manager of Odiorne Wilde Narraway Groome, an upstart advertising agency based in San Francisco.

Narraway's colleagues at the 22-person shop like to call themselves "advertising terrorists" because they charge clients flat fees and present simple sketches rather than elaborate campaigns to land new business. He has this advice for entrepreneurs: "Determine whether you really need an agency, or whether a graphic designer, freelance artist, or copywriter will suffice," said Narraway. "Very often, if you want to run an ad in a local newspaper, radio, or TV station, the sales reps will help you develop your own ad."

If you decide that you need an agency, meet with at least three agencies before you sign with one. Ask for client references and check them carefully before the first meeting.

Public relations, often the most misunderstood form of promoting your business, involves getting your company or products mentioned in the media.

"An effective PR program can bring valuable recognition to your company, because if your product or service is mentioned in the media, it's an implied third-party endorsement," explains Christine Soderbergh, an independent PR consultant based in Pacific Palisades, California.

The key difference between advertising and PR is that with an ad, you own the time and space and can basically say anything you want to; with PR, you can't control the timing, placement, or editorial process.

"Don't ever ask a reporter if you can see the copy before it appears," advises Soderbergh. "And if you call an editor or reporter cold, always ask if they can talk, or if they are on a deadline."

She said it's critical to match the story pitch to the reporter, by following their work and making sure they cover the industry you're involved with.

With public relations, you'll pay a PR person to pitch the story, but won't pay for the story to appear. Independent PR professionals usually charge by the hour or project. Larger PR agencies require a retainer, usually $3,000 to $5,000 a month or more, plus all expenses. One critical issue: There are never any guarantees that your story will be published or broadcast, no matter how hard you or your PR firm may try.

Start a Dog-Related Business

"THERE ARE 59 MILLION DOGS IN THE country—now, there's a market!" says Renee Dougherty, founder of Pet Occasions in Landenberg, Pennsylvania.

Dougherty, who has five dogs, created a birthday party kit for dogs, which sells for $19.99 in pet stores.

"People love their animals and love to celebrate birthdays and other holidays with their pets," she said. "I didn't know the birthdays of two of my dogs, so I just assigned them the birthdays of my best friends."

Her party kit includes doggie hats, loot bags, and a mix for a doggie birthday cake, developed with help from a vet.

"If it takes off, we'll start doing other holidays," said Dougherty.

She borrowed money from her family and savings to get going. She invested quite a bit in colorful business cards and stickers featuring a dog in a birthday hat. Her next step: getting the party kit into pet catalogs.

For more information on Pet Occasions, call (888) DOGLOVR.

Have a Theater Party

WHEN ERIC SCHWAB MOVED HIS ADVERTISING specialties company out of his home, he needed a novel way to entice clients to visit the new location. "We partnered with the Civic Theatre of Central Florida for the opening night preview of *Forever Plaid,*" said Schwab.

He used the plaid theme for everything: the invitations, balloons, and decorations for the Open House/Theater Party. It was scheduled on a Wednesday night for maximum attendance.

While Schwab threw a lively party and raised his company profile, the theater benefited by having an audience full of happy patrons on preview night and by selling ticket subscriptions.

And according to Schwab, not only did lots of people discover his new location, but they also couldn't stop talking about his creative marketing approach.

Invite Associates to a Trade Show

IF EXHIBITING AT OR ATTENDING A TRADE SHOW is on your calendar this year, turn it into a valuable business trip by inviting business associates to meet you there.

As soon as you sign up to attend, go through your database or business card file and make a list of everyone you know who lives within 100 miles of the show. Then invite them to meet you there. You might want to pay their registration fee, if it isn't too exorbitant.

Meeting business associates or prospective customers at a show has several advantages. It saves you an extra trip to their city, for one thing, and if you are exhibiting at the show, they'll see your products and services displayed in a high-profile place. They'll also be able to meet your key staff members and see how you interact with the public. If you can wangle an invitation to speak at a seminar or take part in a panel discussion, better yet. Invite your associates to hear your presentation. What better way to position yourself as a leader in your industry?

If you aren't exhibiting, it's still great to walk the aisles with a colleague and check out the competition. You can brainstorm as you collect information and brochures; you can introduce your guest to others in your industry.

If several clients accept your invitation to meet, turn it into a party by planning a breakfast or dinner to entertain them. Be sure to make reservations early because the city may be overrun with convention attendees.

Attending a trade show, with or without guests, is an essential activity for successful entrepreneurs—it helps you to keep up with the competition and connect with other industry movers and shakers.

Really *Work* a Trade Show

HEDY RATNER, CO-DIRECTOR OF THE WOMEN'S Business Development Center (WBDC) in Chicago, really knows how to work a room. A consummate networker, she has devoted years to helping women entrepreneurs start and grow their businesses.

Here are some of her great tips for making the most of a trip to a trade show:

- Remember why you registered. Ask yourself whether your goal is to find new suppliers or study the competition. "Decide on your goals and be certain to accomplish them before the day ends," said Ratner.
- Dress for success and comfort. "First impressions are important, so dress businesslike," Ratner advises. "You'll meet potential clients, resource people, and perhaps a banker who may one day consider your loan."

  Wear comfortable shoes because you will walk for miles. Ratner also suggests wearing a jacket or dress with two pockets. Put your business cards in one and collect cards in the other.
- Plan your schedule and decide which exhibits you want to visit ahead of time.
- Carry a small tape recorder or notebook to take notes on things you need to follow up on.
- Note seminars, workshops, and other events that occur during the conference. Be sure to attend the key ones.
- Bring lots of business cards and brochures. Don't forget travelers' checks, credit cards, and personal identification.
- Be flexible and leave time for spontaneous meetings with important people. "Trust your instincts to lead you to mentors, models, key contacts, and resources."
- Don't forget to follow up. Sort out the material and cards you collected soon after returning to the office. Record new contacts and remind yourself to take action.

For information on WBDC programs and services, call (312) 853-3477.

Know Your Competition

ENTREPRENEURS LOVE TO BRAG ABOUT BEATING their competition, but the truth is, most small-business owners are too buried in work to keep track of what their competition is up to. But operating your business in a vacuum can lead to its demise.

"You have to start with the basic premise that you need to know what your competition is doing," said Guy Kawasaki, author of *How to Drive Your Competition Crazy*. "So you need to shut off the fax machine and the phone, close the door, and really figure out what you stand for, what your competition is doing, and what they stand for."

Kawasaki, who rejoined Apple Computer after a break to help with their marketing strategy, says there's no excuse not to know everything about your competitors. You can sit at your computer with a modem to find out just about anything by tapping into database services such as Nexis or Dialog or by searching for free information through the Internet and the World Wide Web.

After you fully understand what your competition is doing, figure out where they are vulnerable, he says.

"You're looking for chinks in the armor," said Kawasaki. "You're looking for pockets of dissatisfied customers that you can steal from them."

Kawasaki's book is filled with exercises, tips, strategies, and interviews with people ranging from hotel magnate Steve Wynn to bull-riding champion Charles Sampson.

Meanwhile, here are some ways to check out your competition without spending a lot of money:

- **Go shopping.** If you make or sell a retail product, get out to stores at least once a week. One of the most successful entrepreneurs I know, Kathy Taggares, president and founder of K.T.'s Kitchens, prowls supermarket aisles checking out her private label frozen pizzas and Bob's Big Boy salad dressings. She needs to know where her products are placed, but also wants to see what she's up against.

  To learn more about her great company, *see Great Idea 121*.

- **Subscribe to your industry's trade magazine or newslet-**

ter. Read it from cover to cover when it arrives. I see too many piles of unread trade journals sitting in entrepreneurs' offices. Smart reporters are paid to collect valuable information for you—so read it.

- **Attend a professional meeting at least once a month.** Getting out of your office and meeting competitors face to face is invaluable. People love to brag about what they are doing and often say too much about their upcoming products or services.
- **Go to a major trade show at least once a year.** You may associate trade shows with exhaustion and aching feet, but walking the aisles at an industry show can revitalize or even save your business. Sign up for the seminars, go to the receptions, and talk to everyone you can. Eavesdrop shamelessly during cocktail hour. People talk louder when they are drunk.
- **Relentlessly survey your customers.** Ask them what they like and don't like about doing business with you. Ask the right questions. and they will tell you quite a bit about your company—and your competition. Postcard surveys are cheap, quick, and effective. Send out a stamped postcard with multiple choice or fill-in-the-blank questions. Offer a discount or incentive if they return the card promptly.
- **Assign a staff member to order your competitor's materials**—brochures, catalogs, annual reports, price lists, and so on. Read their ads carefully. Check out their pricing and return policies. Know all you can about the enemy.
- **Order something from your competitor every few months.** This is the best way to find out exactly how they treat their customers. If what they sell is too big or too expensive to buy, visit their showroom.
- **Organize an informal focus group** at your church or synagogue, or with members of an organization. Ask what they like and don't like about your products and your competition's. It may not be scientific, but market research is more art than science.
- **Talk to industry analysts or consultants who serve your industry.** Buy stock in your competitor's firm so you can receive annual reports and other information.

- **Read newspapers and magazines.** Clip out articles relating to your business or assign a staff member to do it on a weekly basis.

  For more about assigning a personal information officer to help keep you informed, see Great Idea 159.

Tap the Growing Hispanic Market

WHEN 10,000 HISPANIC BUSINESS PEOPLE MET in Denver last year for the U.S. Hispanic Chamber of Commerce's 17th annual convention, big and small companies across the country took notice. The huge gathering marked a time when Hispanics began entering the entrepreneurial market in record numbers—and their buying clout began attracting attention from mainstream businesses.

Now is the time to figure out ways to partner with Hispanic-owned businesses or create new marketing campaigns aimed at appealing to Hispanic consumers.

The number of Hispanic-owned businesses is growing along with the Hispanic population, which experts say has tripled during the past 30 years. By the year 2000, the Hispanic population will increase from the current 26 million to 31 million. Hispanics are also growing more affluent, with nearly one million Hispanic households reporting incomes of $50,000 or more, according to the *Hispanic Marketing Handbook.*

"Hispanic entrepreneurs are also increasing in numbers and changing the face of small business," said José Niño, president and CEO of the Washington, D.C.–based Hispanic Chamber of Commerce.

For example, in 1995 1.5 million Hispanic-owned businesses generated an estimated $200 billion in annual revenues. By the year 2000 the number of Hispanic-owned businesses is expected to grow to two million, with collective revenues of $500 billion.

The U.S. Hispanic Chamber, which represents more than 250 chambers in the United States and Puerto Rico, works to foster business growth, but it has also gone on record against congressional efforts to dismantle federal affirmative action programs.

"Hispanic entrepreneurs are growing in numbers, but continue to face numerous obstacles," said Niño. "Eliminating affirmative action programs would have a devastating effect on the Hispanic business community."

Despite the chamber's call for maintaining federal affirmative action programs, many established Hispanic entrepreneurs say they never sought out any special treatment or participated in government programs aimed at providing a leg up.

"We were raised without any idea that we were different or separate from others," said Philip Villalpando, owner of Cam's Shutters in City of Industry, California. "It's not like today, where everyone is waving a flag."

One way to test sales in the Hispanic market is to partner with a Hispanic company. Another way is to repackage your products to appeal to Hispanic tastes. But this takes an investment and careful planning.

Savvy business owners wanting to expand sales into the Hispanic market should always rely on a competent translator. One major Los Angeles Bank had egg on its face a few years ago when a loan campaign aimed at Spanish-speaking clients went awry. When translated into Spanish, the ad copy said something like: "Remember when your mom used to steal money from you? Think of us as your mom."

A mortified bank representative told the ad agency that the newspaper advertising salesperson had messed up the translation. So never trust your translations to an amateur. Be sure to hire someone familiar with the local dialects and who knows the cultural nuances of the specific Latin community you want to reach. Mexicans speak a different type of Spanish and have a far different culture than Salvadoreans or Panamanians, so make sure you carefully target the market.

Many ad agencies now specialize in ethnic marketing, so find a good one in your area and try test-marketing one product or service.

For more information, contact the U.S. Hispanic Chamber of Commerce at (800) USHCC-86.

Become Politically Active

DAL LAMAGNA HAS SOLD MILLIONS OF TWEEZERS. In 1996 he was busy selling himself.

"Hi, I'm Dal LaMagna, and I'm running for Congress," LaMagna said, handing out campaign flyers to sunbathers on Tobay Beach on Long Island. "LaMagna—rhymes with lasagna."

LaMagna, a successful entrepreneur, spent about $200,000 of his own money to unsuccessfully run against Rep. Peter King (R-NY). King represents the affluent 3rd District, which includes Nassau County.

"Tweezerman," as LaMagna is known, said he decided to run for office when the federal government shut down during 1995's acrimonious budget debate.

"I was outraged," he said. "Hey, you're running the largest business in the world. You don't shut it down when you're trying to figure out your budget. Period."

The man his wife Marissa describes as "the Italian Woody Allen" ran on a simple platform: He wants to protect the environment, create jobs, and keep kids off the streets. He's personally against abortion but believes in giving women the right to choose what's right for their families.

Looking back, LaMagna said running for public office represents the American Dream. His grandfather emigrated from Italy and shined shoes for a living. His father worked as a longshoreman and fireman to support his wife and five children.

"I care about humanity, I care about social causes, and I care about giving back," he said.

He never got to Washington, but he doesn't regret his attempt. In fact, he might try to run again. Persistence is what eventually propelled his business to success.

The company he founded 15 years ago with $500 worth of tweezers has been growing at a rate of 30 percent a year.

Although LaMagna has an MBA from Harvard University, he's been involved in a string of entrepreneurial mishaps. In 1969, when teenagers were into free love and rock concerts, he tried turning drive-in movie theaters into discotheques—

a major flop. Other ill-fated ventures included selling lasagna pans and producing a coming-of-age movie that tanked.

In 1982, discouraged and nearly broke, he moved back home and took a $6-an-hour job at an electronics firm. It was there he first saw needlepoint tweezers used to pick up tiny electronic parts.

He remembered how difficult it was to remove a splinter he got when sunbathing nude on a roof. So he bought a few industrial tweezers, repackaged them, and tried selling them to lumberyards for splinter removal. A beauty supply shop owner suggested he find a tweezer that would really pluck eyebrows.

Tweezerman tweezers were a big hit, despite selling for $12 when regular tweezers sold for $3. In 1994 *Time* magazine named his tweezers one of the best products of the year, and sales exploded.

Today Tweezerman markets 60 grooming products and expects to sell close to two million tweezers. The company offers a lifetime guarantee and repairs about 200 tweezers a week free of charge. He expects revenues of the privately held firm to exceed $10 million in 1997.

Make Your 800 Line Ring

AN 800 LINE IS A GREAT WAY TO BOOST SALES, especially if you serve customers in a wide area.

Here are five tips from Pacific Bell with easy ways to generate more calls:

1 **Put your 800 number on every document customers see.** A printer can put your number on existing stationery at a fraction of the cost of reprinting. Or order a brightly colored sticker or stamp that says, "We're pleased to announce a new convenience for customers. Now you can call us toll-free at . . ."

Make sure the sticker or stamp goes on all printed materials—business cards, brochures, catalogs, fax cover sheets, billing statements, and packing materials. Add your 800 number to building or vehicle signs.

2 **Notify your customers of your 800 number.** Call key accounts personally, and follow up with a letter and updated

Rolodex card. If you time your calls to match your customers' purchasing cycle, you also might end up with a reorder.

If you have too many customers to call personally, send brightly colored postcards featuring the 800 number. If postage is a concern, include the card in another mailing, such as a monthly statement or newsletter. Add your 800 number to voice mail greetings. The message could say, "Please make a note of our new toll-free 800 number . . . "

Say the number twice slowly so listeners have time to write it down.

3 **Add your 800 number to print, radio, and television ads as soon as possible.** Make a list of all the directories you're in and find out the closing date for next year's ads. Then have your yellow page ads redesigned to feature your 800 number prominently. Do this now so it's ready when you need it.

4 **Notify all your employees.** They should know who's authorized to use the 800 number and what you want it to accomplish. Your employees can't help you if they don't know the game plan.

5 **Appoint someone as 800 project manager.** Tell them their charter is to make the number start ringing today. Challenge them to be creative but cost-conscious. Consider giving awards or bonuses for increasing 800 calls. Ask for weekly progress reports. Get every employee involved in publicizing the number by sponsoring a contest to see who can come up with the most creative way to use it to get new business. Then award prizes for ideas you use.

Hold an Off-Season Sale

MARTHA MORGAN, OWNER OF MORGAN'S, A women's boutique in Wilmington, Delaware, was broadsided a few years ago when she found out May's department stores was closing two of its downtown Wilmington locations in February. That meant they would offer steep discounts on winter merchandise—direct competition for her small, upscale apparel shop.

Morgan's competitive response strategy was twofold: First, she discounted her winter clothes before Christmas to beat the May's sales, and then she moved right into spring.

In the midst of 1996's brutal winter, she filled her store with fresh flowers and her windows and racks with colorful spring fashions.

She also reached out to the community by organizing a used clothing drive for the local YWCA.

"I encouraged my customers to clean out their closets and make a donation," she said. In return, they received a tax deduction and gift certificates for her merchandise.

"With tax receipts in one hand and my gift certificates in the other, customers felt justified in coming in to shop for their spring wardrobe," she said.

The marketing tactic boosted sales, and Morgan's flourished during that May's store-closing sales.

Publicize Your Food Business

GREAT 108 IDEA

THE POWER OF THE PRESS IS GREATER THAN ever when it comes to driving sales of offbeat specialty foods. Positive publicity sends foodies to the phones to feed their passion for unique food and condiments. With Americans buying an estimated $400 million worth of specialty foods a year by mail, according to the National Association for the Specialty Food Trade in New York City, the field is a gold mine for smaller companies.

A short blurb by a noted food writer, critic, or author often means the difference between success and failure for a start-up. For example, a mention in Florence Fabricant's *New York Times* "Food Notes" column in June 1994 launched Matt and Ted Lee's boiled-peanuts-by-mail business.

"The reason I went for the boiled peanuts was because it was a regional specialty," said Fabricant. "Before the Lee Brothers offered it, boiled peanuts were not available outside a certain region in the South." Fabricant said she receives about two dozen pitches a week from small, specialty food product makers hoping for her attention.

The Lee brothers say they owe their success to journalists like Fabricant. "Publicity is crucial," said Ted Lee. "We've never paid a dime for advertising."

When Ted and Wendy Eidson, founders of Mo Hotta Mo Betta, started their San Luis Obispo, California–based spicy food catalog, they relied on the public library to find the addresses of 200 regional newspapers. They often attach samples of spicy wasabi chips to tempt the palates of the food editors. The Eidsons said 30 to 40 percent of the editors they send information to use it in some way.

The free publicity and growing passion for super-hot foods has fueled sales. The company, with sales under $5 million, is growing at 200 percent a year, Ted Eidson said.

"The catalog business has flattened out at this point," said Eidson. "Now we're diversifying. Last year we started making our own sauces and tamale kits."

Twenty years ago, an article in Delta Airline's *Sky* magazine drew customers from all over the country to Nathalie Dupree's tiny Georgia restaurant. Dupree, an Atlanta-based author and cooking expert, has produced more than 300 shows for PBS and The Food Network. "When an article is written about me, I may get calls for up to five years afterwards," said Dupree, author of *Quick Meals for Busy Days* and many other books.

Dupree, Fabricant, and other food writers and experts realize the impact their coverage can have on a small business. "I don't mention anyone unless I think they can handle the business," Dupree said.

Although success in the specialty food business is largely publicity driven, proper marketing etiquette can be tricky. For instance, don't call to follow up after you send a press release to a food editor. "Assume it got here—and don't pester the editor," said Patricia Mack, food editor for *The Record* in Hackensack, New Jersey. Mack said every week her staff receives hundreds of press releases and about half end up in the trash.

The National Association for the Specialty Food Trade (NASFT) is a membership organization for the industry. They publish a magazine and a mail-order directory and sponsor fancy food shows twice a year.

For information, write to NASFT, 120 Wall St., New York, NY 10005.

Become a Government Contractor

THE FEDERAL GOVERNMENT IS THE WORLD'S LARGEST purchaser of goods and services, so why not get in line? The Federal Marketplace should be your first stop. To get started, check out **www.fedmarket.com**. The site is rich with information on how to market and sell products and services to Uncle Sam.

The SBA's Office of Government Contracting and Minority Enterprise Development are also there to help.

For example, the OGC/MED administers the Prime Contracting Program, which initiates set-asides for government contracts, so small companies get their share of the work. It also helps small companies work their way through the procurement process.

The Subcontracting Assistance Program ensures that small businesses receive the information needed on available work. The recently revised 8(a) Program helps minority-owned small businesses receive federal contracts on a sole-source or limited competition basis.

The Procurement Automated Service System (PASS) is a database with more than 200,000 small companies interested in doing business with the government. PASS provides companies with a quick way to find small suppliers.

Most government agencies have a special department dedicated to helping you do business with them. Ask for the Office of Small and Disadvantaged Business at any federal agency.

The Business Service Centers (BSCs) are located in 12 major cities. These centers offer counseling, bid lists from vendors, and information of all types. Check with your local SBA office for locations.

The Department of Defense, a big spender, operates Procurement Technical Assistance Centers that provide information to businesses interested in selling goods and services to the government. The Air Force also has a special small-business program. It conducts two-day seminars around the country to explain the process through the Air Force Business Education Team.

Susan Gilbert, owner of Interactive Elements, a New York City–based mass-transit consulting firm, landed her first government contract after going through procurement training. She later won the Women's Business Enterprise Award from the Federal Transit Administrator. She continues to work with state, federal, and local transit agencies.

The DOD's Mentor-Protégé Program has matched more than 200 small companies with successful government contractors. The experienced company teaches the ropes to the newcomers.

The SBA also has special programs for veterans, including the Transition Assistance Program (TAP), which helps military personnel start small businesses. The Veteran's Entrepreneurial Training Program is one that provides training to vets.

These are just *some* of the programs established to hook up small business with government contracts: Do some research and see which might apply to your company.

Consider Multilevel Marketing

FRAN LYLES-HARPER WAS A PHYSICIST WORKING on the Space Shuttle's main engines when she attended an in-home art party in 1991. "The art really touched my soul," said Lyles-Harper. "It wasn't only beautiful, but it was quality art at affordable prices."

Lyles-Harper didn't buy anything that night, but agreed to host a showing in her home a few weeks later. Impressed by everyone's response to the art, she signed up with Personal Preference Inc. to sell art on a part-time basis.

For a few years, she kept her day job, selling lithographs and paintings on the side. When she earned $65,000 one year, she decided it was time to sign on full-time.

Janet Madori, founder of Personal Preference Inc., has created a very fair and lucrative business concept, which you could apply to other kinds of products with the right price points and wide consumer appeal. Instead of charging thousands of dollars upfront for the business opportunity, she sets people up in business for under $300 by giving them about $3,000 worth of art and providing extensive training. Art consultants earn a minimum commission of 20 percent, plus monthly bonuses. If you sign up at least two new consultants, your commission and bonuses can reach 34 percent, she said.

In 1997 Madori had 1,500 people selling PPI artwork. PPI's top seller, featuring a beautiful young black woman sitting at a piano, is based on a photograph of a model. "Rhapsody of Dreams" sells for $140, and about 1,200 copies a month fly out the door. Most pieces sell for under $250, custom framed.

PPI, based in a 52,000-square-foot headquarters building in Bolingbrook, Illinois, recently added a 35,000-square-foot extension to keep up with the growth. The 100-employee company sells more than 200,000 pieces a year and generated $22 million in sales in 1997.

Madori continues to grow the company through incentives. In 1997 she set up a program to reward managers who built $1 million sales divisions. She put 20 percent of her company stock in a trust to give to her top salespeople.

"They have ownership and a lifetime override on sales, even after they leave the business."

Personal obstacles in her own life seem to have fueled her desire to help others. She suffered from narcolepsy as a teenager and had to cope with a mentally ill mother who was absent for long periods of time. She never went to college, but proved that anyone can pursue the American Dream.

"About 35 percent of my people are making over $100,000 a year," she said. "One of my best people was a presser in a dry cleaners. There she made $23,000 a year. Last year, at 50 years old, she made over $118,000, has a new company Cadillac, and bought a new home. To see where she's come from and where she's going thrills me. When I heard she used her $20,000 bonus as a down payment on a house, I cried like a baby."

Personal Preference Inc. is located at 800 Remington Blvd., Bolingbrook, IL 60440. Its motto: "A painting is created by the blending of beautiful oils. A company is created by the blending of beautiful people."

Send Pizza to Potential Clients

EVERYBODY LOVES PIZZA. IT'S NOT JUST HOT, gooey, and delicious—it's also a business opportunity. You probably never thought of pizza as a powerful business tool, but it is.

Scott Jackson, founder of the Jackson Design Group in Orlando, Florida, has used pizza as an ice-breaker for many years. He sends potential clients a fresh pizza right before lunchtime. "If you walk into an office with pizza, people are going to smell it and get to the right person, no matter what."

Jackson's pizzas are delivered in a custom-printed box with one slice missing. In the open space it says: "For a larger slice of your market, call Jackson Design Group."

Recipients also find short client-success stories printed under the other slices. Jackson's printer now provides the boxes at no charge because he's getting so much new business from Jackson.

The best news: Jackson said that of the companies he's sent pizza to, about half have signed up with his agency.

A couple of other food ideas: try sending a pair of chocolate shoes or cowboy boots in a box with a note: "I'm trying to get my foot in the door."

A meeting planner from Orlando once sent out the invitation to a baseball-themed fund-raiser on Cracker Jack boxes. It cost 55 cents to mail each box, and they had record-breaking attendance.

Contribute to a Nonprofit Organization

THEY MAKE AN ODD COUPLE, BUT BRIAN MARKS, the Jewish president of an ethnic hair-care company in New Rochelle, New York, and Kathryn Hall, the African-American director of the Sacramento-based Birthing Project USA, found a wonderful way to help each other.

Hall's 10-year-old program, which matches at-risk pregnant women with "sister/friends" who offer moral support and other services, was going broke. "I asked God for help to stabilize the project and keep it going," recalled Hall. "Then out of the clear blue sky came Brian."

"Brian" is Brian Marks, an entrepreneur with a philanthropic bent. Marks serves as president of A.P. Products Ltd., a $30 million-a-year hair-care products company.

"We were looking for a national cause-related partner," said Marks.

By supporting the Birthing Project, Marks said he solidified his relationship with his mostly African-American customers. He said this type of direct involvement with a suitable nonprofit group can help any small business boost its sales and generate goodwill.

A.P., which stands for Africa Pride, is a small, feisty player in the $1 billion ethnic hair- and skin-care products market. The company, with about 100 mostly African-American employees, manufactures products exclusively for black skin and hair.

Since its founding 19 years ago, the company has made a point of strongly supporting community causes.

Marks, a father of two, was in the audience a few years ago when Hall received an award from *Essence* magazine. He said he was touched by the Birthing Project's efforts to help mothers deliver healthy, full-term babies.

After learning of Hall's financial problems, he sent a personal check for $25,000 to keep the Sacramento clinic from closing. Next, he pledged $150,000 over a two-year period to revitalize the program, which has helped more than 5,000 babies in 40 locations across the country.

Although he can't measure exactly how his generosity boosts sales, Marks said supporting community causes also boosts employee morale. Many A.P. employees serve as volunteers in local Birthing Project programs.

Being successful enough to give thousands to charity never crossed Marks's mind when he started in business 15 years ago. His first product, sold with a partner whose father owned a health food store, was called "Indian Hemp."

Although the store sold all kinds of herbs in bulk, one of the biggest sellers was Indian hemp, a Brazilian plant that people brewed into a hair tonic.

Marks and his friend began packaging and selling Indian Hemp to health food stores in ethnic neighborhoods from New York to Baltimore.

"We delivered the product displays in the trunk of our car," said Marks.

Soon, major distributors were calling them for products. Today A.P. has several product lines distributed in several major drug and discount chains. "Allways Natural" products were followed by the "African Pride" and "Ginseng Miracle" lines.

Although Brian Marks keeps a high profile, he says some people are still surprised to learn that the president of a successful ethnic products company is a Jewish guy from Brooklyn.

In 1993 Marks made national headlines when he sued a small black-owned hair-care products company for infringing on his trademarked "African Pride" brand. The suit, which was eventually dropped, prompted activist Rev. Al Sharpton to call for a boycott of A.P. products. Marks countered the criticism by stepping up his advertising in major black magazines and admitting the suit was a mistake.

Hall said she was very aware of the trademark flap when Marks contacted her and offered to rescue the Birthing Project.

"I was very concerned about it," said Hall. "I was a little hesitant to work with him, but now I don't have any problem at all. I just truly love and respect him."

A.P. takes full advantage of its relationship with Hall's group. It uses Birthing Project events to distribute some of the 10 million samples it gives out each year.

Samples are also handed out at book fairs A.P. sponsors with Black Books Galore. Proceeds from book fairs in Washington, D.C., Chicago, Los Angeles, and New York are earmarked for the Birthing Project.

Marks says the relationship with Hall and the Birthing Project is reciprocal.

"When Kathryn spoke at one of our national sales meetings, there were a lot of tears in people's eyes," said Marks.

Although he has a soft spot for babies, Marks is a savvy business owner. He invested $1 million in a state-of-the-art computer system and telecommunications software. Thirty sales reps track product placement and inventory via hand-held computers.

Marks, who admits he doesn't use a computer, runs the company from a deskless office overlooking downtown New Rochelle. He's been approached by venture capitalists and others seeking to grow the company, but so far he's turned them away. He's expanding A.P. exports to Canada, the Caribbean, and Africa.

To contact Birthing Project USA call (916) 558-4812 or write to 1810 "S" St., Sacramento, CA 95814.

How to create a relationship with a nonprofit group

- Find a group that supports a cause compatible with your views and your company's mission.
- Investigate the organization fully to make sure they make good use of contributions.
- Explore ways the organization can help your business and vice versa.

Get Certified as a Minority Supplier

MARGUERITE THOMPSON BROWNE, DIRECTOR OF special projects for San Francisco–based Washington Sportswear Inc., was among the 4,000 people attending the National Minority Supplier Development Council's (NSMDC) 25th annual conference in New York City in October 1997.

"This conference gives you access," said Thompson Browne, whose sportswear company is a certified minority-owned business. Although its products have to stand on their own merit, being certified has opened doors for the apparel firm, which has 140 employees and annual sales of about $5 million.

During the busy trade show, Thompson Browne made a promising contact with members of the Pequot Indian tribe, which owns the Foxwoods Casino in Connecticut.

Thompson Browne's company, which already makes clothes for Sears and Target, is leveraging its minority status to close more deals. She is now hoping to sell a new line of casual clothing to the Pequots.

Last year, minority-owned businesses like Washington Sportswear sold about $30 billion worth of goods and services to major corporations, according to the Manhattan-based NMSDC. That $30 billion represents about 4 percent of total corporate purchases. The national council serves as a matchmaker—working closely with 43 regional supplier councils to match up 15,000 certified minority business owners with 3,500 corporations.

There are local, state, and federal programs that certify minority-owned businesses. A good place to start collecting information is by writing to the NMSDC.

Although the NMSDC said that making personal contacts is critical to landing a contract with a big firm, most big U.S. companies are actively seeking to do business with minority firms in order to meet various government and corporate goals. They also see the economic advantage of catering to minority consumers.

"The buying power of minority groups is $900 billion a

year, and that is a huge opportunity we have to pay attention to," said John Edwardson, president and chief executive officer of United Airlines.

Edwardson said he encourages all United suppliers to seek out and do business with minority-owned firms whenever possible.

Small minority-owned companies also provide a variety of new products to large companies. For example, James Preston, chairman and CEO of Avon Products Inc., said H.K. Enterprises, a small New Jersey firm, developed "Undeniable," one of Avon's best-selling fragrances in the early 1990s.

"We see minority business development today as an investment in our own future," said Preston. He said Avon contracts with 400 minority-owned suppliers, accounting for 12 percent of the cosmetic company's annual purchases. The 12 percent is about three times the national average for corporate purchases from minority suppliers.

One reason Avon is so committed to minority-owned firms is because Avon products, sold by independent representatives, are extremely popular among women of color and their families. Preston said his minority suppliers also provide Avon with insight into the marketplace.

Dealing with minority-owned companies makes good economic sense for any company. Census data indicates that by the year 2050 two of every five Americans will be of minority descent.

The U.S. Small Business Administration and the Commerce Department's Minority Business Development Agency have programs for minority business owners. Minority Enterprise Development Week is celebrated in November every year.

For more information, contact the NMSDC at 15 W. 39th St., 9th floor, New York, NY 10018. You can also try the SBA and your local Commerce Department office.

CHAPTER 4

Developing and Launching Products

THE AMERICAN DREAM OF BECOMING WILDLY successful with a new product or service turns into a nightmare for far too many entrepreneurs—not because their idea is bad, but because they lack a coherent development plan.

Too many business owners consider the launch of a product an event rather than a long, carefully orchestrated process. Saving or borrowing enough money to design and manufacture a prototype of your product is just a baby step along the way to success.

Thousands of entrepreneurs working in back bedrooms, garages, incubators, and industrial parks get through the exciting initial stages of product development, but few manage to get any further before running out of money. Most end up wasting thousands of dollars on products that really should have made it, but didn't, for a variety of reasons.

Based on interviews with hundreds of entrepreneurs, I see that many make the same fatal mistake—they fail to take the time to determine whether or not a market truly exists for their product. In the euphoria of the moment, entrepreneurs are blinded to the reality that many others are launching similar products at the same time. They fail to check out the competition and make sure a niche exists.

Luck and timing also play a huge role in the success of a new product. Who could have predicted that Beanie Babies would become a fad or that kids would spend millions on electronic "pets" from Japan?

You might be reading this and thinking that only big companies with deep pockets can launch products, but in fact many more products are dreamed up by small, innovative companies.

Think about Netscape and the small company that perfected Java software. Think about Liquid Audio, a tiny company revolutionizing the way people buy music over the Internet.

In this chapter, you'll meet a young composer who invented Magnetic Poetry for his own refrigerator, and Frieda Caplan, a Los Angeles woman who brought kiwis to American dinner tables by pioneering the exotic-produce industry. They both started with nothing and ended up with millions.

Sometimes, to succeed, it takes a mixture of novel products and great marketing skills. Check out how Avi Sivan made millions selling the same products through many different channels in Great Idea 122.

The desire to make millions with a new idea keeps the entrepreneurial spirit alive. Through the years, I've interviewed an incredible array of people trying to sell everything from paper toilet-seat covers to kids' soap that smells like bubble gum. With thousands of zany ideas floating around out there, it's no wonder the U.S. Patent and Trademark Office is overburdened with applications, and small inventors are lining up to audition for a time slot on QVC and the Home Shopping Channel.

In this chapter, you'll also learn how to create a working model, license your product, and how two North Dakota women who loved an obscure form of embroidery turned their hobby into a thriving business. You'll meet two women from New Jersey who fell in love with a special type of Italian pottery and ended up importing it for use in gardens and greenhouses across the country.

This batch of great ideas will help you develop a realistic strategy to get your product in shape, out the door, and onto store shelves.

Create a Fad

PEOPLE USED TO STAND IN FRONT OF DAVE KAPELL'S refrigerator for hours, even when they weren't hungry. They were mesmerized by his collection of handmade magnetized words—-an idea that evolved into a major 1990s fad: the Magnetic Poetry kit.

Kapell, a songwriter and cab driver, made the first kit as a way to combat writer's block. He started giving them away to friends.

"Instead of bringing wine to a party, I'd bring the magnetic poetry kits," said Kapell.

He began selling kits at craft fairs and to local retailers. When sales took off, he had 30 people making kits in their homes. He worked 90 hours a week getting the company off the ground.

So far he's sold more than one million kits. Kapell said he knew he had hit the big time when Magnetic Poetry appeared on Jerry Seinfeld's TV apartment refrigerator.

Seinfeld is the perfect customer for the $20 kit. Kapell said his target market is educated, affluent gift-buyers. He sells his kits in museum gift shops and through upscale catalogs. In 1996 sales were about $5 million—not bad for a company that started in 1993 with no sales.

Kapell, who has 50 employees, said he would discourage entrepreneurs from trying too hard to protect their products.

His kits aren't patented, but they are trademarked and copyrighted.

"Little guys should get out there quick and sell the hell out of it," said Kapell. "Don't worry about legal protection—people are paralyzed by it. It costs a lot of bucks to patent something, and it's not important."

He said rushing your product to market is more important than getting bogged down in legalities.

"The big boys aren't going to pay attention or try to compete until you sell millions."

The company also makes other magnetic poetry items, including lunch boxes and coffee mugs with coffee-related magnetic words.

Import Something New and Different

A NEW INDUSTRY WAS SPAWNED 35 YEARS AGO BY a homely fruit then known as the Chinese gooseberry. The palm-sized brown fuzzballs, now called "kiwis," were the basis for Frieda Caplan's wildly successful exotic-produce business.

Before Frieda Caplan began importing fruit and vegetables from around the world, apples, bananas, and oranges were about the only fruits Americans ate. You can now thank Caplan for alfalfa sprouts, macadamia nuts, sugar snap peas, spaghetti squash, and dried blueberries. Frieda's Inc. also popularized the succulent oversized mushrooms called portobellos that sell for up to $7.50 a pound.

Frieda's Inc. brokers about 450 fruits and vegetables from growers around the world. Their number-one seller is jicama, a crunchy root that can be eaten raw with a splash of lime juice.

Caplan began introducing Americans to tastebud-tingling delicacies in 1962. She started the company with a $10,000 bank loan—an enormous amount of money at that time. The vegetable growers welcomed her willingness to distribute their novel produce and helped finance some of her initial start-up costs.

A few years ago, daughters Karen Caplan and Jackie Caplan-Wiggins joined their mother's business, which has about 40 employees. In 1997 the privately held firm posted $20 million in sales. Karen, who joined the family firm in 1986, said she pushed to expand the business. Today about 30 percent of their produce is imported, with the rest grown around the United States.

Importing produce doesn't seem like such a revolutionary concept, but 20 years ago, most grocery store produce departments featured fewer than 100 items. Today the average market stocks about 300—thanks in part to Frieda Caplan's vision.

In addition to offering offbeat fruits and vegetables, Frieda's Inc. has set itself apart from the competition through its use of a distinctive signature purple color in packaging and advertising.

"When mom started, she needed a sign for the store," recalled Karen Caplan. "She had to have it up over the weekend. The guy who painted the sign only had one color in his truck—lavender. Now it's our trademarked purple. It becomes like subliminal advertising. When I show up places, people say things like, 'I really expected to see you in a purple suit.'"

Caplan's employees sign their letters with purple ink. The produce boxes are purple, too.

"A unique design is okay," said Caplan. "But color is especially effective."

Caplan said when she learned to relinquish control and hire more salespeople, sales quickly increased.

The company has also moved into the modern age with a Web site that receives hundred of hits a day. Visit it at: **www.friedas.com**; e-mail is mailorder@friedas.com; or call (800) 241-1771.

Turn Your Hobby into a Successful Business

TURNING YOUR PASSION INTO PROFITS IS EASY when you figure out a way to transform your interests into a business venture. The secret of success is finding others who share your pastime and parlaying their need for supplies into a money-making concept.

For the past 21 years, Roz Watnemo and Sue Meier have leveraged their passion for an obscure form of Norwegian embroidery into a successful retail and mail-order business. In fact, Nordic Needle, based in Fargo, North Dakota, is one of the state's most successful small exporters, honored by state officials and the U.S. Small Business Administration.

College friends Roz and Sue were unlikely entrepreneurs. Looking for something to do, they signed up for a class in Hardanger embroidery, a traditional form of white thread-on-white fabric stitchery used to decorate tablecloths and aprons. Embroidery is especially popular in the Plains states, where winters are long and cold, and people are looking for something to do to pass the time productively.

Tired of driving to Minnesota or sending away to Norway for sewing supplies, the partners decided to sell a few Hardanger necessities. They opened a 400-square-foot shop in downtown Fargo, thinking they'd sell a few yards of fabric to friends.

When they were literally bursting at the seams, about 13 years later, they built a 9,000-square-foot building in a suburban shopping plaza.

The bright, cozy store is a stitcher's paradise. Nearly every inch of floor and wall space is filled with yards of fabric, miles of thread, patterns, samplers, and sewing kits. Multicolored threads from around the world create a fantasy of rainbows.

Their passion for stitchery is shared by many. Nordic Needle boasts 1,500 wholesale customers in 18 countries. About 53,000 retail customers buy supplies, mostly via mail order. About 45 percent of Nordic Needle's sales are generated by their catalogs, 35 percent from wholesale outlets, and 20 percent from their one bustling retail store in Fargo.

Twenty full- and part-time employees—all women who stitch—fill wholesale and retail orders from every continent except Antarctica. In 1994 and 1995 Nordic Needle Corp. was named the state's leading exporter. Sales in 1997 approached $2 million.

Meier and Watnemo, who started their business before they started their families, now have five children between them. They divide the work and profits equally. Their husbands also help out when they can.

Meier, the more outgoing partner, focuses on the wholesale, marketing, and advertising side of the business. She designed their Web site and encourages online sales promotions. Watnemo, the quiet partner, designs all the new patterns and keeps close track of the retail operation.

"I know a lot of partnerships don't go well, but Roz and I are very different from each other, and we complement each other," said Meier.

Watnemo, the Hardanger expert, produces about a dozen new pattern books each year. She designs by hand, but relies on a software program to create the actual pattern graphs.

Here are some tips for turning your hobby into a small business:

- Find out if others who share your passion are looking for equipment or supplies in your town.
- Attend a hobby or craft trade show to check out the trends and competition.
- Subscribe to all the magazines and newsletters that cover your hobby.
- Find out if their subscription list is offered for "rent" and do a test mailing.
- Start small. Offer a few products to test the market.
- Check with your accountant about the IRS rules on tax deductions for hobbies versus businesses.

Form a Strategic Alliance

WHAT HAPPENS WHEN A GOURMET ICE CREAM maker moves into a market near a gourmet cookie baker? A super-delicious handmade ice cream sandwich.

The informal deal between Ronnybrook Farm and Eleni's Cookies came about after the two small businesses moved into the Chelsea Market in the heart of Manhattan.

Eleni Gianopulos, who has been baking cookies professionally for the past four years, began her venture with her own cash and her grandmother's oatmeal cookie recipe. She now sells a variety of delicious cookies in her cheerful, brick-walled bakery.

"When I rented my space in the Chelsea Market, these three big farmers kept coming into the store," Gianopulos recalled. "They wanted to try some cookies."

The "big farmers"—Ronny, Sid, and Rick Osofsky—own Ronnybrook Dairy, which makes homemade-style ice cream from their own milk and cream. Their family-owned dairy farm started making dairy products seven years ago. The farm, located near Rhinebeck, New York, has about a dozen employees. Another six work at the Chelsea Market location in Manhattan.

After munching on Eleni's delicious oatmeal cookies, the dairy guys decided they would taste great wrapped around a chunk of Ronnybrook ice cream. Eleni agreed.

Soon the neighbors began experimenting—mixing other ice cream and fresh-baked cookies.

"The day we opened, we had ginger snaps with ice cream and chocolate cookies with ice cream," said Ronny Osofsky. "We squashed the cookies together. One good idea led to other ideas. But the best idea was that we could all work together."

The ice cream sandwich, selling for $1.50, is available at Chelsea Market, at the Farmer's Market at 14th Street, and on vendor carts in Central Park.

"I think this could really go places," said Ronny. "We might get a machine so the ice cream comes out in a stream on the cookie. This made-by-hand honey-ness is important, but you can do it a little more efficiently."

Become an Exclusive Importer

SOMETIMES BEING THE FIRST TO INTRODUCE A product to the United States is the best way to establish a successful small business. This was the case for Mara Siebert and Lenore Rice, two former high-powered Wall Street players who traded in their briefcases for a new life that includes a New Jersey warehouse full of handmade Italian terra-cotta pottery.

Mara Siebert was on the fast track as a mergers and acquisitions specialist at Chase Manhattan Bank, structuring big leveraged buyouts and hostile corporate takeovers during the 1980s.

Tax attorney Lenore Rice was also on Wall Street during the takeover mania. She was on a partnership track at Shearman & Stirling, a tony law firm. But tired of the rat race and lucky enough to have wealthy husbands, Siebert and Rice decided to quit their jobs to stay home with their young children.

Siebert spent her free time collecting ceramic art and remodeling her home and garden. Rice studied Italian. They became close friends after Rice rented an Italian villa in Tuscany and offered the Sieberts a chance to share the house and expenses with them.

Bored one day when their husbands left to play tennis, the two women wandered into the tiny village of Impruneta to look around. They were immediately dazzled by the town's deep orangey-pink and white-tinged pottery. They began selecting pots to buy for their yards and dragged their husbands into the village to look at the merchandise.

When their husbands agreed the pots were beautiful and durable, they called customs brokers to figure out whether it was feasible to buy a pallet full of pots. Thinking if they couldn't sell them, they would keep them, they spent $3,000 on pots and another $1,000 to ship them by boat to New Jersey.

They began showing the pots and planters to landscape designers and upscale nurseries. It was an immediate hit, and the pottery, which retails from $35 for a small pot to $1,200 for a tree-sized planter, spawned a very successful business.

They invested $5,000 on a high-quality brochure and sold $20,000 during 1994, their first year in business. Sales reached $100,000 in 1995 and grew to close to a million in 1997.

That fateful vacation in the tiny village of Impruneta, Italy, about two hours south of Florence, inspired Siebert and Rice to open a company bearing their names. One big secret of their success was signing exclusive import agreements with four families, giving them the sole U.S. distributorship for Impruneta pottery.

They are so worried about others wooing their suppliers, they won't reveal the last names of their potters. They visit the artists once or twice a year to place more orders and monitor quality.

The business, which began with about $50,000 in inventory, began in the upstairs bedroom of Seibert's home. They now have two employees to help fill orders, which arrive by mail and phone.

They store and ship the pottery from a warehouse in

Short Hills, New Jersey, minimizing breakage with a special foam-making system that protects the pottery.

The company still appears to have a lock on the market.

In 1997 the Biltmore Estate in North Carolina called Siebert and Rice to buy replicas of the original pots purchased by the Vanderbilts in Impruneta.

Floral and interior designers are also contacting the company to have American-style pots made in Italy by Siebert and Rice's artisans.

Be a Location Contrarian

MOST YOUNG, COCKY RESTAURATEURS WOULD rather die than open their cool restaurant in a suburban shopping mall. But Gary Leff, founder of Stir Crazy Enterprises, took a different spin. He headed for the suburbs, and it paid off.

"The first inclination is to open up in the city, and one of the main reasons is ego," said Leff. "The city is sexy, you can see your friends, and the 'big boys' are in the city."

But in downtown Chicago, restaurant owners face fierce competition, high rent, and safety concerns.

"It's also hard to get above the 'noise' in the city," said Leff, who worked as a management consultant for five years before writing a business plan and raising about $5 million from investors to open his restaurant chain. His primary investor is a partner in JMB Realty, a major Chicago-based real-estate firm.

The first three Stir Crazy restaurants are located in upscale shopping malls. Each one cost about $1.3 million to open, and they made money from the start. The first two units generated $5.5 million in revenues the first year. Knowing that many new restaurants fail, Leff spent years doing market research before launching his venture.

"I felt there was a huge gap in the marketplace to do something fresh and fun with Asian food," said Leff.

Stir Crazy isn't cheap; lunch averages $9 to $10 a meal, and dinner is $14. At Stir Crazy restaurants, patrons select a variety of vegetables, meats, and sauces to be stir-fried while they watch. They can also order dishes from an extensive menu.

"Creating your own stir fry is the biggest hit," said Leff, who works with chefs and food consultants to dream up new dishes. "People love it because it gives them a lot of choice; plus, it's fresh, healthful, and fun."

"Contrary to what people say, the suburbs are sophisticated. People who live in the suburbs used to live in the city," said Leff. "We can also stand out because we are going to compete against the restaurant chains that people are sick of."

Leff is now looking to expand and is searching for locations in Boston; Washington, D.C.; Denver, and several areas in Florida.

"We are looking for the best real-estate opportunities," said Leff, adding that it took a year to find the right site for the first Stir Crazy location.

"My mission is to build a multistate chain," he said.

He doesn't envision being the next McDonald's or Red Lobster, but he would like to build 40 units in the next five years and 150 in ten.

"We will be a major player in Asian casual dining," he predicts. Leff's compensation and stake in the company are hinged to performance, so he hopes his predictions are right.

Build a Working Model

YOU MAY HAVE THE MOST BRILLIANT CONCEPT in the world, but raising money to manufacture and market your baby is almost impossible without a working model.

The problem is that too many entrepreneurs fall prey to invention scam artists who promise to introduce them to manufacturers, but often end up stealing their money.

Your challenge is finding a reputable product design firm that won't just perfect your prototype, but will also propose economic options to mass-produce it and bring it to market.

"People think that if they have a patent they are nine-tenths of the way there," said Henry Keck, who has been designing products since the 1950s. "When the inventor says it's 90 percent complete, we say there's 90 percent more to go."

Keck, cofounder of Keck-Craig Inc. in Pasadena, has many well-known product designs to his credit. He's most famous for designing the sleek metal-and-glass flip-top sugar dispenser sitting on millions of restaurant tables around the world.

"We want our products to be well styled and highly marketable," Keck said. He and his partner, Warren Haussler, rely on a staff of six engineers and model makers to design everything from portable eye washers to battery-operated pesticide sprayers. Their tidy model shop is a tinkerer's dream, filled with rows of lathes, presses, mills, and saws.

The veteran industrial designers say that too many inventors make the mistake of patenting their idea before they find out whether or not it can be mass-produced in a cost-effective way.

"People suffer by being stuck to their patents," Keck said. "You can add things to a patent or make changes while it's being processed, but once it's issued, that's it."

Although many big companies, such as Robertshaw Controls and Avery-Dennison, turn to Keck-Craig for design help, the firm serves small entrepreneurs as well.

Small design projects cost $5,000 to $10,000; big jobs can run into hundreds of thousands of dollars, according to Warren Haussler, president. The fees they charge depend upon the amount of time and work needed to design and build a model or prototype. They work with 10 to 20 clients at a time.

Jim Harris, who invented the Shrimp Pro shrimp deveiner, turned to Keck-Craig to bring his dream to reality. His machine, which is sold to restaurants around the world, can devein 60 shrimp a minute. It hit the market in 1995 with the help of a team at Keck-Craig.

"Engineers are an absolute necessity for an entrepreneur," said Harris. "I'm chief visionary officer. The best ideas come from people who are least capable of bringing them to fruition."

Harris said he worked Keck-Craig's model makers and engineers for four months, "yelling and screaming" throughout the process.

"You have to agree to disagree," he said. "That's the most important part of the process. Engineers have a mind-set, and sometimes you have to bring creativity to their mind-set."

Because the machine was so well designed and engineered, Harris said he could cut the retail price in half—from about $1,000 to $500.

Harris advises other entrepreneurs looking for engineers and model makers to ask people with similar but noncompetitive products where they had theirs designed.

"Check out their facilities and the company's résumé. Look at what they've done," he said.

He also cautions inventors to raise money to bring a product to market. This can come to between $150,000 and $300,000, depending on what you are trying to make, especially if you intend to patent your device as he did.

For information on patents, check the U.S. Patent and Trademark Office Web site: **www.uspto.gov**.

Serve the Market's High and Low Ends

ONE OF THE MOST SUCCESSFUL AND CREATIVE entrepreneurs I know built an incredibly lucrative frozen pizza manufacturing business by serving all ends of the pizza market with specific products.

A former potato saleswoman, Kathy Taggares cashed-in her condo, jewelry, and insurance policies in 1989 to buy a nearly defunct salad dressing factory from Marriott Corp. She named the company K.T.'s Kitchens. A few years later, she added pizza crust to her product line. She eventually added a full line of frozen pizza products. In 1997 she made a staggering 125 million pizzas.

With 1997 sales around $55 million, she's definitely doing something right. Taggares has mastered a full spectrum of approaches to marketing her products. This ability to tailor the same product to suit many customers applies to other businesses.

In her case, K.T.'s provides products for the low, middle, and high end of the pizza market by creating lines of different private-label products. The mix is about one-third high, middle, and low price points, Taggares said.

If you think "pizza is pizza," think again. At the low end of the market, she sells pizza in bulk to public schools and the military.

K.T.'s also produces a line of mid-priced pizzas for club stores like Sam's and Costco. At the high end, K.T.'s creates gourmet pizza for Wolfgang Puck. The company also produces its own "Healthy Gourmet" line sold in supermarkets across the country.

Because the ingredients for making any pizza are basically the same, with only the toppings changing, Taggares saves thousands of dollars by buying flour, spices, sauce, and toppings by the container load. The bustling factory, featuring one of the largest commercial freezers in southern California, has the largest refrigerated USDA processing room on the West Coast. K.T.'s runs several production lines at once; some workers are making big, low-cost pizzas for Costco, while across the way, others are carefully hand-stretching crusts for Wolfgang Puck.

"The biggest benefit of a diversified product mix is to spread my risk," said Taggares. "At first, I didn't have enough money to develop and market my own brand, so I got into food service, selling to schools and doing private label packing for others."

Maintaining multiple product lines has another strong advantage: "It helps even out the sales year-round," she explained. "During the summers, school business is down, but club store business is way up."

She's hoping her own brand will generate strong sales, but not scare away her long-standing customers.

"Now that we are more established, we are going out with our own brand, but we still need the sales volume from the other sides of the business," said Taggares.

I asked Taggares if her multiple product approach would work for other entrepreneurs.

"It depends on the flexibility of your product line," she said. "We can serve pretty much every segment of the market with the same type of equipment. It wouldn't work if you needed different equipment to make different products."

Launch New Products with a Media Blitz

GREAT 122 IDEA

AVI SIVAN, A FORMER ISRAELI COMMANDO AND stuntman, gives new meaning to the expression "media blitz."

Through an aggressive and expensive combination of magazine advertising, infomercials, and direct mail, Sivan has created a marketing machine for his personal care products sold under the "IGIA" brand. His company is called Tactica International.

"His simultaneous multimedia push is unusual," said John Kogler, founder of Jordan Whitney Inc., which monitors the billion-dollar-plus infomercial industry. "I think it's unique."

Kogler's Tustin, California–based firm publishes several direct response television reports and newsletters. In the fall of 1997, IGIA's hair removal system ranked among the top 10 on Jordan Whitney's list of top 15 direct response ads. IGIA's blemish remover ranked eleventh on the same list.

Kogler said Sivan takes advantage of the fact that the infomercial industry "has become a lot more dependent on retail to sell a variety of consumer products." Many consumers who are reluctant to give their credit card numbers over the phone may want a product they've seen demonstrated on TV, but prefer to buy it in a store.

"A product that gets into stores because of TV will sell six to 10 times as much in the retail stores as it does on TV," explained Kogler.

Although Tactica International Inc.'s intense marketing campaigns drive sales, they also created customer service problems, including late deliveries and slow refunds. Around Christmas in 1996, the Manhattan-based company fell way behind on deliveries, prompting consumers to file hundreds of complaints.

Sivan said every complaint was taken care of, and everyone whose "Active Air Advanced Beauty System" was delayed was sent $20 worth of face cream free as an apology.

"We looked at it as good trouble," said Sivan. "We were overwhelmed with orders for that product."

Sivan, an intense 34-year-old entrepreneur, said he learned how to market personal care products to women when he worked for EPI Products USA, the ill-fated Santa Monica–based company that grew to $200 million in sales before it filed for bankruptcy in 1990 amid lawsuits and other legal troubles. Epilady, a hair removal product invented on a kibbutz in Israel, was infamous for painfully removing hair, but it still sold by the thousands.

Sivan worked with and was once engaged to one of the Krok sisters, who ran the company with their father, South African businessman Solomon Krok.

Determined to learn from Epilady's mistakes, Sivan found a British inventor who developed a less painful tweezing method. The IGIA hair removal system sells for $120.

"It's a huge success in the department stores," said Orly Zoran, who worked with Sivan at EPI Products and handles sales and marketing for IGIA products.

Zoran, who specializes in launching and marketing new consumer products, said thousands of beauty magazine ads and huge TV budgets make Sivan's hair removal product a hit. Sales also skyrocketed after Sivan spent more than $2 million on slick ads inserted into a department store's monthly statements.

By the fall of 1997, Sivan said, he had sold 800,000 units with another 300,000 on back order. One retail industry expert credits Sivan with "rejuvenating the whole hair removal industry."

Privately held Tactica, with 1997 sales approaching $100 million, is managed by a small team of people working on the 74th floor of the Empire State Building. Moving his company into an American landmark is significant for Sivan, who grew up in a poor family in Israel. At nine, he started delivering laundry to earn money to pay for his own bar mitzvah.

At 14, he ran away from home and joined a kibbutz. He later served in the Israeli Army. In the early 1980s, he was the only survivor of a secret mission into Lebanon and spent six months in a hospital recovering from gunshot wounds.

After working for EPI Products and watching it grow, prosper, and collapse, Sivan said, "I knew there was a huge opportunity because the market for hair removal products is enormous."

Now his challenge is to not repeat EPI's mistakes.

"My name and credibility are very important to me," said Sivan, who works from 6 AM to 11 PM most days. Sivan says his entrepreneurial hero is Richard Branson, founder of Virgin Records and Virgin Airlines, who is expanding his empire into banks and soft drinks.

"We get 50 to 60 pitches a month," said Sivan. "We have a focus group to filter the products, but I make the final decisions."

Meanwhile, Sivan has these tips for anyone interested in following his aggressive marketing model:

- Develop a product that appeals to the masses. It has to be unique and not a "me, too" product.
- Find a product with markup of five times the wholesale price. If it costs you $20, you want to sell it for $100.
- Register copyrights and trademark your product to protect it from knock-offs.
- Encourage inventors to present you with new ideas.

Do a Deal with a Big Company

FOR A SMALL-BUSINESS OWNER, DOING A DEAL with a giant corporation is thrilling, intimidating, and scary. But the opportunities are out there. Big companies of all kinds are hungry for the nimble thinking and new products created by entrepreneurs.

The first challenge is making contact with someone at the big company who is interested in what you have to offer. Sometimes this takes weeks, but once in a while the big company finds you.

That's what happened to Santa Monica–based Roundhouse Products, which designs patented CD storage systems for itself and others. Four years ago, Roundhouse signed a lucrative licensing and design agreement with office products giant Avery Dennison.

Jon Williamson, senior product manager for new products at Avery, said he was in the process of designing a CD storage system when he found Roundhouse's products and said, "this is it."

"They bring a freshness that I can't always get in a larger company," said Williamson. "I'm constantly intrigued by their intelligence and how quickly they can get something to market."

The relationship, which ended in 1997, benefited both companies. When it was growing, Roundhouse benefited from Avery's tremendous retail distribution clout, while Avery took advantage of Roundhouse's design talents and speed in executing new ideas.

Neither company would disclose the exact financial details of the agreement, but both said it was positive for everyone involved.

"When Avery came to us, we had a good strong patent position and something exciting to offer," said Howard Sherman, Roundhouse's chief executive officer. Roundhouses's

Tips for dealing with large companies

- Find the right person to contact and be persistent until you reach them.
- Present the gist of your idea in a clear, concise manner.
- Be well prepared for your first meeting so you make a positive impression.
- Surround yourself with experienced advisers including your attorney and accountant.
- Be patient. Things take longer to be decided at big companies.

sales have been so strong, they no longer need Avery's help. Sherman joined Roundhouse to bring some management expertise to the founders, who have a strong background in design but little financial expertise.

Roundhouse, founded in 1989 as a design consultancy, produced its first products in 1991. It currently has 40 employees and annual sales in excess of $10 million.

"Two guys from Art Center in Pasadena basically invented and patented a system for storing CDs," said Sherman. The company's patented "Roladisc" system eliminates the need for the bulky plastic jewel cases by storing CDs in plastic sleeves. In fact, customers are encouraged to send back the plastic cases to Roundhouse for recycling.

Roundhouse also has a significant business relationship with a division of Sony to develop another line of customized CD storage products.

"We didn't care about their size," said Carl Walter, senior vice president of operations for Sony Signatures in San Francisco. "What was important to us was that we felt they were very creative. They had a very innovative product that we liked."

That joint venture agreement covered a line of CD storage cases featuring famous artists including Neil Diamond, Santana, Kiss, Janis Joplin, and Bob Dylan.

Roundhouse's Sherman said one challenge in dealing with a big company is not to appear too anxious or naive, even when you are so eager to do the deal. "It was very exciting for us when we first met with Avery," he said. "But we all had to wear our poker faces."

He said another big challenge is timing. People who work for big companies often can't believe how quickly a small company can turn something around. Although they had a letter of intent drafted in a few days, it took 10 months to sign a formal contract with Avery. Being patient and persistent are both important, Sherman said.

"You also need to persevere and be flexible as the players change within a corporation," Sherman advised.

Roundhouse's relationships with big companies have

been successful in more ways than just profits, Sherman said. One great advantage is that Avery's lawyers could help defend against any patent infringements. As the company moves forward and sales skyrocket, he's happy to have worked with major corporate partners.

Have Your Product Mandated for Use by an Official Group

IN 1988, MIAMI RADIO SALESMAN EDUARDO Barea read about a mandatory uniform policy about to be implemented in local public schools. That day a great idea took hold: He would get into the school uniform business.

This father of four founded Ibiley School Uniforms Inc. and immediately began pitching the benefits of uniforms to parents, kids, and teachers. He truly believes that wearing school uniforms reduces peer pressure and truancy and encourages better behavior. His fervent pitch to school board members worked: In the first year, he sold uniforms to 14 schools.

Barea, who was named the Small-Business Person of the Year from Florida in 1997, has sales of $6 million and 200 employees during the peak summer buying season.

His greatest challenge is still the seasonal nature of the business and being able to keep the cash flowing year-round. In 1994, at the suggestion of his banker, Barea applied for a $500,000 line of credit through the SBA's Greenline program and got it. He continues to grow his business by attending PTA meetings and lobbying for more schools to adopt the mandatory uniform policy.

Currently dozens of schools require students to wear uniforms, and Barea is providing a major percentage of them.

Up the coast, a New York firm is also benefiting from government mandates. Maurice King, founder of King Research Inc. in Brooklyn, pioneered a mandated product strategy in the late 1940s. King, who developed Barbicide, the bright-blue disinfectant for haircutters, traveled around the country with his younger brother, James, meeting with state health officials to extol the virtues of his sanitizing product.

"Sure enough, the state officials began to pass rules that there be a disinfectant [in barber shops] and in some cases, they said, 'Sure, Mr. King, but can you suggest a product?'" recalls Maurice's son, Ben King.

"'Why, yes!' my father replied. 'Barbicide! It's germicidal and fungicidal'—and Barbicide got written into a number of the rule books being created," says Ben King, who now serves as chief executive officer and president of the small family business.

As more and more states issued regulations requiring barbers to soak their barbering tools, Barbicide sales grew. Although the product is mentioned by name in only two state rule books, it still flourishes.

In 1997 sales were about $5 million. The company celebrated its 50th anniversary with a party at the Smithsonian Institution's National Museum of American History and presented the museum with a jar of Barbicide—and a donation. Maurice King, who died of a heart attack in 1988, would have gotten a big kick out of the ceremony, which included, of course, a barbershop quartet.

King's 25 employees make 20 different products, including talcs, hospital disinfectants, and creams. But bright, almost-neon blue Barbicide is still the flagship brand.

"My father's secret joke was that he had a rash condition on his scalp and whenever barbers pricked him, it hurt like the devil," says Ben King. "When he developed Barbicide, he decided to name it as such because it translated into 'kill the barber.' I don't think he ever put that into his advertising."

So think about a way to encourage an official government agency or organization to mandate that people buy your product or service. Then work hard to build your marketing strategy around the requirements.

Find a Need and Fill It

WHEN NELLIE MAY SUTTON WAS DIAGNOSED with Alzheimer's disease in 1985, her son Joseph began searching for a place where she could live safely and comfortably. After checking out nursing homes and elder care services, Sutton decided to rent a ranch-style house and hire a caregiver to take care of his mother. He then found four other Alzheimer's patients to fill the extra bedrooms, and a novel business concept was born.

"I opened my first home to care for my mother—no other reason," said Sutton, founder of Sutton Homes, based in Englewood, Colorado. Sutton sells franchises to entrepreneurs who want to operate homes for the elderly around the country. Serving America's aging is providing tremendous opportunities for savvy entrepreneurs like Sutton.

About 19 million Americans have a family member suffering from the progressive, degenerative disease that affects memory. Many Alzheimer's patients require round-the-clock attention and supervision. Smaller group homes are often more suitable for Alzheimer's patients, who find nursing homes, with their many activities and visitors, too hectic and confusing, according to Joe Sutton.

Gladys Thankachan, a Los Angeles gerontologist and hospital administrator, said small units of five to seven residents are more friendly and accommodating than large institutional facilities for people in the early stages of Alzheimer's. However, she said, independent "board and care" homes such as Sutton's can be difficult to regulate. Yet given the increasing geriatric population, she said, such homes are a step in the right direction, "if we can make sure the standard of care is appropriate."

Although anyone can apply for a license to operate a board and care facility in most states, Sutton teaches people how to operate the homes in a professional manner. Sutton has franchisees operating almost 50 Sutton Homes in the United States.

Potential Sutton Homes franchisees make an initial investment of $250,000 for the minimum of three homes, to $450,000 for a nine-home package. That amount covers leasing the homes, renovating them, and paying for the staff for about a year. Franchisees also pay Sutton a 7 percent royalty on revenues, plus a 1 percent marketing fee.

Once franchisees are up and running, several homes can generate profits into the six-figure range, according to David Coker, vice president of franchise development for Sutton Homes.

Sutton said he tries to balance business savvy with elder care. He insists the services be top-notch but affordable. Sutton Homes provide franchisees with a week of training in Colorado, plus several days in their hometowns. The company also encourages franchisees to hire professionals to staff and manage the homes.

Sutton realized there are thousands of Americans dealing with the same stress he faced in finding a safe place for his mother. For him, Sutton Homes filled a personal need and, at the same time, produced a real business opportunity.

For more information, contact Alzheimer's Association National Headquarters, 919 Michigan Avenue, Suite 1000, Chicago, IL 60611, (800) 272-3900; Sutton Homes at (303) 220-7989; or the U.S. Department on Aging Information line: (800) 222-2225.

Open Your Store in a Market

AMERICANS HAVE LOVED SHOPPING IN MARKETS since before there was America. The first farmer's market opened in Alexandria, Virginia, in the 1750s. Today the U.S. Department of Agriculture reports there are about 3,500 farmer's markets across the country. Thousands more flea markets and other ventures sell everything from junk jewelry to jam.

Opening your business in an established market setting has tremendous advantages. The rent and utilities are often more affordable than stand-alone retail space. Plus, the landlord takes on part of the responsibility for attracting customers through signage and advertising.

You can also find safety and encouragement in numbers.

You won't feel so alone when you can wander next door and visit with your neighboring merchant.

Before you run out and rent space, here are some tips:

- **Go shopping.** Visit all the markets in your area. Some are open every day; others open only on the weekends. You want to make sure your merchandise fits the clientele.
- **Check out the competition.** Make sure your product or service fills a need in that particular market. You don't want to be the fourth bakery in a market.
- **Speak with the other vendors.** Ask them how the landlord treats them and whether he or she keeps promises made to tenants.
- **Check out the appearance and maintenance.** Are the public areas and restrooms kept clean? Is there adequate and well-lit parking for customers? Are security guards provided by the management? How will you secure your space when the market is closed?
- **Ask to see the advertising materials or brochures put out by the landlord.** Be clear about the kind of advertising they pay for and whether there are any restrictions on doing your own advertising.
- **Find out how you will be charged for your space.** Some open-air markets charge by the running foot; other, more permanent markets tend to charge by the square foot. Make sure you understand exactly what you are paying for, including utilities. Will you need to buy liability insurance? Will you be paying a percentage of sales to the management?
- **Spend some time in the market to get a feel for the ambiance.** You will be spending many long hours in this place, so you want to be sure it feels right.

If you are ever in New York City, visit one of my favorites—the Chelsea Market. Built in an old Nabisco factory, it is one of the nicest markets I've ever wandered through. The architecture is unique and captures the feeling of the old stone factory. The stores sell everything from discount produce to gourmet baked goods. There's a florist, a fish market, and a basket store, among others. It's located at 9th Avenue at 15th Street. Check it out.

Turn Your Anger into Energy

CARMEN MUÑOZ KNOWS HOW TOUGH IT IS TO make it in a man's world. She's been in the automotive parts business for more than 35 years, starting out as the sole saleswoman for a small firm in the Detroit area. In 1984, when the owner's son took over the business, she was called into his office.

"He told me I was making too much money for a woman, especially 'a Mexican woman,'" recalls Muñoz. She was so stunned, she asked him to repeat what he said—slowly.

He did. She'll never forget Thursday, March 13, 1984, the life-changing day she quit her job.

The following Monday, she started her own company to compete with the misguided son. She's never looked back, although she did laugh a little when her former employer shut down 18 months after she left.

"Anger is a marvelous thing," said Muñoz. "You can use the energy to propel you to accomplish major feats."

Muñoz, winner of Avon's 1997 Women of Enterprise Award, became chairman of the board of GSC Industries Inc. in 1996, when her company was acquired by another automotive firm. Based in Detroit, with offices in Livonia and Indianapolis, GSC's 220 employees make precision parts for transmissions. Clearly, one would hope that it not take being insulted and harassed to motivate women (or men, for that matter) to excel in business, but—let's face it—sometimes it takes an extreme situation to move you toward a better future and to clarify the potential in front of you. Even anger can be used in a positive way, if you let it.

Set Up a Cart in a Mall

VETERAN SILVERSMITH KENT MCCUSTION USED to travel to about 50 craft shows a year, often driving hundreds of miles to shows around Illinois. In 1997 he cut back to six or seven shows, because the Colorado Silversmith's kiosk he opened in the Northwoods Mall in 1996 is doing so well.

So far, he's sold more than $100,000 worth of jewelry, with some silver buckles and necklaces selling for $500 each.

McCustion, who designs and produces his own jewelry in addition to selling Navajo, Zuni, and Hopi pieces, said he planned on operating the 20-by-8-foot kiosk just during the holiday shopping season. But business is so strong, he has no plans to leave the mall.

Colorful kiosks and carts featuring unique merchandise have become fixtures in American malls. The first were set up in Boston's Quincy Market in 1976 when local developers set out to rejuvenate the city's ailing downtown area.

Today, about 80 percent of America's 1,800 enclosed and regional shopping malls have so-called "temporary tenants," according to industry experts.

Kiosks and carts have tremendous benefits for small-business owners and mall operators: Entrepreneurs are able to display their wares in a prime, high foot-traffic setting with little investment; malls benefit from a wider variety of interesting merchandise and extra rent.

"The mall doesn't have to take a risk on a long-term lease," said Mark Schoifet, spokesman for the International Council of Shopping Centers. "For the retailer, there's access to a lot of customers that they would not otherwise have."

Major mall developers, such as the Indianapolis-based Simon De Bartolo Group, aggressively promote their temporary tenant program. Jim Allen, vice president of retail development, said the company's malls, which often have between 10 and 40 carts per mall, rely on carts to add color and variety, as well as to generate income. Allen said while some cart operators move in just to capitalize on the busy holiday gift-buying season, many more remain year-round.

Danny Vaswani, a longtime Simon De Bartolo mall tenant, said the secret of success is to offer something "the anchor stores are not offering."

He began selling perfume from his Cleopatra carts in two El Paso malls four years ago. Most of the European fragrances he sells from his carts are not available elsewhere in the mall, and some retail for as much as $100.

"By selling in shopping malls with this kind of arrangement, you can come in with a small investment," he said. Initially he paid $2,500 to get into the mall, not counting the cost of inventory. Now he pays $1,300 a month rent for every cart he operates.

"But rent for in-line stores can be four times the rent for carts or kiosks," said Vaswani, who has become a cart magnate. He now operates carts in four malls in five cities.

He's expanded beyond perfume to sell Dippin' Dots ice cream and tee-shirts. All together, he said, his carts generate annual sales of more than $1 million.

"The pushcarts used to act as incubators for a potential market," said Jennifer Ciotti, manager of specialty retail for Boston's Faneuil Hall. "Now the retailer is a professional specialty retailer who opens more and more carts. It's become reputable and very sophisticated."

Unlike the pushcarts of yesterday, today's carts feature phone lines, elaborate lighting, and computerized inventory systems. Vendors can accept credit cards and orders via computers, Ciotti said.

Minnesota's Mall of America is not only America's biggest mall, but it operates the largest specialty leasing program in the nation. There were about 100 temporary tenants in the mall in the fall of 1997.

"The temporary tenants are really the gems of the mall," said Theresa McFarland, spokeswoman for the mall.

Tips for making the move to a mall

- Visit malls in your area to check out the competition and foot-traffic.
- Meet with the specialty retail manager to discuss what merchandise they are looking for.
- If possible, work for someone else before you invest in your own cart.
- Speak to the other vendors to find out what life in a mall is really like.
- Make sure your cart is attractive, well lit, and functional.

Kathy Rusche, director of the mall's temporary leasing program, said they set very high standards for vendors. All temporary tenants must pay $1,500 in "key money," which pays for a store designer to design and build a cart with the right look.

"We want to make sure the curb appeal is there for the customers," said Rusche.

Temporary tenants can expect to pay a premium for space at a consumer wonderland like the Mall of America. Last year, 40 million shoppers visited the mall, which boasts an amusement park in one section.

Cart rental rates are $2,300 a month or 15 percent of monthly sales, whichever is greater, Rusche said.

Turn Your Passion into Profits

GEOFFREY BERLINER IS A TINKERER. HE BEGAN tinkering with old watches, pens, and lighters when he was at Harvard Divinity School in the late 1980s. "I like to bring things back to life," he explained.

As a student in Cambridge, he frequented a pipe and tobacco shop that had a collection of vintage pens and antiques in the back room. He began collecting old pens for around $25 each because he couldn't afford to buy old watches.

"Those pens warmed me up," said Berliner, who intended to be a college professor, but became a paralegal when he moved back to New York City.

In New York he began haunting flea markets and antique stores, buying and repairing pens, some more than 100 years old.

"I began machining some of my own parts and finding parts from old junker pens," he said. "I was still collecting and working out of my apartment."

His fame as a "pen doctor" grew. He began writing articles on pen repair for *Pen World* magazine and became a director of the Pen Collectors of America. "I've always liked the idea of living in another century," said Berliner. "Pens slow you down—they're very deliberate. Computers make you do everything quicker."

In 1994, when it was apparent there was a real market for his products and repair services, he moved his business out of his apartment into a 1,000-square-foot space in the Flatiron District of Manhattan.

And as he became busier, he couldn't keep up with demand. He met his future partner, Bernard Isaacson, at a flea market, and they became friends. Isaacson eventually gave up his job as a hospital administrator to work full-time at Berliner Pen. Today their cozy shop sells both antique and contemporary pens. They also have a pen museum, a Web site, and a quarterly magazine, *Penfinder.*

"We are a full-service pen shop," said Berliner, who sells pens ranging from $35 to $20,000. "You've got to spend at least $300 on a quality pen."

Berliner said sales are between $500,000 and $1 million a year. At some point, he'd like to design his own line of pens, "but who has the time?"

Berliner has this advice for entrepreneurs who want to turn their hobby into a business: "Enjoy what you're doing, and the money will follow," he said, adding that being ethical when you parlay your passion into a business is essential. Why? Because you want to develop long-term relationships with collectors and customers.

Berliner Pen is located at 928 Broadway, Suite 604, New York, NY 10010; (212) 614-3020.

Develop a High-Tech Solution to a Problem

CONCERNS REGARDING INFANT ABDUCTION FROM hospitals have created a hot market for infant security systems. Several small high-tech equipment manufacturers are competing to sell high-tech systems to nervous hospital administrators.

While there are no exact figures on the market for infant security systems, the United States has about 3,500 birthing centers handling about 4.1 million births a year. About 1,000 hospitals are big enough to afford high-tech security systems, according to industry experts. They are willing to pay for tracking and alarm systems because one abducted baby can result in a multimillion-dollar lawsuit.

"The financial loss to a hospital could be in the realm of about $55 million," said Bernard Shore, vice president of Dynaflow in Syosset, New York. That's how much a sympathetic judge may think a newborn baby's life is worth to the distraught parents, Shore said. Dynaflow, which seven years ago began making electronic bracelets used to keep track of adult patients, entered the infant security market in 1996 with a system that costs about $30,000. Shore said increased publicity about infant abduction and pressure from the Joint Commission on Accreditation of Health Care Organizations to increase hospital security has prompted many entrepreneurial companies to enter the market.

Between 1983 and 1997, 161 infants were reported abducted, according to the National Center for Missing and Exploited Children. Of that total, 94 were taken from health care facilities—52 from the mother's hospital room. The good news is that 89 were recovered, but the negative publicity has made protecting babies a top priority for hospitals.

"Most of the feedback we get is peace of mind," said Joseph Gulinello, director of Interfaith Hospital's security and safety division. He said Dynaflow's infant security system at the Brooklyn hospital generates very positive feedback from parents and medical personnel.

"People say, 'this institution obviously cares about us, and I can close my eyes and go to sleep and know that there is an integrated system that is going to help keep my baby safe.'"

Dynaflow systems are installed in about 40 hospitals, mostly in the Northeast. Many hospitals are in high-crime areas where babies must be protected from drug-addicted mothers or fathers trying to take a baby out of the nursery where it's being held by social workers.

Small electronic devices on bracelets attached to the baby's ankle trigger an alarm signal if the baby is taken out of the authorized area. The system also disables elevators and exit doors to prevent escape.

CHAPTER 5

People

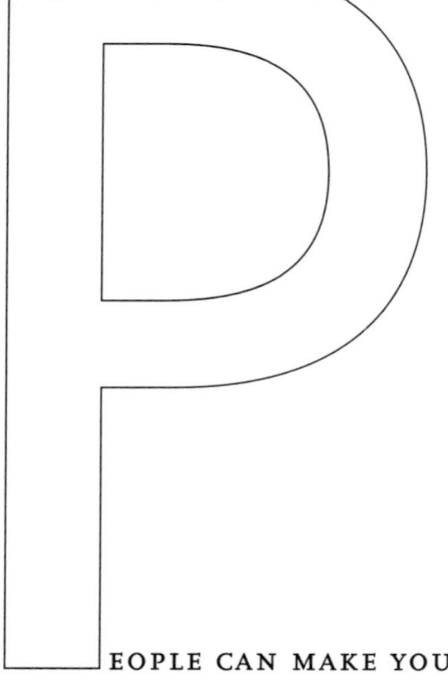

EOPLE CAN MAKE YOUR BUSINESS AND personal life miserable or magical.

If it's magic you want, surround yourself with talented, confident, and resourceful people. It's a secret of success to swear by in life and in business.

The challenge is to find the right mix of people in a very competitive economic environment. National unemployment rates, at this writing, are at an all-time low. Talented workers, especially in health care and high technology, have their pick of good jobs virtually anywhere in this country—or abroad.

This means small-business owners have to compete for talent with not only local competitors, but also with bigger companies offering fat salaries, cushy benefits, and expensive perks.

It's tough, but you can build and grow a terrific team if you try some of these great ideas to attract, develop, and retain good employees. In this chapter, you'll learn how to find great applicants, how to interview and screen them, hire them, discipline them, promote them, and even fire them.

As an employer since 1991, I've learned the hard way how to deal with personnel issues. Through the years, I've handled a disruptive office romance, incompetent assistants, a talented but moody researcher, an insecure business partner, an insane client, and a variety of other wackos.

At times, when my head is about to explode, I think about the good old days when it was just me, my cat, and my computer in a cozy corner of my den in Sun Valley, California.

But of course you can't go back. You have to learn to manage yourself and then lead and manage the people around you.

Above all, I've found that good communication is critical to managing staff. Life is so much less stressful when you are honest and clear about your expectations. Spell them out. Write them down. Scrawl them in crayon on the wall, but tell people exactly what you expect them to do, how you want them to do it, and when you need to have it done.

I realize that everyone communicates differently. Being a writer, I like to write notes filled with instructions. The problem is, my husband, Joe, and our kids, Jeanne and Evan, absolutely hate receiving them.

"Just *tell* me what you want me to do," admonishes Jeanne, my teen-aged daughter. "Don't write it down."

"You'll be leaving notes on our graves," jokes Evan, our precocious fifth grader. He's probably right.

Once you've established a clear style of communication, master the art of motivation and delegation. If people don't feel truly appreciated, they won't work hard for you. They'll be unhappy and quit or force you to fire them. And if they don't feel trusted, they won't overachieve. It's that simple.

Human beings crave personal feedback and reward. Without those, our work suffers and we feel meaningless. So you have to figure out how to evaluate and respond positively—or negatively—to the work people do for you every day.

Sometimes a simple "Thanks, good job" is all someone needs to hear. Sometimes you need to do more, including giving some sort of financial reward or perk. A day off with pay is one of the best ways to thank someone for their extra effort or for meeting a tough deadline.

This chapter includes a variety of ways to deal with the people you work with, whether they are clients, customers, employees, or vendors. You'll learn how to let your clients participate in the hiring process and how to hire an interim executive. There are great ideas about training, teaching English to employees, recruiting, and giving your business a tough personnel audit. My friends at Disney share their ideas about customer service. You'll also learn what to do if an employee turns violent on the job.

So remember: You are only as good as the people you work with.

Cast a Wide Net to Attract Good Employees

ONE OF THE GREATEST CHALLENGES FOR SMALL-business owners is to recruit, train, and retain good workers. It's very tough for a small company, especially in the bootstrapping start-up phase, to compete with bigger companies when it comes to offering competitive salaries and attractive benefits.

But it's essential to focus on hiring the best people from the very beginning. Hiring mistakes are costly.

A big company can afford a few duds on the payroll, but a small business doesn't have the time or financial resources to waste on a poor hire.

Here are some low-cost ways to recruit good workers:

- **Tell your customers and vendors that you're hiring.** They know your business and can tell you the kind of people they would like to work with.
- **Call other small-business owners and ask if they've interviewed any good people they haven't hired.** This isn't as strange as it sounds. Many times people wish they could hire someone but they don't have the budget or the timing isn't quite right.
- **Consider hiring older and younger workers.** Students and retired people are a tremendous resource for small businesses *(see Great Ideas 137 and 138)*. Contact your local business school, community college, or even high school to find a competent student. Students have all sorts of talents and are eager for real-world job experience.

  I found a terrific research assistant through the job board at a nearby journalism school. Inquire about internship programs that offer students class credit for work experience. Sometimes students are willing to work for free if they can get school credit for the job. If not, a good intern is worth paying well.

  Retired managers and executives not only have tremendous experience and knowledge, but also are often willing to work at a lower rate of pay. Contact your trade or professional association or local chamber of commerce, and rely on word-of-mouth.

- **Advertise in the local newspaper or in trade publications** before you spend a lot of money on advertising in major papers. If you want to launch a national search, the *Wall Street Journal* and the *National Business Employment Weekly* are good places to start. Advertise in trade journals or weeklies serving your industry.
- **Contact your state Employment Development Department.** The state can help you find job candidates in many fields. The state also offers training programs and tax incentives for hiring new people, so check out what's available.

Write Clear Job Descriptions

IN THE INTEREST OF CLARITY AND GOOD COMmunication, it's a great idea to outline specific job responsibilities for everyone on your staff. This helps avoid confusion and boosts productivity. It also helps cross-train workers to cover for each other.

If you don't think you need to do this, just ask your staff to tell you exactly what they are expected to do every day. You may be very surprised at the contrast between what you *think* you hired them to do and what they are actually doing.

Be sure to update your job descriptions every six months and whenever you hire new people or consultants.

We are a very small company, but our responsibilities are very clear:

JANE APPLEGATE: Manage the big picture. Write weekly *Succeeding in Small Business®* column; write monthly *Women's Issues* column for the *Costco Connection* magazine; answer questions for Micro Talk on the Microsoft Web site; write two monthly *Tips & Tricks* columns for Hewlett Packard. Research and prepare speeches; plan national book tour with Brooke Halpin; work on proprietary consulting projects.

DONNA BUCKLEY: Manage the Applegate Group office; coordinate Jane's schedule; answer the phones and handle the mail; screen story ideas; fact-check and return calls for Jane. Keep the office equipment and supplies in order; run business-related errands. Keep Jane in line and laugh at her jokes.

JOE APPLEGATE: Part-time financial manager; full-time ethical director. Review all projects from an ethical perspective; provide guidance and moral support to Jane. Keep the home fires burning.

RESEARCHERS AND FREELANCE PRODUCERS: Interview sources; collect background information; and provide detailed notes for Jane's columns and articles.

Other cast members

CARLA CAESAR: President of Egg Entertainment in New York City: Serve as Jane's producer for all video projects.

BROOKE HALPIN: President of Halpin House West: Coordinates and manages all public relations activities and corporate relationships. Serve as a liaison between Jane and the outside world.

JOSETTE CRISOSTOMO: Freelance bookkeeper.

Know What *Not* to Ask Job Applicants

WHEN 100 SMALL-BUSINESS OWNERS WERE asked if they had ever asked a job applicant any of the the following questions during an interview, all of them said "yes."

1. Have you ever filed a workers' compensation claim?
2. Do you have any physical problems or injuries?
3. How many days were you sick last year?
4. Are you currently taking any medication?
5. Have you ever been treated for drug abuse?

The problem is, under the Americans with Disabilities Act, it's illegal to ask applicants these questions, according to Morlee Rothchild, head of the labor and employment practices section at the law firm of Kahn, Kleinman, Yanowitz and Arnson in Cleveland, Ohio.

"Small companies are especially at risk when it comes to complying with the ADA and other employment-related laws," said Rothchild.

They are often too busy to keep up with current regulations, which makes them vulnerable to lawsuits and complaints. And remember, ignorance of the law is no defense if a prospective employee decides to sue you.

"When interviewing to fill a particular position, you must ask questions relevant to the prospective employee's ability to perform the essential functions of the job," Rothchild said.

For more information on conducting effective, legal interviews, read *Hire, Manage & Retain Employees for Your Small Business,* edited by Joel Handelsman. It's part of the CCH Business Owner's Toolkit. Call CCH at (800) 248-3248.

Recruit Good Employees

A SMALL BUSINESS CAN'T AFFORD TO MAKE POOR hiring choices. Yet small-business owners too often hire the first person who drifts through the door, even for key jobs.

Casting the widest net possible before hiring is one approach, but it often pays to bring in professional help. Why? Because in a small, expanding business, your people-power means the difference between success and failure.

Many entrepreneurs believe they can't afford the professional services of an executive recruiter. But consider how critical a savvy sales manager or controller can be to the future of your business.

Executive recruiters, long retained by big companies to find just the right person, also work with many smaller firms. Their fee—traditionally $33\frac{1}{3}$ percent of the total first year's salary plus all expenses—may sound steep, but think of it as an investment.

You should begin a search with local networking, classified advertising, and word-of-mouth, but that's often not enough to attract the very best candidates.

"We create a strategy for the hunt," said Brad Marks, chairman and chief executive officer of Brad Marks International in Century City, California.

Marks, a veteran executive recruiter, has placed many top executives in the entertainment industry. A former executive at Walt Disney Co. and ABC, he's been helping companies find just the right person since 1982.

Marks, who works with four women colleagues, is particularly known for placing high-level women in a traditionally male-dominated field.

"I have a distinct desire on my part to find the best executive for the position, and in many cases that turns out to be a woman," said Marks.

According to an industry report, 24 percent of the news directors in the top 10 media markets are women. Two-thirds of all news writers and producers are women, and 41 percent of all middle managers at radio and television stations are female.

Marks said a willingness to consider women for high-level jobs began in the 1980s, when the leveraged buyouts of Hollywood studios took many out of family hands and put them under corporate control.

Marks, who encouraged KNBC in Los Angeles to hire Carole Black as general manager and placed Dawn Tarnofsky at Lifetime, said his type of work can be very "cloak and dagger," especially when he is replacing people who don't know they are about to lose their jobs.

He said the executive search process has several steps. After meeting with clients to determine exactly what kind of person they need, he and his team begin searching for suitable candidates. It can often take up to 10 weeks to track down and interview people. Marks then narrows the field to about 20 people who are interviewed by him and his associates. After careful evaluation, the top five people are scheduled to meet with the client.

Hopefully, one will be a perfect fit. If you need to hire a key manager, consider paying for professional help.

Look Far and Wide for the Best Person

FINDING THE RIGHT PERSON TO HELP RUN YOUR small business may mean hiring an out-of-towner and paying to relocate that person.

Relocation involves a myriad of financial and emotional issues for both you and your employee. It's a complex and expensive process.

Finding a comparable and comfortable place to live is important, but a positive relocation depends on many factors, according to Maryanne Rainone, vice president of Heyman Associates, a Manhattan executive search firm.

"We talk to thousands of job candidates, and you get to know what kind of things are red lights for a prospective employee," said Rainone.

She said it's important to ask job candidates if they've thought about relocation even before the first interview. If their résumés show they've gone to school and worked in only one state, they are probably not good candidates for a major move.

"Make sure the candidate is open to moving before you get too interested, because sometimes companies fall in love with one person and end up comparing everyone to the candidate they can't get," she said.

By law, you can't ask a job candidate if they are married or have children, but you can ask if they have any family issues affecting a relocation. At this point, most people will tell you whether they need a good nursery school or a nursing home for their mother.

"Elder care is a big issue now and one of the primary reasons people can't leave where they are," said Rainone.

Even if you aren't using an executive search firm, Rainone suggests calling a relocation consultant to collect vital information about schools, real-estate prices, and quality-of-life issues in your town. She also recommends looking locally before you look elsewhere. You may be able to hire a wonderful person by offering a higher salary, rather than paying all the relocation expenses to hire an out-of-towner.

Being aware of spousal issues is also important to a successful relocation. If the trailing spouse will have a tough time finding work or adjusting to life in your town, the relocation could prove to be a disaster, Rainone warns.

Remember, you are not just recruiting one person—you are recruiting an entire family.

Work with People You Like

JOHN CHUANG, FOUNDER OF BOSTON-BASED MacTemps Inc., matches candidates with Mac and Windows expertise with companies that need temporary support. He has some contrarian advice for entrepreneurs growing their businesses.

"You've heard that two things you never want to do with friends is lend them money and go into business with them," said Chuang. "But the reality is that people who go into ventures with people they know and trust are one step ahead of the game."

Chuang attributes the success of his high-tech professional temporary agency to the fact that he went into business with friends from college and graduate school.

They set out to serve a small base of computer-literate customers in Boston, but ended up creating a business that now has offices from Atlanta to Tokyo and places about 2,000 temps a week.

Chuang said working with people you know lets you work around their strengths and weaknesses. You also communicate better with people you like, and this can be a real advantage over working with strangers, he said.

"Hiring trusted friends cuts down on the time spent interviewing and screening," he said. "You know who you trust, and it takes some of the guesswork out of the process."

Sharing the same sense of humor can also help you ride the entrepreneurial roller-coaster.

"We used humor to weather the tough times," said Chuang.

Best of all, "if you have to work late, you'd rather be with your friends than a room full of strangers."

Hire Seniors as Employees

ONE OF THE BEST SALESPEOPLE I EVER DEALT with was a tiny woman in her late seventies. A few weeks before we moved into our beautiful, pre-war apartment, my husband, Joe, and I wandered into a suburban Westchester County lighting store, long shopping list in hand. We were immediately dazzled and baffled by the vast selection of fixtures.

Gratefully, we were met by a pixie. Barely five feet tall and smartly dressed, Ann introduced herself, clipboard in hand. I must admit I was surprised to see a woman of her age still working in sales.

But she was absolutely amazing. She quickly steered us around the store from the ceiling fan room, to the chandelier department, the brass table lamp section, and back to the sales counter. She answered all of our questions about quality, wattage, and installation, standing on tiptoe to reach the cords to illuminate the fixtures.

Ann knew everything there was to know about light fixtures. She spent more than an hour with us, writing up an order totaling hundreds of dollars—including the appropriate light bulbs.

Dealing with Ann reinforced my belief that experienced older people can be an incredible asset to your business. No matter what you do, consider hiring at least one senior worker, at least part-time. Seniors not only have a lifetime of experiences, but they also like flexible hours and probably won't demand a fat paycheck.

One summer, when I was just starting my business, I had two great seniors working with me: my grandparents, Jean and George Coan. They were staying with my parents in the sleepy San Fernando Valley and feeling very bored when I showed up with a huge box of fan mail. At the time, I was offering a free resource guide, and we had received thousands of requests from my newspaper readers. I handed the mail over to them to open, sort, and stuff.

I relied on my grandparents because I couldn't afford to hire anyone to deal with the mail; plus, it was the perfect job for them. George got a kick out of reading the fan mail and questions from readers. Jean was content to slice open the piles of envelopes and be on the brochure-stuffing team.

For that same project, I recruited my now dearly departed Aunt Pearl Weissman. Although she was busy tutoring foreign-born students and volunteering at the local Democratic Party headquarters, she would make time to stuff a few hundred envelopes with brochures every week. I'd visit with her and my uncle Sam for a while, then return a few days later to pick up the finished work at their Santa Monica apartment.

Consider how you can tap into the wisdom and skill of older workers. Don't reject candidates because they have gray hair and wrinkles. Hire them.

Hire Teenagers

GREAT 138 IDEA

IN RESPONSE TO THE SHIFTING ECONOMY, SEVEN out of 10 high school students want to start a business, according to a Gallup Poll released in 1994. The primary motivation is to be their own boss, not to earn a lot of money.

Although there are no firm statistics on how many of America's 27 million teens run small businesses, the numbers are well into the thousands and growing, according to those involved in training young entrepreneurs. Teens are selling handmade crafts, moving furniture, detailing cars, and designing clothes, among other ventures. But not all teenagers have a natural entrepreneurial bent.

"We have to train kids not just how to get a job, but how to make a job," said Joline Godfrey, founder of An Income of Her Own, a nonprofit educational organization devoted to teaching teenage girls about business.

Despite this strong interest, 86 percent of the teens surveyed said they lacked the skills needed to start even the simplest business. The study, commissioned by the Center for Entrepreneurial Leadership at the Ewing Marion Kauffman Foundation in Kansas City, Missouri, also found that most of the students were taught little or nothing about running a small business.

This thirst for practical information has fueled the growth of several organizations aimed at training young entrepreneurs. An Income of Her Own, with offices in New York and San Francisco, operates summer camps, sponsors seminars, and organizes a national business plan competition for girls.

Other groups are serving low-income youth or business owners' children with a variety of training programs. Steve Mariotti, founder of the National Foundation for Teaching Entrepreneurship in Manhattan, said his group reaches out to economically disadvantaged teenagers in 14 cities. The program boasts 12,000 graduates, a $5 million budget, and 200 corporate sponsors.

"Economic illiteracy is an intellectual handicap in a capitalist society," Mariotti said. "It's life-threatening for the poor."

Mariotti, co-author of *The Young Entrepreneur's Guide to Starting and Running a Business,* said teens who participate in the foundation's classes are taught the practical marketing and financial skills needed to make it in the business world.

Many teens get into business because their parents are entrepreneurs. Katy Meyer of Carlisle, Massachusetts, launched her silk scarf business after she won a national business plan competition in 1993 sponsored by An Income of Her Own. She learned silk painting at an art camp and has been perfecting her technique ever since. The 10th-grader has sold scores of scarves, ranging in price from $100 to $500. She also created 10 wall hangings for a Massachusetts medical center as part of design project managed by her mother, an interior designer.

What better way to support aspiring teen business owners than to hire one as an intern or part-time worker? This can serve to fill a labor void in your business and also add a new, younger perspective to your team. Are you thinking of aiming your products at the teen market? Why not get your teen employee involved in the initiative?

If you're interested in hiring a teenager, start by contacting one of these organizations for more information: An Income of Her Own, at (805) 646-1215; and the National Foundation for Teaching Entrepreneurship at (212) 232-3333.

Use the BATH System for Hiring

JAY GOLTZ HAS BEEN AN ENTREPRENEUR SINCE he got out of school in the 1970s. He's learned a lot about hiring and now has about 140 employees at his framing and home-and-garden stores in Chicago.

He's found through the years that hiring good people is the toughest challenge for business owners.

"Seventy-five percent of good management is hiring the right people in the first place," said Goltz, author of *The Street-Smart Entrepreneur* (Addicus; $14.95).

Although former employers are reluctant to provide references, try asking them if they would rehire the person. This is one good way to get an honest opinion.

Another way to gauge your current hiring strategy is to consider this hypothetical situation: An employee comes in this morning to tell you they have to quit because they are moving to California. Do you say "yippee!" or would you be sad to see them go? If you're happy that they are leaving, Goltz says they are clearly not the best person for the job.

Goltz helps other entrepreneurs by holding seminars he calls "Boss School." He spends a lot of time explaining how to hire and screen workers. His process is called the BATH test and here's how it works:

- **"B" is for buy into your concept.** Tell prospective employees what your company is all about. You want to fit square pegs into square holes.
- **"A" is for ability.** Find people who have done this job before.
- **"T" is for team playing.** Will they tell you what is on their mind? You can spend your whole life playing psychoanalyst with your employees—and it's a waste of time.
- **"H" is for hungry.** "I need people who are hungry and want to work," he says.

Since he's begun using his BATH system of hiring, his turnover rate has dropped to 10 percent.

Goltz also likes to do a "gang interview." He meets with groups of applicants to tell them about the business. Some folks ask where the bathroom is and run off. But, he says, it's better to scare off the wrong candidates at the beginning.

"Working here is like the Tilt-A-Whirl ride at a carnival," said Goltz. "Some want to go on again . . . others stagger off and vomit. You either love to work here, or you get shaken up."

Perform a Personnel Checkup

BUSINESS OWNERS USED TO GETTING ROUTINE dental and medical checkups would benefit similarly by giving their *businesses* a periodic personnel checkup.

The reason: Every year, thousands of unhappily terminated employees sue their former employers. Their complaints, justified or not, cost small-business owners millions of dollars in legal fees, emotional distress, and lost productivity. While many problems are easily avoided if you follow the rules governing employment, there are so many complex regulations on the books, it's tough to keep up.

As her fast-growing public relations firm approached 50 employees, Ellen LaNicca, chief executive officer of Patrice Tanaka & Co., felt she needed expert help. Many state and federal employee regulations kick in at the 50-employee level, and she wanted to be sure she was in full compliance.

LaNicca turned to Peter Skeie, an attorney and cofounder of The Personnel Department Inc., to sort through the morass of laws she had to deal with. Skeie and his partner, Craig Chatfield, left their jobs at Fortune 500 companies to set up their own human resources consulting service in New York City.

"Peter is part diplomat, part human resources legal counsel, and part troubleshooter," said LaNicca. "He helped us through the process of restructuring jobs and creating separation packages for employees being let go."

Skeie helped LaNicca review all the company's personnel practices, including revising the employee policy manual and job applications. She still calls him whenever she needs advice.

"From the beginning, we wanted to have the best working environment possible," said LaNicca. In addition to providing traditional medical benefits and flexible scheduling, the firm has a meditation room to help employees "de-stress."

Skeie said most small business aren't as employee-friendly as LaNicca's, but they all face similar people problems.

"We realized small companies have the same employment liability as Fortune 500 companies," said Skeie. "We set out to provide that kind of support on an outsource basis."

He admits that serving entrepreneurial companies has been a challenge because smaller employers are reluctant to bring in outsiders. To make their services more affordable, Skeie and Chatfield have developed "The Personnel Department in a Box." The $3,500 system contains all the policies and forms a company needs. It includes templates for writing a personnel manual, warning letters, and new hire letters. The "box" also helps companies do their own systematic personnel audit aimed at fixing problems before they turn into major disasters.

"Failure to document problems as they occur is at the top of the list," said Skeie. "It's much better to take a half hour and document employee problems, because if you don't write them down, it's much harder to defend yourself later in court."

He said too many small-business owners tolerate high levels of poor performance from employees because they don't know what to do. "Eventually, a straw breaks the camel's back, and they fire the person," said Skeie. "But then they get sued because this person who has become accustomed to doing virtually nothing gets fired and wants revenge."

Not knowing labor law is no defense when an employer gets sued by an irate former employee. Employers are expected to keep up with all the changes and new requirements, but many don't.

"Another mistake made by business owners is having incomplete policies and procedures," said Skeie. "You can get in trouble if it can be proved there's been a lack of attention to employment-related issues."

Plain old management misconduct is another serious problem.

"Employers make stupid but innocent mistakes," he said. "They probably don't mean anything discriminatory by asking whether you are going to get married and have children, but it's against the law."

Jack Farnan, vice president of human resources at Comstream Corp., in San Diego, California, worked with The Personnel Department when his firm applied for employment practices liability insurance. Reliance National Insurance Co., which issues the coverage, requires a detailed personnel practices audit before it issues a policy. These special insurance policies cover legal fees when a company is sued by an employee or former employee. Some policies also cover the damage awards.

"It would behoove any human resources professional to periodically do a self-audit," said Farnan. "But having an objective third party come in sure makes it easy."

Here are a couple of new books worth checking out to get you up to speed on employment law.

Slash Your Workers' Comp Costs, by Thomas Lundberg and Lynn Tylczak, offers lots of practical tips and a clear explanation of workers' comp regulations (Amacom; $27.95).

The American Bar Association Guide to Workplace Law is written in plain English. It covers a variety of topics from sexual harassment to hiring and firing (Times Books; $14.00).

The Personnel Department is based in Manhattan at 310 Madison Ave., Suite 1223, New York, NY 10017; (212) 818-0666.

Hire a Welfare Recipient

YOU CAN COMPLAIN ABOUT WELFARE RECIPIENTS spending your tax dollars, or you can do something about it by offering an entry-level job to one person on the public dole.

With training programs and support in the form of public transportation vouchers or help with childcare, thousands of welfare recipients are joining the working class—some for the first time in their lives. You might think your business is too small to give someone on welfare a chance, but in today's tight job market, you can find untapped talent—as well as doing a good deed.

A few years ago, my father hired two brothers to work for his small nail products company. One brother was a recovering drug addict; the other was on and off welfare. I admit that when I heard what he had done, I was surprised that he would take that kind of a risk. But they turned out to be tremendously loyal and competent workers.

Sure, they had their share of personal problems, but most days they showed up and worked hard, mixing flammable chemicals and loading 55-gallon drums on trucks. My dad became sort of a surrogate father to them. By treating them with respect and setting high standards, he helped them get their lives together.

My dad, who sold the business in 1997, remembers being promised some sort of state tax subsidy in exchange for hiring the brothers, but it never materialized. He kept them on the payroll anyway.

There are a variety of state, local, and federal programs available to help business owners hire welfare recipients. On the national level, the Welfare to Work Partnership, based in Washington, D.C., provides a variety of resources.

By 1998, more than 2,500 big and small companies had joined the Partnership, an independent, nonpartisan group of businesses pledging to hire welfare recipients without displacing other workers.

Businesses across America are stepping up to the plate to hire people from public assistance, said Wisconsin Gov. Tommy Thompson. More than 350 companies have signed the pledge in Wisconsin alone. Thompson, a popular Republican, has been a pioneer in welfare reform. By eliminating cash payments to welfare recipients at few years ago, he slashed Wisconsin's welfare rolls by 70 percent. Before his time, welfare was so easy to qualify for in Wisconsin, Thompson said bus companies were selling discount tickets so people from Chicago could sign up for benefits in Wisconsin.

Today, Wisconsin's welfare recipients must take part in some sort of training program or work in a sheltered workshop to receive any public assistance. The state also provides money to business owners who hire former welfare recipients.

Dozens of governors have joined Thompson's and the Partnership's efforts to reduce the welfare rolls.

"Our success in implementing comprehensive welfare reform throughout the nation will be largely dependent on our ability to forge powerful ties between the public sector and employers," said Gov. Tom Carper, a Delaware Democrat.

The Partnership's bipartisan approach has attracted support from America's blue-chip companies, including United Airlines, Monsanto, Marriott International, The Limited, Time Warner, Burger King Corp., Sprint, and United Parcel Service of America. United Airlines chief executive officer Gerald Greenwald serves as chairman of the Partnership board.

For more information on how to hire a welfare recipient, contact the Welfare to Work Partnership, 1250 Connecticut Ave., NW, Suite 610, Washington, DC 20036-2603; (202) 955-3005. The Partnership's Web site can be found at: **www.welfaretowork.org**.

Consider Telecommuting as an Option

TELECOMMUTING HAS TREMENDOUS BENEFITS for workers and employers, but only if it's handled right. For employers, telecommuting can boost the productivity of workers who are independent self-starters. Motivated employees who live far from their offices can accomplish more by eliminating a long and stressful commute.

Here are some tips if you are considering telecommuting as an option for your business:

- Determine whether the work can be done offsite. If the staff person is responsible for writing proposals or crunching numbers all day, telecommuting is a viable option. If he or she is managing a team of salespeople, it probably won't work.
- Figure out what equipment, software, and furniture you'll need to provide for your remote workers and whether it's

worth the investment.

- Determine which of your employees are best suited to working at home. In many cases, employees ask to telecommute as a way to spend more time with their young children or to care for a sick relative.
- Set up a probationary period to see if telecommuting works. Begin with one or two days a week—this gives you a chance to work out the kinks. Then try it for a month or two. Tell your telecommuters that this arrangement is considered experimental and could end at any time.
- Be sure telecommuters understand that keeping company files and information confidential and safe is essential. This is one case where if the "dog ate the homework," it could be disastrous.
- Stay home and telecommute at least one day a week yourself. Many busy managers I know swear by this. Have your office transfer calls to your home. If working at home is not a good option, check into assigning workers to telecommuting centers opening up around the country.

Tailor Benefits to Employees' Needs

IN THE SMALL-BUSINESS WORLD, ONE SIZE definitely does not fit all. Every company has a distinct group of employees with varying personal lives, professional goals, and priorities.

While big companies prefer to offer the same insurance benefits and options to everyone, small companies have an advantage in being able to tailor benefits to their employees' specific needs. In many cases, your employees are covered by their spouses' corporate benefits, and you won't want to duplicate coverage.

If your business is really small, you might consider giving each employee a fixed amount of money each month that they can use to buy a particular benefit. A single person may want dental insurance, but a young mother might prefer that you help her pay for child care. Another employee might want legal insurance if they have legal problems relating to property or investments.

There is a wide array of insurance benefits and programs available to employers. One option is to hire a benefits consultant to tailor what is called a "cafeteria" program of benefits to your employees' needs. You'll also need professional help to figure out whether to pay for employee benefits with pre-tax or after-tax dollars.

Basically, as long as you spend the same amount of money on each employee, you'll stay out of trouble. Even $150 a month goes a long way toward buying one single person's coverage in a health maintenance organization (HMO) or other group insurance program.

Remember, some of the best benefits you can offer employees may not cost you much money at all. Flexible scheduling is one of the ways small-business owners can retain good workers and boost morale. It doesn't cost you any more money to stagger work hours to fit your employees' needs.

If some people really want to be home when their children get home from school, why not let them work from 6 AM to 2 PM? This works especially well if you are a West Coast company dealing with East Coast clients. Job-sharing is another perk to consider. Often two working mothers or fathers will ask to split a job and split the benefits that go with that job.

When you think about benefits, don't just think about insurance. Think of ways to address your employees' specific needs; chances are, they will serve your business better in the long run.

Offer Classes in English as a Second Language

IT'S NO SURPRISE TO ME THAT TWO OF THE nation's most successful entrepreneurs offer free, onsite English as a second language (ESL) classes to employees.

David Giuliani, president of the Optiva Corp., and the Small Business Administration's 1997 Small-Business Person of the Year, faced a major challenge at his fast-growing toothbrush company.

Employees at the Bellevue, Washington, firm speak 15 different languages, so Optiva, which makes Sonicare toothbrushes, decided to host free lunchtime English classes. "Taking good care of employees is required for good business," said Giuliani.

Through the years, scores of employees have taken advantage of the free classes. Their improved English skills lead to improved productivity and better communication throughout the company.

Marsha Serlin, president of United Scrap in Chicago, also provides onsite ESL classes to the mostly Spanish-speaking workers at her recycling business.

Serlin said she benefits from a skilled, English-speaking workforce. "Many of my workers, who started here with nothing a few years ago, are now able to buy their own homes," she said.

If you think your multilingual workforce would benefit from ESL classes, call your local community college or continuing education program to find out how much it will cost.

Teaching English to employees is a great way to invest in your company's future.

Find Out How Disney Does It

NO ONE IS SURPRISED WHEN AN ENTREPRENEUR heads to Harvard, New York University, or USC for a management training program, but eyebrows raise when they sign up for a course at Walt Disney World's Disney Institute in Orlando, Florida.

More than 60,000 people a year attend these classes, which offer a behind-the-scenes look at the Disney management philosophy. In the past three years, small-business owners with fewer than 50 employees represented 44 percent of attendees, say Disney officials.

"Walt Disney was probably one of the premier entrepreneurs of all time." said Valerie Oberle, vice president of Disney University Professional Development Programs. In fact, Disney's company was started in a garage, with next to no capital.

Oberle said Disney began sharing its management philosophy 11 years ago, after the company was profiled in Tom Peters' *In Search of Excellence.*

From that point on, she said, business owners and managers were anxious to find out how Disney managed the 40,000 people in its Florida parks alone. People pay about $2,500 to attend a three-and-a-half-day course in leadership, people management, orientation design, and quality service. Disney characters are heavily used throughout the course.

"Before the Disney course, we hired people if they were breathing," said Michael Collands, chief executive officer of Perfect Response, a customer service company based in Willoughby, Ohio. "Now we screen thoroughly."

Collands, who also has an office in San Diego County, has taken three Disney courses so far. His company, which helps auto dealers improve customer service, once had a tough time recruiting and retaining good employees. Based on what he learned at Disney, Collands now requires all job candidates to read a company newsletter before they are handed a job application. After reading about company policies and requirements, Collands said 15 percent leave without applying. Those who are eventually hired go through an intense one-and-a-half-day orientation.

"Our morale is up 2,000 percent," said Collands. "Everyone has pulled together. Before, employees took my ideas and executed them if I stood over them; now they take my great ideas and make them 10 times better."

Collands, who has 30 employees and annual sales of about $3 million, said he registered for the Disney program instead of a university course because all of the Disney employees he's met seem happy.

"Most people will tell you what their job is when you ask them, but when you ask Disney employees, there's a twinkle in their eyes," he said.

Lamar Berry, chairman of New Orleans–based International Marketing Systems, says he sends hundreds of clients a year to Disney University. Berry also works with Disney U. officials to develop special programs for his clients.

"There is a tremendous benefit to going to an icon and seeing how that culture is maintained," said Berry. He said it's easy for his clients to adapt Disney's culture to their businesses in other industries, including hospitals and oil companies.

Bob Van Dyk, chief executive officer of Van Dyk Health Care Inc. in Ridgewood, New Jersey, said he first attended a Disney program when he was working for a large, nonprofit health care company. Since then, he's gone out on his own to operate two nursing homes with 220 employees and sales of $9 million.

He said he liked the way Disney employees feel "like a big family."

"After hearing about Disney's approach to management, I realized how applicable it was to my own business," said Van Dyk, who has attended three Disney programs.

To learn more about the Disney Institute, call (407) 828-4411.

Other entrepreneurial management programs to consider are:

- **Harvard Business School's Owner/President Management Program.** This nine-week, full-time residential program consists of three three-week segments.

  Participants take one session a year for three years. The fee is $13,750 per session. Harvard Business School spokesman Jim Aisner said about 2,400 people have gone through the program in recent years.

  For information, contact the Harvard Business School at (800) HBS-5577; e-mail to executive_education@hbs .edu. Or visit Harvard's Web site: **www.exed.hbs.edu**/.
- **New York University, Stern School of Business: Executive Development Programs.** For information, write to Stern School of Business, 44 West 4th St., room 451, New York, N.Y. 10012, or call (212) 998-0270.
- **University of Southern California; Entrepreneurial Program,** School of Business Administration, Bridge Hall 1, Los Angeles, CA 90089-1421. Voice mail menu: (213) 740-0641.
- **University of California, Los Angeles.** For information, write to UCLA Management Development Program, 110 Westwood Plaza, suite C-305, Los Angeles, CA 90095.

Ask Good Clients to Meet Key Hires

GREAT 146 IDEA

WHEN IT COMES TO HIRING KEY EMPLOYEES LIKE new sales or account manager, marketing chief, graphic designer, or executive assistant, it makes sense to go that extra step. Introduce your top candidates to the clients they will work with if they get the job. This serves several important purposes. First of all, it gives the prospective employee an opportunity to meet your most important clients. It emphasizes the client relationship by involving them in the hiring process. It also gives you the benefit of another expert opinion on your candidate.

Don't make a big deal about the meeting. Be clear that it's an informal thing. You just want to drop by with your candidate to give everyone the chance to chat. Try to leave them alone for a few minutes so they have time for a short conversation. Give them time to form an impression of each other.

You should realize that there are small risks involved with this courtesy call. If your client feels negative about the person, and you end up hiring him or her, the new employee will have to work extra-hard to build the relationship. On the flip side, if your client is very impressed, you might risk losing that person to the client at some point.

But I believe the risks are worth it.

When I was looking for a new research associate, I planned to introduce the top candidate to my then biggest client, my colleagues at Bloomberg Television. But, as it turned out, they had already met, as she had previously interned at Bloomberg.

Because of that, I was able to judge the quality of her work firsthand. It worked out well for everyone. They benefited from her familiarity with Bloomberg and her expertise in scouting locations and helping to produce segments for our small-business show.

So, consider the benefits of introducing top job candidates to important clients. It will add considerably to your peace of mind when you are ready to make that job offer.

Work with a Great Labor Attorney

"YOU WILL BE ASSAULTED, ABUSED, OR SUED BY an employee; it's only a question of when and how," declares Robert Millman, a feisty labor attorney and partner at Littler Mendelson in Los Angeles.

"Small-business owners, in particular, are being hit very hard by employment laws, even if they only have five employees," said Millman, who has been defending and protecting companies from their angry, derisive employees for more than 20 years.

Business owners eagerly buy liability insurance to protect themselves from fires and floods, yet they don't spend time or money getting up to speed on employment laws.

"The most dangerous thing you face in your small business is not a fire or your truck driver wiping out a family of six," he said. "The most dangerous thing is one of your employees suing you."

That's why employment liability insurance, despite its high premium and high deductibles, is the hottest-selling business insurance of the '90s, Millman said. Although a policy can prevent a lengthy legal battle from bankrupting your firm, you usually don't get to choose your own lawyers to represent you. And the policy may not cover all costs.

Millman, who cheerily describes himself as a "cheesehead" from Wisconsin, said he's "seen it all" during his lengthy career representing management on labor issues.

He said far too many small-business owners get terrible legal advice and end up spending $500,000 on a case that should have settled for $10,000. Most of the time the bad advice comes from attorneys who want to run up their bills. Millman avoids this by charging clients a flat fee for handling some of the most challenging matters.

His firm, with 350 people and offices around the country, has been a pioneer in training and education for employers. He said the scariest issue is workplace violence because you are liable if someone hurts or kills someone else at your business.

"There are so many telltale signs," said Millman, adding

that good employees rarely show up one day for work and go berserk. There is always a pattern of negative behavior and clear signals that employers must learn to spot.

"A company is going to face severe liability if someone is sending out signals, and they don't do something about it," warned Millman.

His firm offers a variety of reports and materials on how to do employee background checks, write legal employment contracts, and conduct disciplinary investigations. They also publish national and state-by-state reference guides on employment law.

Littler Mendelson also created "Winning through Prevention," a $99 board game made by the makers of Trivial Pursuit™, which helps employers learn how to avoid personnel land mines.

For a list of related products and their prices, write to Littler Mendelson, P.O. Box 45547, San Francisco, CA 94145-0547, or call (415) 399-8440.

Hire an Interim Executive

GREAT 148 IDEA

BIG AND SMALL BUSINESSES ARE TURNING TO temporary executives more and more to fill important positions. While the number of traditional clerical temps is declining, the professional and technical segment of the temporary staffing industry is growing by about 5 percent a year, industry experts say. In 1996 professionals represented about 25 percent of the total interim workforce.

"With temporary staffing, you get a level of executive you may not be able to afford long-term," said Bruce Steinberg, spokesman for the Alexandria, Virginia–based National Association of Temporary and Staffing Services (NATSS).

Steinberg said the temporary staffing companies provide small businesses with skilled executives they probably couldn't attract, screen, or hire on their own. Another benefit: The staffing company handles all the employee-related paperwork, benefits, and payroll taxes.

With thousands of skilled executives tossed into the labor

pool by downsizing, executive temps often have between 15 and 30 years' experience in their industry to offer your firm.

"Small businesses may want a professional with very specific skills or experience—a financial strategist, a marketing consultant, or someone who has taken a company public," said Marilou Myrick, president and CEO of ProResource Inc., a staffing company in Cleveland, Ohio. Myrick said her clients are usually billed between $1,500 and $2,500 for a week's worth of service by one of her temporary executives or professionals.

Jean Ban, executive vice president at Chicago-based Paladin Inc., said, "our temps are highly focused, flexible people who can hit the ground running."

Paladin Inc. sets itself apart by placing high-level creative temps, specialists in public relations, marketing, and communications. After intense interviews and reference checks, the company has built a pool of 5,000 "flex execs." When a client puts in a request, Paladin sends along two or three candidates who fit the bill. Then the client chooses the best person for the job and often pays up to $200 an hour for the executive's expertise.

Finding the right short-term help isn't cheap. Executive staffing companies take a significant cut for themselves—as much as 30 percent of billings go to the matchmaking service. They are the employers of record; they pay the employer's contribution to FICA and Medicare and provide state and federal unemployment insurance coverage.

Be aware that putting a temporary newcomer into a position of authority can be a challenge.

When the home health care agency director at Mindy Jacobsen's Idaho hospital said she'd be taking a six-month leave of absence, Jacobsen needed someone with special skills to supervise the agency's 40 employees on a short-term basis.

Jacobsen, chief operating and chief clinical officer at Columbia West Valley Medical Center in Caldwell, Idaho, called Healthcare Concepts in Memphis, Tennessee, a company specializing in short-term, high-level temps. Within a few months, Jacobsen had located an interim director who filled in for the missing director until she returned.

It's very important to prepare your permanent staff before the arrival of a new temporary manager or director. Jacobsen met with her employees to fill them in.

"I told them she would provide them with support and guidance, and I assured them it was a temporary arrangement."

There are quite a few challenges to stepping into a company at a top level.

Janet Sodaro, a Paladin associate with expertise as a marketing manager, was hired to help an insurance company launch a new product. A three-month stint turned into two years, during which she orchestrated a four million-piece direct mail program.

"Because I'm not really staff but I'm not a consultant, either, I have to know when to let go of certain issues and when to press on others," said Sodaro. She says her presence in the company frees up permanent employees to think about long-term strategy while she plows ahead with the marketing tasks at hand.

Offer to Train Your Employees

GREAT 149 IDEA

SPENDING ON TRAINING AND EDUCATION PAYS off big for you and your employees. For a modest sum, your employees can learn a new skill, build confidence, and boost productivity. Subsequently, you and your business benefit from happier, healthier, and more energetic workers.

Ask your employees what skills they would like to learn or develop. If you are doing business globally, maybe they would like to study a foreign language or brush up their conversational skills for a language they already know.

Maybe taking a weekly yoga or tai chi class would relieve stress. Learning a new graphic design or financial spreadsheet program might make their life easier.

Assign someone on your staff to collect catalogs, brochures, and class schedules from local community colleges, extension programs, the Learning Annex, Learning Tree University, and other adult education programs in your area.

Figure out how much you want to spend on a quarterly, semiannual, and annual basis. If money is tight, you might provide a one-time $100 bonus to pay for books and materials. Or if you can afford it, reward your key managers with a day-long seminar of their choice. Most seminars cost under $300.

Once you've decided to offer training as a perk, be fair, and don't play favorites. You can establish a policy making these educational perks available only after six months or a year of service. Be sure to keep track of who is taking which classes and encourage people to share their experiences and knowledge with coworkers.

An alternative to sending workers offsite for educational programs is to hire your own trainers. Another option is to hire a trainer and split the cost with other small-business owners whose employees also need training.

Finally, take advantage of your state's extensive and affordable community college system. For just a few dollars a course, your employees will learn valuable skills that they will bring to work every day.

Offer Employees the Right Incentives

GREAT 150 IDEA

IF YOU THINK GLITZY TRIPS TO ATLANTIC CITY OR Las Vegas are great sales motivators for your employees, think again.

When offered the choice between a trip or money, 44 percent of the employees polled preferred the financial reward, while 39 percent said they would take a trip by themselves or with a family member. Only 5 percent would choose to take a trip with coworkers, according to a survey commissioned by American Express Gift Cheques, Amex's gift certificate division.

A $50 gift certificate is preferred by a four-to-one margin over any other type of monetary appreciation, the survey also found. Only 14 percent of respondents preferred $50 worth of tickets to a concert, show, or sporting event, and fewer than one in 10 wanted to be treated to a lunch worth $50.

But cash rewards, in the long run, may not be enough to keep employees satisfied.

"Money is a powerful incentive, but it has its limitations if it's the only incentive," said Dr. Barrie Greiff, a psychiatrist consultant at Harvard University Health Services in Cambridge, Massachusetts, who consults with big and small companies.

Greiff said taking time to express your appreciation for a job well done means a lot more than money to many employees.

"You want to create a profile of incentives," said Greiff. "You want to give employees an interesting work environment, a talented team, opportunities to stretch and grow, and adequate vacation time."

He said too many employers are reluctant to express their feelings to employees, whether they are positive or negative.

"It takes a certain degree of skill and candidness—and people are uncomfortable being candid," said Greiff.

He favors what he calls "360-degree communication." Twice a year, you should evaluate employees and let them evaluate you as the boss.

"If the ultimate goal is to improve the performance of the company, then feedback is a valuable tool," Greiff said.

He said it's important to take time to really think about business relationships and ways to improve communication. "You have to maintain the pulse of the organization," he advises. He said one of his clients was in shock after losing four key employees at his 12-person firm. They quit and took the client list because they felt they could do a better job serving clients themselves. The owner was disheartened, but decided not to take legal action and, instead, just pick up the pieces.

"You have to make sure there are more than economic rewards and that people are challenged," Greiff said, adding that if you do decide to give a monetary reward, try a gift certificate, because cash is "just spent at the supermarket."

Deal Carefully with Issues of Workplace Violence

WHAT WOULD YOU DO IF YOUR SALES MANAGER walked into work one morning with a black eye? What do you say when your secretary shows up with a split lip and puffy, swollen eyes? Do you ask what happened? Do you pretend nothing is wrong?

A battered employee is impossible to ignore.

No one likes to invade an employee's privacy, but too often domestic violence adversely affects you and your business. Smaller businesses, which usually operate more like a close-knit family, are profoundly affected when an employee is in trouble.

Chances are that at some point, you will experience the devastating effects of domestic violence. Every year, about one million women are attacked by someone they know. And according to a report by the U.S. Department of Labor's Women's Bureaus, battered women can't help but bring their problems with them to the office.

A recent study of women who are victims of domestic violence found that 96 percent experienced some problems at work. More than 60 percent were late for work; 70 percent reported having a tough time concentrating on their tasks. A distracted or unmotivated employee poses a personnel problem, but a battered and emotionally overwrought employee can turn into an emotional and financial disaster.

While corporations have formal employee assistance programs, small-business owners, who can't even afford basic insurance benefits, rarely have such programs in place. In fact, only 15 percent of small businesses offer some sort of employee assistance program, according to the Bureau of Labor Statistics.

But you obviously have to do something when an injured or emotionally upset employee appears at your office door.

The first step may be to provide basic medical attention at a local clinic. Referring the employee to a social service agency that provides counseling on a sliding-scale basis may also be a short-term solution. As an employer, you have to be careful not to cross the line and demand the details, but being truly compassionate rarely gets anyone in trouble. In many cases, a battered spouse only feels safe at work, so your place of business becomes her only haven.

Domestic violence is an economic issue, whether you like it or not.

Troubled employees rarely leave their problems at home. You may have to deal with coworkers' fear and be forced to increase security. If coworkers are afraid of the batterer, it can turn into a sensitive companywide problem, especially if people know the husband or boyfriend. (Most domestic violence cases involve men battering women, but there are definitely women who physically abuse their husbands.)

In California, employers can seek a temporary restraining order on behalf of an employee if the person has been threatened with violence that could take place at work. This provision, in a piece of pioneering legislation, is part of the Workplace Violence Safety Act. Make sure you know what laws apply in your state.

If domestic violence is affecting your business, don't be an ostrich.

Here are some of the many resources available to help:

- You can contact the National Workplace Resource Center on Domestic Violence in San Francisco, 383 Rhode Island St., suite 304, San Francisco, CA 94103-5133; (415) 252-8900.
- The U.S. Department of Justice has a special office set up to deal with violence against women: Violence against Women Office, Room 5302, 10th & Constitution Ave., NW, Washington, DC 20530.
- The Occupational Safety and Health Administration (OSHA) also deals with workplace violence of all kinds.
- The NOW Legal Defense and Education Fund is another resource for employers, located at 99 Hudson St., New York, NY 10013; (212) 925-6635.
- A 24-hour, toll-free national domestic violence hotline (800-799-SAFE) provides counseling and referrals to a variety of services including medical care and shelters.

Take Your Sexual Harassment Policy Seriously

IN JUNE 1997, A FEDERAL JURY AWARDED $6.6 million to a woman who was subjected to regular sexual taunts from her coworkers at a car dealership.

Sexual harassment is serious business. That's why even the smallest company should have a written policy in place, according to Lawrence Rogak, an Oceanside, New York, attorney who specializes in the subject.

According to federal regulations, a company is responsible for sexual harassment in the workplace "where the employer (or its agents or supervisory employees) knows or should have known of the conduct."

If you think telling sexual jokes or touching employees is funny, it's not. Of all working women, 40 to 60 percent have reported being subjected to some sort of sexual harassment on the job, according to the American Psychological Association. Complaints from men or women on your payroll should never be taken lightly. The last thing you need is an expensive and time-consuming lawsuit.

Here are some tips from Rogak and others:

- Draft and distribute a clear policy prohibiting sexual harassment at your company. Ask employees to acknowledge in writing that they have received and read it and understand the ramifications of violating it.
- Document any sexual harassment complaints in writing. Create a paper trail that contains details of the alleged event.
- Question any witnesses to the alleged event and document their account.
- Consult an experienced attorney if your employee threatens to file a formal complaint.
- Remember, under federal law, an employer is automatically liable for an employee's behavior in the workplace, unless you can prove that you wrote and distributed a policy prohibiting sexual harassment.

Rely on Temps or Leased Workers

WITH UNEMPLOYMENT LEVELS AT RECORD LOWS across the country, finding skilled workers is a small-business owner's nightmare. Talented people, especially in the high-tech arena, are fielding multiple job offers. In a seller's market, top people demand high salaries, incredible benefits, and perks. Big companies can afford to woo them, but what can you do to compete for talent?

Don't despair. There are millions of terrific people who, for one reason or another, prefer to work for a variety of firms. So they register with temporary agencies or employee leasing firms. Temping also has a strong appeal to people who are between jobs or people who just need a fresh start after a bad work experience, maternity leave, or a move across country.

Unlike the strictly clerical or secretarial agencies of the past, modern temp agencies attract top talent and frequently specialize in specific industries. There are agencies that place accountants, software engineers, marketing executives, construction managers, graphic designers, and medical doctors.

No matter what kind of work you require, you can find a temporary worker to fit the bill. The greatest advantage to hiring a temp is that because they are on someone else's payroll, you don't have to worry about benefits or payroll taxes. If the person doesn't work out, you just call the agency and they quickly disappear. The best agencies will replace problem workers on the same day if you call early enough in the morning.

Before I could afford a part-time secretary, when we had special projects I always hired temporary workers. One challenge for me years ago was that I worked from home in a remodeled garage. Although it was a fully equipped office, most agencies I called wouldn't send anyone to a residential neighborhood. I found one company that would, and I was a grateful and loyal client for years.

It's easy to contact the big companies in the business. Olsten, Manpower, Kelly Services, and Adia are among the best-known companies. In fact, Manpower ranked number one in 1996 with $7.5 billion in worldwide sales.

If you can't find what you need locally or by referral, you can contact Staffing Industry Analysts, a research group that tracks the industry: 2235 Grant Road #3, Los Altos, CA 94024; (650) 903-9494. Or check out their Web site: **www.sireport.com**.

Another alternative is leased workers. Leased workers are hired with a more permanent situation in mind. It works like this: You sign an agreement with an employee leasing company and pay a fee, which is usually a percentage of the total payroll. The leasing company then hires the kind of people you need, puts them on their payroll, and "leases" them back to you.

The advantage of leasing is that most of the time-consuming personnel and administrative aspects of staffing are handled by the leasing company.

Another great thing about leasing is that you can easily convert your existing employees to leased workers if you are tired of dealing with all the paperwork.

"A client company has the flexibility to lease all or a portion of their work force, even top management," according to a brochure from Personnel Coordinators in Fair Lawn, New Jersey.

Companies like Personnel Coordinators can take care of everything from filing payroll tax reports to setting up direct deposit for checks, pension plans, credit unions, and employee reward programs. They also perform background checks on applicants, comply with all state and federal hiring regulations, and legally terminate problem employees.

The Department of Health and Human Services estimates the average manager spends about 15 percent of his or her time on employee-related administrative tasks. If you can think of better ways to spend your time and are tired of dealing with the hassles of hiring and firing people, look into employee leasing.

Consider Remote Workers

LLOYD HENRY, FOUNDER AND PRESIDENT OF Biotech Marketing Inc., which buys and sells used and refurbished hospital equipment, prefers to hire salespeople without meeting them.

"The important thing to me is that the person relates well on a personal basis over the phone," said Henry. "Often I'm more convinced by what I hear than what I see. After five or six phone conversations, you can tell what people are made of."

That's good, because Henry rarely ever sees his employees, except for his wife, Anita, who handles marketing and customer service from their company headquarters based in their Margate, Florida, home. The company relies on independent sales reps in Atlanta, Denver, Indianapolis, and Los Angeles.

Henry has grown his business despite the lack of in-person contact with his colleagues. "Many of our customers are rural hospitals, so the bulk of sales work is done over the phone, anyway," says Henry. "One customer is located 80 miles from the nearest McDonald's."

Managing remote employees is fast becoming one of the true business art forms of the '90s. And it will continue into the next century as skilled workers demand flexibility and mobility.

Finding responsible and motivated remote workers is easier than you think. Corporate downsizing has left hundreds of thousands of middle-aged, tech-savvy professionals looking for new ways to work and live. Many of them are reluctant to relocate for family reasons and are looking for high-level, home-based job opportunities.

"After the last five years of corporate layoffs, a lot of people are finding the best way to excel is to work on their own terms," said Tom Miller, vice president of research at the Emerging Technologies Research Group in Ithaca, New York, which studies the impact of technology and work on culture.

"Many of these people are tempted by the ease of

computer networking to break out of the corporate rat race and consult. From a management perspective, the key is to find people who are good self-starters," Miller said.

Entrepreneurs like Lloyd Henry, who buys used equipment from hospitals, refurbishes it, and resells it to other hospitals, are hungry to hire mature and independent self-starters. But putting together a virtual team is not as easy as it sounds.

"We've had a few personnel changes," said Henry, who started the business four years ago after burning out as a financial consultant who spent months on the road.

"Some of our people just couldn't keep up with the learning curve and didn't pan out. All were laid off by larger organizations and didn't realize that working remotely takes a tremendous amount of discipline."

More difficult than managing remote employees is managing some of his hospital customers' expectations. "They're used to salespeople coming around to take them out to lunch," said Henry. "We don't do that, but we do provide a much higher level of service. We can have an engineer on the phone in a minute."

For all the media coverage on sophisticated technology, the plain old telephone—with its host of services—is the backbone of Biotech Marketing's infrastructure. A toll-free 800 number is answered at the Margate headquarters. The company's monthly phone bill averages $3,000 to $4,000.

Conference calls between the field representative, customer, or vendor, and the Margate headquarters are common. All his people can forward calls to one another; they can also patch another rep into a call when needed.

Henry and his wife have seven incoming lines; other staffers have two or three lines each. Henry generates price quotes and faxes or e-mails them to field reps. The reps all have personal computers and color printers to create sales presentations.

It's a plain-vanilla setup with the advantages of a quick start-up, a short learning curve for employees, and no need for a high-tech network manager or Internet guru.

Still, Henry admits his remote workers miss "the

water-cooler interaction." But his secret of success is "hiring professional, mature people."

"We're all 45 years old or older. We've been through the rat race. Now we're at a point in our lives where we want to look at the quality of life. Our associate in Denver, for instance, loves to ski. There's no reason he can't work thousands of miles from our main office here in Florida."

Tips for Recruiting Executives

GREGORY H. WINGFIELD, PRESIDENT OF THE Greater Richmond Partnership Inc., suggests the following guidelines for recruiting small-business executives:

- **Make certain the executive is not a dyed-in-the-wool corporate player.** Those spoiled by the trappings of a huge support staff and a battalion of secretaries may resent having to roll up their sleeves and write a marketing plan.
- **Look for decisive individuals capable of making choices without the support of blue-ribbon committees.** The bureaucratic gamesmanship that goes with the turf in a giant corporation cannot be tolerated in smaller firms where speed and agility are vital weapons. The owner's top aide must have the self-confidence to act.
- **Seek those executives with an entrepreneurial flair.** Managers experienced in working for other small firms may fit the bill. They are likely to have the right skills and can withstand the economic pressures that are a way of life in small companies. An ideal candidate will relish the opportunity to net a large bonus while simultaneously accepting the risk of no bonus at all. He or she must be a bit of a gambler.
- **Stop short of hiring former entrepreneurs on the rebound from their own losing ventures.** Most will want to call all the shots and will seek to introduce the same management tactics that failed in the past.
- **The best bet is to look for someone who is not looking for a job.** That way, you raise the odds of finding a winner. Come up with a strong-enough salary and benefits package to lure away a well-established executive presently contributing to

another firm. The last thing you want is for your company to be a haven for those executives seeking any kind of work that comes along.

- **Be wary of the "small business is a family affair" syndrome.** Although hiring brothers and sisters may be a kind gesture, it should be done only if the individual is the most qualified person for the job.
- **Look for those who lead by example rather than by force.** The team effort is too important in small business for the executive to alienate workers, prompting good people to resign. It is a good idea to check references to establish evidence of a solid track record in companies like yours.
- **Consider asking executive recruiters and business associates for referrals.** It's important to use all of your contacts to locate a pool of suitable candidates.

Send Flowers to an Employee's Spouse

BEING ON THE ROAD AWAY FROM HOME CAN BE A drag. But when you get to spend time with people like Dr. Allan Weis, it's worth the trip. Weis and I met a few years ago when we were part of a traveling faculty hired by IBM to speak to entrepreneurs.

Weis, credited as one of the key developers of the technical backbone of the Internet, has founded several small, high-tech companies. Through the years, he has learned how to keep employees happy, especially when they are working long hours on complex, technical projects.

One of his most inventive morale-boosters is to send a bouquet of fresh flowers to the wives of busy employees as a special thank-you gesture.

"I never send roses," said Weis. "That's too emotional."

He said the flowers serve several purposes: They cheer up the upset spouse and show his appreciation for the extra effort put in by his staff.

CHAPTER 6

Time Management

TIME IS MONEY” IS A VERY OLD CLICHÉ, BUT it’s still true. If you waste time, you waste money and add major stress to your busy life.

Most successful entrepreneurs work incredibly long hours. There are some people, though, who manage to accomplish so much more than the rest of us—and in less time. So what’s their secret?

They are relentless delegators. They let go of all the things they know they don’t need to do themselves, like answer the phone, open the mail, and fill out FedEx forms. They have skilled support people manage their schedules, deal with paperwork, return phone calls, host nonessential staff meetings, and make travel arrangements.

Savvy entrepreneurs take full advantage of voice mail and e-mail. They leave long, detailed messages and instructions late at night when they are sure no one will answer the phone. They answer e-mail in batches and don't continually sign on to check messages during the day when they should be working on more important projects.

They have wonderful administrative assistants who keep track of all the details that bog down busy entrepreneurs. A good assistant screens calls, deals with most requests for information, and knows when to interrupt. A good assistant keeps the space around you clear so you can concentrate on doing the strategic work and making the money.

I admit, it took me years to learn not to micromanage the details of projects I assigned to my employees. By peering over shoulders and second-guessing work, I was wasting both my time and theirs. And, of course, doing that cost me money in addition to hurting productivity and morale.

I urge you to try the time-saving ideas in this

chapter. For instance, I use index cards to keep track of daily tasks and calls. I rely on a Month-at-a-Glance calendar, which comes highly recommended by time-management expert Ruth Klein. It's easier to plan your schedule and keep track of big projects and deadlines when you have the whole month on view in front of you.

I work hard to maintain a schedule of "in days" and "out days." On "in days," I stay in the office all day and work. I return phone calls, and I write articles, memos, or proposals. On my "out days," I set up several appointments in a row and spend the day in New York City or wherever else I happen to be working.

When I'm in transit, I try to meditate and rest; I spend time considering larger issues rather than engaging in busywork. I find it much too distracting to concentrate on airplanes, especially in first or business class where fellow passengers tend to talk very loudly on the phone or to each other. Plus, as much as I love my IBM laptop, it's heavy, and I don't enjoy lugging it around airports.

Other time-savers to implement include returning phone calls in batches and letting the voice mail take messages when you're alone in the office. I go through all the new story pitches and mail once or twice a week, rather than every day.

And I work at least part of one weekend day, so I can spend evenings at home with my husband and children.

The following great ideas are meant to get you started on a new path. For more detailed information, read any book by Ruth Klein, Barbara Hemphill, Stephanie Culp, or Susan Silver. They are experts in this field, and their books will help streamline your life.

As you'll see from reading this chapter, I asked every expert I know for great ideas that anyone can use, no matter what kind of business you're in.

Your first challenge, right now, is to make time to read them!

Take This Time-Management Quiz

MARKETING CONSULTANT RUTH KLEIN HELPS clients manage their time, which of course then allows them to work more effectively and make more money. She sent along this provocative little time-management quiz to help you determine how well you organize your day. Spend a minute or two thinking about your answers.

Which of these statements below are true in your life?

1 You send or receive more Federal Express mail than ordinary mail.

2 You bring an overflowing binder or briefcase with "stuff you have to do" on a one- or two-day trip.

3 Your cell phone bill is half your office rent.

4 Most of your conversations begin with, "I'm sorry I didn't get back to you sooner, but . . ."

5 You dream about e-mail more than you dream about humans.

6 While on vacation, you spend more time around the fax machine than around the pool.

If you agree with most of these statements, you need to get a grip and get your life organized. For help, read on and find more great ideas for better time management.

Get Organized—Right Now

EVERY SUCCESSFUL ENTREPRENEUR TRIES TO BE well-organized in order to maximize every minute of the day. If you believe getting organized is just for the compulsively neat, add up the time you spend every day hunting around for misplaced files or documents. You'll be shocked at how much time and money your messy desk costs your business.

Hiring a professional organizer is one way to go, but be prepared to pay between $50 and $150 an hour. It's also not that difficult to do it yourself. Start by reading *Taming the Paper Tiger,* by Barbara Hemphill, and using the companion software product.

Meanwhile, get started right now:

1 **Schedule a weekend or two to totally clean up your office.** If necessary, pay employees overtime to help you tackle the mess. Get into the right mood by playing your favorite music. Bring in plenty of snacks, soft drinks, cleaning supplies, and lots of big trash bags.

2 **Take everything off your desk and set things on the floor.** Throw away any piece of paper that you haven't touched for a month. Next, go through your "in" basket and distribute everything you can.

3 **Scan through those stacks of magazines and newspapers.** Tear out articles that you absolutely must read. Recycle the rest.

4 **Clean out every file in your filing cabinets.** Ask your employees to do the same with their files, too. Be ruthless. You don't need paper copies of everything that is in your computer as long as the files are properly backed up and stored offsite.

5 **Remember, your desk is work space, not an exhibit area.** Clear off all the plants, family pictures, toys, and gadgets.

6 **Once you've dumped the accumulated trash, figure out what nifty supplies will help you stay organized.** Everyone has a different style of organization. Wander around a big office-supply store. Do you like to see project files hanging on the wall? Would colored files help you keep better track of projects? Use filing cabinets for storage, not for active projects.

7 **Sort through your piles of business cards.** Throw out the ones you'll never use. Then put the remaining ones in a Rolodex file or a business card album, or scan them into a business card database.

8 **Buy a calendar that works for you.**Keep one master calendar for yourself. Multiple calendars create confusion. Do you like one that shows the whole week, the whole month, or each day individually? I use a book-sized calendar that shows the entire month on two pages. When I'm traveling or have a lot of appointments, I transfer my daily schedule to an index card. Index cards are cheap and easy organizing tools. Save the cards if you want a daily journal.

9 **Once you've cleaned up your office, try to keep it neat by avoiding the paper pile-up.** Sort the mail into categories: bills, personal letters, marketing materials, and so on. Throw out the junk mail right away. Put the bills in a file and keep them in a safe place for check writing. Pass along as much mail as you can to key employees. Write notes and action steps right on the letters or information.

10 **Try scheduling what I call "in days" and "out days"** *(see Great Idea 160)*. Schedule back-to-back appointments for your "out days" and stay out all day, if need be. But on your "in days," stay in and work hard.

11 **Set aside an hour or two every day to return phone calls.** Take advantage of voice mail to leave after-hour messages. Don't be afraid to let your assistant or your voice mail pick up your phone. You'll never get any work done if you take every call that comes in.

12 **Promise yourself that you'll try to stay organized for at least a month.** Then take it one day at a time.

Hire a Personal Information Officer

THE INFORMATION SUPERHIGHWAY LEADS TO information overload for many busy entrepreneurs. With so much to do, it's difficult to find the time to keep up with all the Web sites, books, magazines, and professional journals we know we should be reading.

One solution with multiple benefits is to ask your assistant or a key staffer to serve as your "personal information officer," or PIO.

Your PIO benefits by being well informed and learning about your world, while you save time by reading only the material you absolutely must read. This system takes a little time and planning, but it will save you many hours over the long run.

First, decide which magazines, newspapers, and Web sites provide valuable information and insights for your particular business. If your daily newspapers are piling up unread, get started by pulling out the business section and recycling the rest.

If you don't subscribe to your industry's top trade journal, subscribe right away.

Once you've made a "must-read" list of publications, go online and use search engines to find the Web sites that should be visited at least once a week (don't forget to include **janeapplegate.com**). "Bookmark" these sites or put them in "Favorites" so you can reach them quickly when you or your assistant sign on.

Collect a stack of current publications and sit down with your assistant to point out which articles are of particular interest to you. Note which columns (including my weekly newspaper column) you want clipped out every week. Some people want their assistant to highlight key paragraphs, as well.

Create a "To Read" file for the clippings or computer printouts. Urge your PIO to be selective. You won't be saving much time if they clip dozens of articles every week.

In addition to articles and editorials about your particular industry and those that affect your business, your PIO should look for articles about the United States and world economies, unemployment, and interest rates. These may also be very helpful to your decision-making process.

While your PIO's job is to fill up your "To Read" file, your job is to empty it out at least once a week. Carry the file with you and get into the habit of reading in line at the bank or the movies or while riding the train, bus, or subway. Try reading for a half hour in bed before you pick up the novel you're reading for pleasure.

I read in hotel lobbies and offices while waiting for appointments. Once it becomes a habit, you'll look for times to do some quick reading.

If you prefer to listen to the news highlights, you might want to contact the Newstrack Executive Tape Service in Pitman, New Jersey. Newstrack hires professional announcers to record a variety of business columns clipped from publications around the United States. For information on Newstrack, call (800) 334-5771.

The final step is deciding what to save and what to toss out. Save only the articles you know you will refer to again and discard the rest.

I have long contended that a lack of pertinent information, rather than a lack of money, leads to business failure. Uninformed business owners invariably make poor business decisions.

Plan "In" Days and "Out" Days

AS MY BUSINESS FLOURISHED AND MY LIFE became busier and busier, I needed a better way to structure my time. I came up with this plan when I was working out of my home office in Sun Valley, California. Sun Valley is a rural community about 25 miles from downtown Los Angeles. We ended up there because our daughter Jeanne was devoted to horses, and we needed to live in a horse community with horse property. I also loved raising chickens for the fresh eggs.

Unfortunately, it's not easy to get from Sun Valley to anywhere in Los Angeles. Because traffic is such a nightmare no matter when you travel in L.A., setting up one appointment across town meant I would be gone for most of the day.

I found that the best way to break up my week was to schedule "in" days and "out" days. On my "in" days, I never left the office, except maybe to drive someone to school or run to the supermarket. I spent the day writing, returning calls, working on project proposals, dealing with paperwork, and basically digging out.

On my "out" days, I scheduled back-to-back appointments in one area. I would book a breakfast appointment, an interview at lunch, a meeting with Brooke Halpin, my friend and marketing guru, a trip to my acupuncturist, and anything else I could squeeze in. I'd be gone from very early in the morning until late into the evening, staying out as long as it took to complete my work. Halfway through the day, I would check in with my assistant and return calls.

I still use this system, although we live in New York now. This plan is really effective, especially if you travel a lot and need quiet time in your office between trips to accomplish the work.

If you have a similarly hectic lifestyle, it might help you, too, to organize your time and get more accomplished.

Beat Your Deadlines

JANICE GAY, A FREELANCE DESKTOP PUBLISHER IN Florida, shared this great idea during a brainstorming session a few years ago. It's simple but smart.

"I move my deadline up a few days earlier than the date I quoted the client," she said. "Then I meet my personal deadline. The client is surprised and pleased that I turned out a quality product ahead of schedule, and I always get return business."

This is a great idea because it sets you apart from the rest of the business world, which is thick with folks who beg for deadline extensions. Better yet, it exceeds your clients' expectations and costs you absolutely nothing.

I like to set internal and external deadlines for projects. With so many different projects under way at one time, it helps to stagger the deadlines so things are not all due at the same time. Setting earlier deadlines also helps avert last-minute disasters.

Moving the deadline up a few days gives you peace of mind. If a computer crashes, the printer freaks, or someone calls in sick, you won't fall behind.

Making a promise and keeping it sounds so simple, but too often, it's the exception and not the rule.

Throw Away Your Expensive Time-Management System

I DON'T KNOW ABOUT YOU, BUT I HAVE A COLLECTION of pricey organizers—all gathering dust. I hate to throw them out because they are so darn expensive. But I've tried them all: the big chunky notebooks, the planners, the runners, the memo managers—all for naught.

They were too complicated for me to keep up with, and I consider myself a pretty smart woman. I finally went back to one of the oldest—and cheapest—organizing tricks, the lowly index card.

Yep. A top corporate executive was the first person I saw pull an index card out of his shirt pocket. Every morning, his secretary handed him a card with the highlights of his day neatly typed. It included addresses, phone numbers, and a few details to remind him of what he had to say during important meetings.

"I save them for a few weeks as a record, then I toss them out," he confided.

Of course, you can save a year's worth in a plastic recipe box and have your whole year on record, if you insist.

I must admit, I've backslid through the years and spent another few hundred bucks on organizers. My last was a $199 digital memo-minder. My son has subsequently inherited it and is waiting to take it apart and see how it works as soon as I give him the go-ahead.

I combine use of the three-by-five-inch index cards with a simple monthly planner sent to me as a gift from a wigmaker I profiled on a Bloomberg television show. It's perfect.

The calendar, which is very light and portable, helps me keep track of the big picture. The cards keep my days in order.

Try using index cards for a few weeks and see if you aren't ready to toss out that heavy, expensive leather notebook you lug around.

Follow These Five Quick Time-Management Tips

GREAT 163 IDEA

TIME-MANAGEMENT GURU PETER GORDON offered these five tips; I knew I had to pass them along to you.

1 **Start with the big picture.** Ask yourself what you want to accomplish, where you are trying to go, and what the most important things are for you to do. "This type of clear thinking will give you a solid foundation for goal setting, prioritizing, and establishing a clear sense of direction," said Gordon.

2 **Use one planning and organizing system.** "Consolidate your various calendars, schedules, and to-do lists into a single planning system. Eliminate those floating notes and scraps of paper," said Gordon. "Integrate phone numbers into your system for quick reference."

3 **Invest the time to plan each day.** "Review and prioritize your to-do list, blocking out time for the most important tasks," said Gordon. He suggests choosing the most "distract-free" time to do your daily planning.

4 **Make appointments with yourself.** Schedule time to do certain mundane tasks, especially ones you don't like to do. Gordon says this is a great way to avoid procrastination and just get them finished.

5 **Batch the little things.** When it comes to going through your "in" basket, answering e-mail, or filing, do it all together, advises Gordon. "For maximum efficiency, batch tasks together and handle them all at once, whenever possible."

Getting yourself more organized seems like a daunting task, but once you do it, it will change your life.

CHAPTER 7

Technology and Telecommunications

I ADMIT THAT I AM NO HIGH-TECH GURU, but any book full of great ideas has to include vital tips on making the most of affordable equipment and technology.

Even the worst technophobe has to deal with it. You can't be in business without the right stuff, especially when computer and communications equipment has never been faster, better, and cheaper. Affordable technology truly levels the playing field, giving any company the chance to act as competitive and professional as much bigger firms with greater resources.

Most entrepreneurs rely on others to guide them when it comes to choosing and maintaining their computers and software. In fact, 36 percent of small-business owners surveyed by Hewlett Packard in 1997 said they rely on outside tech consultants to repair computer problems. Forty-four percent said they call consultants for routine maintenance.

Computers are great, but they're not cheap. Companies with fewer than 20 employees spend an average of $292 a month on computer maintenance. Companies with 50 to 100 employees spend an average of $1,019 a month, according to the HP survey.

Although 81 percent of those surveyed said access to free or low-cost technical support is critical when they decide what brand to purchase, only 5 percent said they use the manufacturer's tech support for routine maintenance; 14 percent use it for troubleshooting.

Anyone who has ever waited on hold for 35 minutes or more trying to speak with a human tech-support person wouldn't be surprised at these figures.

Despite needing help with maintenance and

installation, 43 percent of those surveyed classified themselves as "smooth operators" when it came to their computer systems. A mere 3 percent felt they were "clueless."

For this chapter, I've relied on several colleagues to share inside tips. Mie-Yun Lee, a syndicated columnist and publisher of the monthly *Business Consumer Guide,* suggests some great equipment to buy for your business.

Amy Berger, founder of Berger Technology Research, follows the ever-changing communications technology market and keeps me posted. She helped with the section on communications options.

This chapter includes a variety of ideas to help you, whether you barely know how to use your voice mail or are running a $50 million software company.

My emphasis is on telecommunications, because to me, good communication is the core of every successful business. We've also found a few new things to whet your appetite for the future of business technology.

So check out ways to link your computer to your telephone, how to train your employees online, what to buy for the busy entrepreneur on the run, how to sell your products online, and many more great ideas to get your small business moving into the year 2000.

Five Great Things to Buy

GREAT 164 IDEA

BEFORE YOU CAN BE TRULY HIGH-TECH, YOUR business needs to have the right equipment and be set up properly.

Here are the five things your office probably doesn't have but should, according to business equipment expert Mie-Yun Lee:

1 **Computer backup system.** It's easy to think your computers will never crash or be damaged by water or fire or be hit by a virus. But it could—and probably will—happen.

Prevent the despair you'll feel when a disaster strikes by buying a backup system. Look for a tape-based system to minimize storage costs. You want a system that can store key data from all your current and future computer systems.

Brands to look for include Exabyte, Hewlett-Packard, and (for Macs) APS Technologies. Lee also suggests practicing recovering your data before you actually need to do it. And be sure to back up files every week, if not every day.

2 **Router: Rather than buying modems for every computer you add to the office, buy a router.** These devices serve as an officewide modem for everyone, with access available to all networked computers.

A router can save you money, because all modem usage can be consolidated to just a couple of phone lines instead of requiring a separate line for each modem. This devise can also eliminate unsightly telephone wires snaking around the office. A router can connect to regular phone lines, ISDN, and dedicated lines. Try 3Com or Ascend for PC-based routers; Farallon is a good source for Mac routers.

3 **Color printer: A splash of color can make your important documents more memorable.** A color ink-jet printer is good for basic printing. Whatever printer you choose, make sure you buy a four-color, not three-color, model. Four-color models have a reservoir that holds black ink, while three-color ones combine various colors to approximate black.

Also, make sure you reload or refill cartridges separately. Otherwise, when you run out of one color, you will be forced to throw out the entire cartridge.

Consider brands like Epson, Canon, or Hewlett-Packard for printers and cartridges.

4 **Computer-height desks.** Computers sitting atop standard-issue desks often spell trouble for employees. Many suffer aching hands or carpal tunnel syndrome, a serious repetitive stress problem *(see Great Idea 14)*. To alleviate the discomfort, buy lower desks or desks that adjust to computer keyboard height.

You can retrofit desks by adding a keyboard platform that is adjustable. If you use a mouse, make sure the platform is wide enough to hold both the keyboard and the mouse. Remember, part of working in the information age means having the right office equipment to accommodate the new technology.

5 **Employee 800 number.** If you have employees calling in

from the road, try installing a toll-free 800/888 number instead of issuing calling cards. You can save money in the long run, and employees will have fewer numbers to dial when they are on the run. Many telephone service providers offer toll-free service. You can also equip the 800 number with account codes to prevent employees from using the 800 number for personal calls.

For more ideas from Mie-Yun, read her book, *The Essential Business Buyers Guide,* available for $18.95 from Sourcebooks.

Find the Right Communications Technology for Your Business

WHEN IT CAME TIME TO CONSIDER THE BEST kinds of communications technology for my business, I turned to an expert I can trust: my sister Amy Berger, founder of Berger Technology Research in Fremont, California.

Communicating with your customers is the most important thing for small-business owners. Here are some key devices and services to consider:

- **Cellular telephones.** There are four different kinds of cellular telephones on the market: analog, digital, dual-mode, and PCS. Analog phones have been around for about a decade and are given away by many companies when you sign up for service. Dual-mode phones accommodate both analog and traditional digital service, which works well if you live in analog-only areas of the country.

Digital phones are being superseded by PCS telephones. PCS stands for "personal communications services." PCS relies on radio frequencies that the FCC made available within the past few years. PCS frequencies are not available nationwide, so make sure they are in your area before you buy a phone. PCS handsets sell for about $150.

There are many, many companies providing a confusing array of cellular phone services. Do your homework and ask other business owners which providers they use before signing a long-term service contract.

- **Multifunction boxes.** In 1996 a new telecommunications product was created. It looks like a printer with a scanner, but it can do four things: fax, print, copy, and scan. For about $1,000 retail, it's a great deal for a small office. Hewlett Packard and Canon make these affordable multifunctional machines.
- **Two-way pagers.** PageNet and Skytel sell pagers that can answer a message. With new technology and radio frequencies, users can send an alphanumeric message and receive a reply. Some pagers can hook up to your voice mail system for continual access to incoming phone calls. Again, there are many, many models and service providers, so look for reliability and solid equipment. GTE Communications also offers a great text pager, which I use.
- **Internet service providers.** There are more than 5,000 Internet service providers in the world, ranging from tiny businesses to AT&T, UUNET, and PSINet. The Internet provides access to unlimited information, e-mail, and electronic commerce. You can also link to individual customers' Web sites and find all sorts of specialized business-support groups.
- **Personal digital assistants (PDAs).** These devices are the size of a small book or large waffle. They typically have a small screen and a writing device—much like the Etch-A-Sketch you played with as a kid. Most PDAs have some kind of mini-keyboard and modem. They are portable companions to your personal computer, not a replacement, and must be hooked up by a wire or wireless communication.

  What you create on a PDA can easily be downloaded into your PC. PDAs are good for people on the go who don't want to lug around a laptop. PDAs are made by US Robotics, Casio, Apple Computer, Sony, and Hewlett Packard.
- **Fax/modem card.** For less than $150, you can buy a 33.6 kpbs modem/fax card that you can put into your PC. This dual-function device allows you to send and receive faxes, e-mail, and computer files. You need to leave your PC turned on to enjoy the benefits of a fax/modem card.
- **Wireless modems.** Another technology to consider is wireless communications devices, which transmit information to

the nearest radio tower, then rely on land lines to connect a provider who relays the information to the client's database. RAM Mobile Data, in Woodbridge, New Jersey, provides this type of service. This works well when you have lots of sales reps on the road who need to place orders with a quick turnaround.

Train Your Employees Online

IN THE RUSH TO UPGRADE COMPUTERS AND BUY new software, many business owners forget that people need to be taught how to use the software before they can begin to be more productive.

Yet employees can lose up to three weeks of work time tackling computer problems on their own, according to a recent survey of 400 PC users by SCO, a British software firm, and Harris Research. In fact, the first month after a new software program is introduced, employees spend an average of 100 minutes a week trying to figure out how to use it. "The latest software isn't empowering these users, it's disrupting their workday," said Geoff Seabrook of SCO.

One alternative to sending your employees to community college classes or hiring private instructors is to look into customized training provided online.

"I don't like to be instructed. I like to work on my own," said Barbara Epstein, who recently spent about an hour a day teaching herself how to use Microsoft spreadsheet and database programs with an online tutoring service.

Epstein is the site manager for the Physick House, a historic mansion built in 1786 and located in Philadelphia's downtown historic district. She now uses her personal computer to schedule tours, catalog antiques, and do the bookkeeping.

Because her job keeps her so busy, taking classes was not an attractive option. Instead, she taught herself how to use the programs via LearnItOnline, a tutoring service offered by Ziff-Davis Education on the World Wide Web.

"I really don't enjoy reading instruction books," said Epstein. "This has given me confidence with the computer."

Because it operates 24 hours a day, LearnItOnline and other services like it allow people to work at their own pace and set their own training schedules. It's like having a virtual tutor who never sleeps and isn't on the payroll.

"The second half of 1997 is witnessing an explosion in the Web-based training market," said Bill Rosenthal, president of Ziff-Davis Education, which entered the market in March 1997. "The people who benefit most from this are often the people who are most scared of being online," said Dina Wood, a spokeswoman for Hand Technologies in Austin, Texas.

Hand, which sells computers to small companies and individuals, has been offering LearnItOnline services to customers on a trial basis. The company, which has 1,000 sales consultants nationwide, now plans to offer the program to clients across the country.

Ziff-Davis relies on computer resellers and popular Web sites to market the service, paying its partners a 10 percent referral fee for every new subscriber they sign up. You can check out the site at **www.learnitonline.com**.

Because everyone learns differently, the online tutorials include audio instruction as well as visual demonstrations.

Tips for training employees

SAVVY ENTREPRENEURS invest time and money training their employees. Here's how to get started:

1. Ask your employees what software programs they think would boost productivity before you buy anything new.
2. Schedule time during the day for training, whether it's online or with an instructor.
3. Encourage employees to practice their new computer skills on company time and after hours.
4. Share the expense of hiring a trainer with another small-business owner in your area.
5. Call your local community college district for information on the variety of affordable classes available for employees.

You can pick up the basics of a program or learn more advanced functions. Then you can practice everything you've just learned.

Meanwhile, back in Philadelphia, Epstein said her main complaint about her online tutoring was that the audio portion of the lesson takes several minutes to download. But she said it's worth waiting for the voice to explain to her exactly what she should do to master the program.

By the year 2001, worldwide revenues for the information-technology training and education market are expected to reach $27 billion, according to International Data Corp. Investing in training has become necessary because nearly one-fifth of the top U.S. information technology executives rated the lack of skilled people as the most serious constraint to the growth of their businesses, according to Ellen Julian, IDC's research manager.

Link Your Telephone and Computer

COMPUTER TELEPHONE INTEGRATION (CTI) IS A great idea for anyone who is on the phone with lots of clients or customers all day. A decade ago, big companies installed this kind of system for $100,000. Today you can put one in for $1,000 to $10,000, depending on your system requirements.

The first step in setting up CTI is to sign up for Caller ID from your local phone company. Next, you need a fast and accurate database software program, such as Goldmine, and whatever other related software programs you need to do your work.

Here's how it works: When a call comes through, the Caller ID information checks to see whether the phone number is already in your database. If it is, a screen pops up with the caller's name, date you first did business together, and all sorts of personal information that you've stored in the database. You not only know who is calling, but can mentally prepare to answer their questions. You are a step ahead of your caller within seconds. If the number is unknown, a blank form to fill out appears on your screen.

A CTI system is great for accountants, brokers, consultants, and anyone else who has to keep track of constantly changing information and people.

Set Up a Teleconference

GREAT 168 IDEA

IF YOU ARE STRESSED OUT AND TIRED OF AIRPORTS, bad airline food, and the expense of traveling, consider joining the modern age.

Videoconferencing, once available only to major megabuck corporations, is now accessible and affordable for smaller companies. Best of all, you don't need any equipment to conduct a multisite discussion. Although many other companies offer videoconferencing services, Kinko's, the small-business owner's friend, offers videoconferencing services at more than 200 locations.

If everyone on your conference call goes to a Kinko's, the cost is $150 per hour per site with a half hour minimum. Multiple Kinko's sites are $205 per site; it's $180 per hour if you use a non-Kinko's location at one end.

In addition to broadcasting your image, you can transmit graphics, slides, videotape, and computer data. "It's the second-best thing to being there," said Kinko's spokeswoman Laura McCormick.

Here are some tips from Kinko's on making your videoconference a success:

- Arrange the conference in advance and make sure everyone knows what needs to be accomplished.
- Send out an agenda and other materials prior to the conference.
- Remember, time is money, so prioritize your points and choose one person to act as chairperson at each location.
- Avoid wearing bright red, white, plaids, stripes, or prints, because they are distracting and create visual problems on camera.
- Speak naturally and clearly. Pause briefly at the end of your remark because there is a slight lag-time in transmission.
- Don't cough into the microphone or hold side conversations during the session.

- Let everyone know when you are about to show graphics.
- Identify yourself from time to time so everyone can keep track of the participants.

For more information and to make reservations, contact a Kinko's in your area.

Make the Most of Voice Mail

EVEN THE WORST TECHNOPHOBES LOVE VOICE mail. For me, it's the greatest technology ever invented. The ability to change your outgoing message every day, receive multiple messages while you're on the phone, and call in for messages from anywhere on the planet is an irreplaceable part of doing business today. I don't pretend to understand all the intricacies of how it works, but I know I couldn't work without it.

The problem is, many people don't take full advantage of the system. It takes only a few seconds to change your message whenever necessary. Busy entrepreneurs can impress clients and customers by telling them whether they are in or out of the office every day and when callers can expect a return call. This really cuts down on telephone tag.

After I leave a detailed message, I also mention the best time to reach me. Voice mail is especially wonderful when you are dealing across multiple time zones and internationally. Through the years, I have negotiated, planned, managed, and completed six-figure projects without ever meeting certain members of the client's team.

When people know how to use voice mail like a pro, it can really speed things up. Sometimes just forwarding a message to the right person for a reply can get a problem solved quickly.

It may seem basic, but when you leave a message, remember to give your name, your company name, your phone number, and the best time to reach you.

If you've chosen a more elaborate voice mail system with different mail boxes for each employee or department, it's important to make it easy for callers to find the right extension or to reach a human being. I truly believe businesses lose millions of dollars in sales because frustrated callers hang up when they can't maneuver through a tricky voice mail system.

In addition to voice mail, if you expect to put callers on hold, you might consider installing a "messages on hold" feature. These systems allow you to do everything from play popular music to review your business hours—all while people are waiting to get through to a person *(see Great Idea 76)*.

Messages on hold are annoying if they are on a short, repetitive loop. The best ones, used by many big companies, tell callers exactly how much more time they have to wait for service.

Because the industry is evolving so fast, it may pay to hire a telecommunications consultant before choosing a voice mail system. But whatever system you order, use it well—to make life easier for everyone who deals with you.

Perform a Technology Checkup

WITH THE COST OF TECHNOLOGY PLUMMETING, there's no excuse not to have the best hardware and software available. The right technology not only makes your life easier, but it also boosts morale and productivity and improves customer service.

One way to figure out exactly what you need to purchase is to take this quick technology checkup. My three-step checkup helps you determine whether you are serving yourself, your employees, and your customers well. It will also help you match the equipment you need with the work you must accomplish every day.

1 **Determine your own technology preferences.** Busy entrepreneurs rely on quick, clear communication to keep up with all their responsibilities. Ask yourself how you prefer to communicate with people: Is it via e-mail? Voice mail? Fax or pager? Even the most computerphobic entrepreneurs are slowly realizing that the PC is their most powerful business tool. Decide whether you need a laptop computer. Or maybe you prefer to work in the office and transmit files via modem?

Determining what kind of equipment is necessary to do your work sets the stage for the way the rest of your employees, vendors, and customers deal with your company.

Once you've figured out what is needed, make a "wish list" of things to buy. Decide whether single-purpose or multipurpose equipment best fits your needs. Take a stroll through a showroom to become acquainted with what's on the market.

2 **Speak with key employees about their technology requirements.** You can't make smart purchasing decisions without feedback from your people on the front lines.

Add your employees' equipment requests to the company "wish list." They may not need much. Maybe they'd like a color printer to add pizzazz to sales materials. Perhaps they need faster personal computers or networking capabilities. Assign one interested person to begin researching prices and equipment specifications. Speak to other business owners and ask for their personal recommendations. Most people are very happy to share what they like and don't like about the hardware and software they use.

3 **Poll your customers and vendors.** A quick, efficient way to collect information is to send out a prepaid, perforated, two-part postcard. Most quick printers can help you design one.

Keep the questions short: Do they prefer to fax orders or phone them in? Would they order more if they could order online?

Find out if they need an after-hours phone number, an e-mail address, or fax-back service. Ask them if your brochures and catalogs are providing them with all the necessary information. Most customers will be happy to take a few minutes to let you know what's right and wrong about their dealings with your firm.

Add the customer requests to your wish list before you set your budget and priorities.

While you probably can't afford to run out and purchase everything on the list right away, at least you can get started. Then set a time to do this checkup again at the same time next year so you can see what progress you've made.

Use a Digital Camera for Your Web Site

IN THE SUMMER OF 1997, JOHN AND BETSY Powel, owners of Salt Marsh Pottery, skipped the Atlanta gift trade show they had attended for years. It just didn't seem worth spending $8,000 to participate in the show, which generated only $16,000 worth of orders.

Still, they didn't want to lose the business. So they printed and mailed colored "sell" sheets to the trade show attendees. Soon after, they booked $16,000 worth of orders, and the phone is still ringing.

The Powels produced the sheets themselves in a couple of days using a digital camera, computer, and ink-jet color printer. The camera cost about $1,000; they also use it to shoot product photos for their Web site.

Steve Morgenstern, author of *Grow Your Business with Desktop Publishing,* said rather than using run-of-the-mill clip art to convey ideas, small businesses can put their products on display fast.

"The combination of digital cameras and computers to print or electronically publish color photos is the second publishing revolution for small businesses, following desktop publishing, made possible by laser printers and computers," said Morgenstern.

Digital cameras are filmless. Like other digital media, digital cameras allow you to view, erase, or edit images before you print. They work just like regular auto-focus, point-and-shoot cameras. But after you shoot, you view the image on the back side of the camera. If it's not just right, you can erase it and take another shot.

To edit the image, you connect the camera to your computer via a cable. There are a variety of software programs ranging in price and capability, so shop around. Adobe's PhotoShop is widely used, but is a bit pricey for small-business owners. With the right software in place, you can adjust the brightness, contrast, and size. Once you've concocted the best image, you print it out with a laser or color ink-jet printer. With a modem, you can send the image by e-mail to a customer or post it on your own Web site.

Professional-quality digital cameras, like those used by *Sports Illustrated* photographers, start at $15,000, and go up. But digital auto-focus cameras for the layman cost less than $1,000. A good ink-jet printer can be had for under $300; however, the special high-gloss paper you need for images costs about 75 cents a sheet.

There is a downside: While digital images are quicker and easier to manipulate than traditional film images, the quality is still not as good as film if you want to produce a high-end catalog or advertisement. And professional photographers will tell you that digital images pale compared to those they shoot on film.

Morgenstern also cautions: "Unless you use an expensive laser printer, the quality of photographic output doesn't match the clarity of a drugstore snapshot reprint."

Some advantages of going digital

- No per-picture expense. After you buy the camera, there are no film or development costs. You can fire away, free of charge.
- Immediate results. Wonder whether you got the shot? Just hook the camera up to your computer or view the results instantly on the camera's built-in LCD panel.
- Easy integration into digital media. With desktop publishing tools, digital cameras provide powerful graphic ammunition with minimal fuss and bother.
- Easy transmission via fax or modem. With a digital camera, you can grab a picture and quickly send it by e-mail or print a copy and fax it.

Scan Your Business Cards

YOUR ROLODEX IS A GOLD MINE, BUT FLIPPING through it and keeping it up to date is a hassle.

Insurance broker Richard Butwin, of Great Neck, New York, said his greatest idea was to buy a CardScan system. Through the miracles of modern technology, you pop a business card into the scanner, and within minutes the data is read and stored. Then, when you are ready, the software transfers the information into whatever contact management software you use.

The company says the system is great for salespeople, executives, assistants—anyone who has to keep track of lots of people. CardScan's basic software costs $99; the deluxe system with scanner and software is $299. For more information, call CardScan at (800) 316-4183, or visit their Web site at **www.cardscan.com**.

Create a Web Site

CREATING YOUR OWN WEB SITE IS A COMPLEX and demanding project that can cost you money instead of making you money—if you don't do it right. Before you plan your site, determine whether you can afford to create and maintain it. You can't just put it out there in cyberspace and forget about it. At least once a week, you should be adding fresh information, offers, and incentives to visit your site. You also need to make sure that your customers and clients are Web-savvy. If they aren't yet going online to find information or make purchases, there's a chance you may be wasting your time and money.

Here are some steps to get you started:

1 **Go online to check out a variety of Web sites belonging to big and small companies.** This is the best way to figure out exactly what you like and don't like. Some sites are very elaborate, with all sorts of graphics and animation. Some are very simple and elegant. Mark the sites you like so you can share them with a designer.

2 **Outline all the elements you would like to include on**

your own site. Carefully list the information you want to share with your customers or clients. Ask yourself: Do you need to include product information and a price list? An order form? Will you be putting your catalog online? Will you feature some sort of schedule to track product releases or shipments?

3 **Make a list of the sections and estimate how many pages of text they will take up.** Most Web site estimates are based on the number of pages or screens.

4 **Once you've outlined all of the sections you want on your site, make appointments to meet with at least two or three designers.** Ask your friends or colleagues to recommend good Web site designers. Or better yet, call the companies whose sites you liked best and ask them for the name and phone number of their designer. Before you set up an appointment to meet with a designer, ask for some references and call them. Meet only with the people who come highly recommended. You don't want to waste time getting an estimate from someone who is difficult to work with, doesn't meet deadlines, or has a bad reputation.

5 **At the first meeting, ask the designer to go online and show you some of the work they've done for other clients.** Before you show them what you want done, get clear answers to these questions:

- *Will they do all the work themselves, or farm it out to others?*
- *How and when do they expect to be paid? Do they require a deposit up front?*
- *How much do they charge to update and maintain a site? Most designers have an hourly rate for these services.*
- *Will they find you a host server and help set up your site?*

6 **After you get answers to the above questions, ask for a written, detailed estimate**—including a "site map" which shows you how all the pages will flow from the home page.

7 **Remember, development prices will vary considerably, depending on what you want.** Developing a new Web site can cost as little as $2,500 or as much as $200,000, depending on the complexity. Many online services offer very low-cost personal sites to members, but if you are in business,

you probably want to have a more professional-looking site. When you receive the estimates, make careful comparisons. Be sure to factor in the cost of the server and any setup fees.

8 **Watch out for padding or hidden costs.** Don't be afraid to ask questions to really understand everything you'll be paying for.

9 **When your site is finished, be sure to obtain a disk or CD-ROM with your completed site from your designer.** Remember, the designer doesn't own the site, you do. Having a copy in hand will protect you from losing all the work should you decide to hire someone else down the line.

10 **Start out simple.** Nothing should be more than two clicks from the home page. Aim for a very clean, elegant design; you can always add animated graphics later, if you need to.

11 **Check out these books before getting started:** *Creating Killer Web Sites: The Art of Third-Generation Site Design,* by David S. Siegel (Hayden Books; $14.00), and *How to Make a Fortune on the Internet,* by Martha Siegel (HarperCollins; $14.00).

Computerize Your Service Business

BEFORE VETERAN TAILOR AND DRY CLEANER YOON Lim bought the Manor Cleaners in Pelham Manor, New York, whenever I forgot my yellow dry cleaning receipt, I had to sign my name in a worn spiral notebook to confirm that I had collected my clothes.

That old-fashioned system ended abruptly one day in October 1997. When the door opened at 8 AM, there stood two shiny computer stations set into slick blue-and-white Formica counters. Manor Cleaners had gone high-tech overnight.

Lim, who owns two other dry cleaning businesses in Westchester County, said he spent about $5,000 for each customized computer. The system, which he has installed in all three stores, is designed specifically for dry cleaning businesses. Each keyboard key is coded to record a shirt, coat, dress, or bedspread.

The prices ring up automatically, and the system prints

out a crisp, two-part, detailed receipt—one for the store, the other for customers. We may keep losing our receipts, but Lim's staff will never lose track of our clothes or what we owe him.

Lim said he couldn't operate the business without help from his new computers. No matter what kind of small business you own, you can buy a customized computer system. If you operate a pet store, construction company, restaurant, law firm, insurance office, or a chain of beauty salons, you can find a customized system to track inventory, log point-of-purchase sales information, generate invoices, and trigger reorders.

You can buy systems from many big companies, including IBM, the granddaddy of customized systems, or hire a local hardware consultant to put together a system from scratch.

According to a 1997 survey by Microsoft, there are about 200,000 independent computer dealers who create customized systems for business owners just like you. Although about 20 percent of them disappear or go out of business every year, most stick around long enough to get your system up and running.

The advantages of having a customized system are many. You get exactly what you need—nothing more. The software is written for your particular industry and is frequently updated.

The best way to find the right software is to contact your trade or professional association and ask for a list of software vendors serving your industry. If you don't belong to a group, now is the time to join.

If you think your business is too esoteric to have software written for it, think again. My friend and neighbor, Debra Orlando, designs store interiors for Esteé Lauder stores around the world. In her cozy attic, she works on a Macintosh computer loaded with special CAD-CAM software for interior designers. She sends a disk to the architects and contractors, who download her files to print out detailed construction plans.

Orlando rarely meets face to face with her colleagues, but she manages to do very high-level design work from her home-based studio. Her computer systems allows her to spend more time with her preschool daughter, Kara, and to be home when her 10-year-old son, Peter, gets home from school.

So no matter what kind of small business you run, consider looking beyond what's available off the shelf to find exactly the kind of hardware and software you need to succeed.

Buy a High-Tech Postage Meter

THE DAYS OF LUGGING A HEAVY POSTAGE METER to the post office for a refill are almost over. By March 31, 1999, the U.S. Postal Service is outlawing the mechanical postage meters used by most small businesses. This means the 750,000 businesses that use them need to move quickly into the modern age. The Postal Service is phasing out the mechanical meters to eliminate tampering fraud estimated to cost taxpayers about $100 million a year.

Luckily, the new digital postage meter is much more efficient. It can download postage via modem in less than a minute for a small fee.

There are four companies marketing products on the Postal Service's authorized list: Postalia Inc., Ascom Hasler Mailing Systems Inc., Neopost, and Pitney Bowes.

Pitney Bowes, the granddaddy of postal equipment, has a "Personal Post Office" product designed specifically for small businesses. The sleek, digital postage meter can download postage via a modem in about 20 seconds, 24 hours a day. The software can print up to 10 envelopes a minute, design envelopes, manage addresses, and tell you how much postage a letter or package needs.

"Mail is the engine of commerce for small firms, but it's time-consuming," said Mike Stecyk, vice president and general manager of Pitney Bowes small office/home office division. "Pitney Bowes is reinventing the way small businesses generate mail. We understand there is more to mailing than just putting postage on an envelope."

Stecyk said a recent company-sponsored survey found that 85 percent of small businesses surveyed are still licking stamps and preparing mail by hand—this is a big waste of time and money. The company also has a Mail Marketer CD-ROM, which provides a direct mail tutorial, and DirectNET, a mailing service that allows small companies to modem mailings to Pitney Bowes for distribution.

For information on Pitney Bowes products, call the company at (800) 640-7058, or check out their Web site at: **www.pitneybowes.com**.

Prepare Your Computer for 2000

YOU WOULD HAVE TO BE DEAD NOT TO BE AWARE that computer systems are going to need some help coping with the date change on January 1, 2000. Yet Peter de Jager, a consultant and developer of the Year 2000 Internet Information Center (**www.year2000.com**), said that even by late 1997, fewer than 35 percent of American companies were dealing with the problem, and only 10 percent of European countries had done anything at all.

The whole problem is based on the way software code was written 25 or 30 years ago. Computer code consists of zeros and ones—and will apparently go crazy when it has to deal with two zeros in the date. The "00 problem" is worse for mainframe computers, but PC and Macintosh users will also have to upgrade much of the software they use.

If you believe the computer gurus, the cost of fixing this glitch is staggering. The Gartner Group, a well-respected think tank, predicts it could cost $600 billion to update the world's computers. Boston's Software Productivity Research puts the price tag at a mind-boggling $3.6 trillion.

To learn what I could about the challenge, I attended a Year 2000 conference sponsored by Cruttenden Roth, a small but aggressive Newport Beach, California, investment banking firm. The meeting featured representatives from dozens of publicly held high-tech companies, all determined to make a fortune fixing the "millennium bug."

The computer experts explained how massive mainframe "legacy" computer systems need their code converted line by line. They spoke of "factories" full of technicians being set up around the world to convert round-the-clock. The companies involved plan to charge as much as eight cents per line—with billions of lines of code in total.

If you have a mainframe computer system, I would hope you have a crack team of information systems experts already handling this problem. If you are smart enough to buy this book, you are smart enough to hire someone to prepare your computers for the new century.

If you own a small company that relies mainly on PCs, you are also pretty lucky. Most popular computer software programs are already programmed to deal with the 00 date change, but find out for sure how to avoid nasty surprises on New Year's Eve 1999. Many off-the-shelf programs will be easily upgraded, but you'll probably have to pay for those upgrades.

The experts say middle-sized companies with a mix of computers will probably have the toughest time with the Year 2000 problem.

In addition to computers, don't forget to reprogram any computer-driven manufacturing equipment and electronic devices that rely on dates to keep track of information. Bar coders, scanners, and those nifty handheld devices used by UPS will all have to be upgraded.

But rather than panicking, spend some time right now figuring out exactly what needs to be done to get your business ready for the millennium. If you get busy today, you can spend the rest of the '90s planning the best New Year's Eve celebration ever, rather than fretting over an impending computer crash.

Use E-Fax

RATHER THAN ELIMINATING PAPERWORK, personal computers generate massive piles of paper. Sure, we e-mail files around the world, but most of us then print out a copy and stick it in a file somewhere.

Still, the main advantage of using electronic mail to transmit information is that it can save you time and money. For example, using the Internet to fax can be substantially cheaper than using traditional phone lines, even if you delay documents until the long-distance rates drop.

There are scores of companies around the world now providing electronic fax services. Here are a couple of them:

- **E-Fax Communication** reported that if you send 500 one-page documents by first-class mail, the postage will cost $160; good-quality letterhead and envelopes will cost about $175; and labor to prepare the envelopes is $130.

  If you decide instead to go the fax broadcast route, you can send the mailing list and the information to their service bureau. The charge for transmitting to 500 locations is about $85, or 17 cents each, according to E-Fax. For more information on E-Fax, call them at (800) 252-0360.
- **.Comfax** is another firm that opened its doors in 1997. .comfax (pronounced "dot-comfax") offers Internet fax services to big and small companies. The service allows documents to be sent from any Windows-based PC over the Internet at a savings of about 50 percent over traditional faxing.

  ".comfax is both the Volkswagen and Mercedes Benz of faxing," said Ben Fader, chief executive officer and president. "You don't have to be a Fortune 500 company to enjoy low prices."

  Free .comfax software lets you send 1,000 faxes—or just one—for about 10 cents a minute anywhere in the United States. International rates vary by country.

  The software also sets up a "virtual fax in-box" that receives faxes when you are away from the office. Each user is assigned a personal phone number for receiving faxes. You can view or print your faxes wherever you are or forward them on. To check out .comfax services, go to their Web site at **www.comfax.com**.

Sell Products Online

WOULD YOU SPEND $23,000 WHILE SITTING AT your computer? Well, someone actually paid that much for a $3 gold piece minted in 1884, during an antique coin auction hosted by Numismatists Online in November 1997. The site, managed by San Francisco–based Hobby Markets Online, has received more than 100,000 bids in more than 1,000 auctions.

"Soon, 4,000 coin dealers will be online, and our growth will be out of sight!" said Jonathan Hubbard, cofounder and president of the Web marketing firm. Founded in 1995, **www.hobbymarkets.com** was established to serve the collectibles market. Rare coin sales alone were about $4 million in 1997. The company collects a commission on all sales and is one of the lucky Internet companies turning a profit.

After some Internet security–related cold feet, consumers seem to be feeling more comfortable shopping online, so it's time to figure out if you should be selling via the World Wide Web. In 1997 worldwide online retail sales topped $10 billion, and sales are expected to hit $200 billion in 2001, according to International Data Corp. Although there are still some technical problems and psychological resistance, consumers seem to have fewer complaints about buying online, and many become repeat shoppers. You can't beat the convenience of shopping online if you know where to go.

Ronny Yakov, founder of Colorbank Digital Sources Inc. in Manhattan, approached several clients to create ShopFast (**www.shopfast.com**), a shopping site for upscale items such as Belgian chocolate, seaweed-based beauty products, and golf equipment.

"The companies maintain their individual identity, but if you make a purchase on one of the sites, you can get a discount if you buy something else from another," said Yakov.

He doesn't charge anything to design the sites, but earns a percentage of sales. "We leave all the pricing decisions to the clients, but we like to work with companies that have a strong ability to deliver the goods," said Yakov.

His sites' eclectic mix of music, clothes, software, flowers, toys, movies, and beauty and recreational products seems to be working. "It's growing tremendously from month to month," he said. "People are feeling more comfortable about using credit cards over the Internet."

For those still reluctant to release credit card information, ShopFast offers the ability to call an 800 number, fax an order, or use electronic funds transfer.

Savvy Web-preneurs tell me that it's important to offer a variety of payment options so you don't scare customers away. Although financial transactions over the Net are usually secure, there have been problems. But if you've ever ordered things over the phone, you know that there are hassles with catalog shopping, as well.

Here are some things to consider before offering products online:

- Do your clients or customers use the Internet? If they don't, it's not worth setting up shop online.
- Can you display your wares through simple photographs or illustrations?
- Can you provide enough product information online for people to make an intelligent buying decision?
- Is your fulfillment process in place? Do you accept credit cards?
- Do you have someone on your staff who is Web-savvy and can process online orders?
- Can you test-market your products on someone else's site before investing in your own?

If you answered "yes" to at least four of the questions, it's worth looking into online sales.

CHAPTER 8

Customer Service

I LAUGHED WHEN SOMEONE ONCE SAID TO me, "Business is great, except for the people." It's true, but without people you won't have a business, so your job is to provide the best customer service possible.

We all know that one unhappy customer blabs to 10 others about how awful you or your staff has treated them, but a happy customer rarely passes along the good news.

Your challenge is to get your good customers to generate a positive buzz about your business. They will, *if* you give them excellent service and a reason to recommend you.

It sounds easier than it is. Providing really good customer service takes time, money, and extraordinary patience. It means putting yourself out there to take the good news with the bad. And it means taking responsibility for making sure no complaint goes unresolved.

My husband, Joe, is a great customer. He refuses to put up with poor service or shoddy products. In a typical week, he returned a broken cordless phone to Staples and got a full refund from the manager, even though a clerk said it was impossible because we had thrown the box away. "I had the receipt, so they had to give me my money back," he explained.

He returned a broken plastic dimmer knob to the manufacturer and received a nice brass one in the mail a few days later. He's found that being a squeaky wheel really works—most of the time.

But don't wait for complaints to set your services in order—having a courteous and consistent customer service policy will win you a lot of new business. The burden is on you, the business owner, to keep customers loyal.

No chapter on customer service would be complete without mentioning Nordstrom, the Cadillac of customer service-oriented companies. Their employee handbook is just a five-by-eight-inch gray card that reads:

> *We're glad to have you with our company.*
>
> *Our number one goal is to provide outstanding customer service. Set both your personal and professional goals high. We have great confidence in your ability to achieve them.*
>
> *Rule #1:* Use your good judgment in all situations. *There will be no additional rules. Please feel free to ask your department manager, store manager, or division general manager any question at any time.*

Pretty cool. But it takes a total commitment to customer service and a special, almost cultish approach to pull it off. If you want to know more about how Nordstrom customer service can't be beat, read *The Nordstrom Way*, by Robert Spector and Patrick McCarthy.

When I asked my former research associate, Mimi Schultz, for her favorite customer service-oriented company, she said it was Mindspring, a new online service. She likes the way they give her a $10 credit toward one month's service every time she refers a new customer. So far, she's signed up her roommates, several other friends, and me.

In this chapter I cover how to survey customers to find out what they really think about your business. You'll learn how to take advantage of "mystery shoppers," and how taking your product or service to your customer's home or business can really boost sales. There's also a new retail training center that's teaching clerks to do more than ring up a sale.

As tough as it is to be pleasant and patient some days, remember that if you put people first, more business will follow.

Take This Customer-Service Quiz

GREAT 179 IDEA

TAKE THIS CUSTOMER-SERVICE QUIZ TO FIND OUT whether you are treating your customers the way you, yourself, would like to be treated.

1 **Do you really know who your customers are and whether you are responsive to their changing needs?** If you are unsure, create a database to collect information on their purchasing habits, likes, wants, and business practices. Be sure to update the database on a regular basis.

2 **When a customer returns a product, are they treated the same way as when they purchased that product? How do you handle complaints?** Use the same courtesy and level of service when a customer is returning a product as you did when he or she bought it. Treat complaints as a way to improve your business and generate goodwill.

3 **Are telephone calls answered promptly and returned the same day? Do customers and clients complain that your phone lines are constantly busy?** Customers expect a quick response. Return phone calls the same day, if possible. And when customers call, they should never get a busy signal. Voice mail can help you, but it should never replace a human at the other end of the line.

4 **If your product comes with a guarantee, are you honoring that guarantee?** If a customer thinks the product is guaranteed, but finds too many loopholes that void it, you could be perceived as dishonest. Honor all product guarantees, even if the conditions are not fully met. Nordstrom takes back any item, with no questions asked.

5 **Does your staff really know how to serve your customers?** Make sure everyone on your staff knows exactly what kind of service to provide. Review their performance and reward employees for providing good customer service.

Hire a Mystery Shopper

GREAT 180 IDEA

CAROL CHERRY MAY MAKE HER LIVING FROM shopping, but you won't catch her at the local mall browsing for a gift.

"I hate shopping. I can't remember the last time I've been to a mall," said Cherry, owner and president of Atlanta-based Shop'n Chek Inc., one of the nation's largest mystery shopping companies. Businesses hire her firm to see if employees are providing good customer service.

Cherry founded the company in 1974, and today it has about 50,000 freelance shoppers in the United States and abroad. They visit restaurants, department stores, gas stations, bowling alleys, and anywhere else people shop, eat, or play.

"This industry can really help a small business, especially one with two locations when the owner can't be in two places at once," said Cherry, whose client list reads like a *Who's Who* of American business. (Client confidentiality precludes her naming any names.)

Cherry said the industry began years ago as a way for big retailers to learn why certain appliances weren't selling. Then employers started hiring outsiders to make sure employees weren't stealing from them. But so-called honesty shopping, Cherry said, has been outlawed in most states unless it's performed by licensed private investigators.

Mystery shoppers, however, are regular folks who are observant and like to deal with people. They are paid per assignment, which involves filling out a detailed questionnaire immediately after a visit. They note how they were greeted by salespeople. They examine the way merchandise is displayed and how salespeople handle their questions, complaints, and returns. Mystery shoppers will also check to see if employees offer information about special promotions or explain company services properly.

A good mystery shopping service will spend time learning about your business and how you expect your employees to behave. And it will be objective.

Mystery shoppers set their own hours and do the work

more for fun than money. A shopper might earn $10 to $20 for a night at a local bowling alley.

Many services specialize. For example, Melinda Brody & Associates in Orlando, Florida, focuses on tourism, travel, and home building. Brody, who worked as an apartment leasing agent and sales trainer, knows the real-estate business, and so she focuses on that. Her partner, Marilyn Whelan, works on the hotel accounts.

One of their company's specialties is checking on real-estate salespeople. Home builders get permission to tape their salespeople while they are speaking with customers. The salesperson never knows whether that nice couple looking to buy a condo are real customers or one of Brody's mystery shopping teams.

In its work with hotel chains and resorts around Florida, the group relies on a statewide network of 500 freelance shoppers. The 10-year-old company had its best year yet in 1997— its sales approached $1 million.

In most cities, mystery shoppers are listed in the Yellow Pages under "shopping services."

Don't Make Your Customers Angry

ONE OF THE SMARTEST BUSINESS PEOPLE I KNOW is my grandfather, George Coan. He finally retired after 66 years in the retail business. Yes, 66 years!

Coan started his retail career as a teenager, selling clothes on the Lower East Side of New York City. Movie-star handsome and always a snappy dresser, he worked his way up to store manager and eventually served as vice president of personnel for a major East Coast men's clothing chain.

Soon after he retired and moved to North Miami, he sold leisure wear in a tiny boutique in his condominium complex. At 92, he's still my best clipping service and a top adviser. He offered this great idea based on his experience waiting on thousands of customers.

"Whatever you do, don't make your customer angry."

It sounds simple, but so many things in a retail setting can upset a customer. For example, if you make a customer wait too long while you look for their size or obtain a credit approval, they grow impatient.

If your salespeople are rude, act bored, or are careless, you will alienate customers. Nothing is worse than waiting for a salesclerk to finish a chatty conversation with a colleague or cooling your heels while they blab away on a personal call. Customers are gold to any business. If you do things to upset them, they may walk away and never return. You want every person's visit to your store to be a pleasure, not a nightmare.

With so many alternatives to retail shopping, including mail order and electronic commerce on the World Wide Web, do everything you can to keep your customers coming back, checkbook in hand.

Make House Calls

GREAT 182 IDEA

IN THIS HIGH-TECH, CONSTANTLY BUSTLING world, a little personal service goes a long, long way. Visiting your clients or customers at their homes or in their neighborhood gives some businesses a definite edge over the competition.

Mary Heyob and her husband, Tom, sell crop insurance in the Midwest. Nadya, a Balinese-based clothing designer, meets her clients in hotel suites across America. First Union National Bank of Maryland sends bankers to set up branches in retirement homes. And London-based Norton & Townsend tailors visit well-off and well-dressed men in their homes and offices.

Although they all sell vastly different products, they attribute much of their success to meeting their customers' needs on their own turf.

"We see 95 percent of our customers on their farms, all over the state," said Mary Heyob, who serves as office manager and bookkeeper for the Pro Crop Insurance Agency.

Because the sale of crop insurance is totally regulated by the Federal Crop Insurance Corp., the prices are set by the government. This means the only way the Heyobs can set themselves apart is by providing terrific service. They know their customers' needs and meet with them on farms throughout Indiana and western Ohio.

Keeping thousands of customers happy is what Nadya does best. Originally from Chicago, the one-name designer fell in love with Bali while vacationing there in 1978. By 1980 she started hiring artists and seamstresses to create her unique, comfortable batiked or hand-painted cotton and rayon clothing.

On a 1997 visit to New York City, she told me she had 125 people working in two locations, with annual sales in excess of $1 million.

Nadya spends about six months creating new lines of clothing, then she hits the road—selling her wares across America. She keeps her overhead low by setting up shop in hotel suites in Los Angeles; Washington, D.C.; San Francisco; Boston; Chicago; and Irvine, California.

Her trunk sales are more party than high-pressure sales event. She serves sparkling water, fruit, cheese, and crackers. Models drift around the suite, showing off her fashions. Assistants help select and fit customers.

For more information, go online to Nadya's Web site at **www.Nadya.com**.

While banking services are not as glamorous as Balinese fashions, smart banks are sending bankers to nursing homes to serve elderly customers. A branch in Maryland's Edenwald retirement facility has 500 square feet with about 170 safety deposit boxes.

Jim Bowe, vice president of American Seniors Housing Association, told the *Washington Business Journal* that seniors are attractive bank customers for several reasons. They have consistent income and have to maintain a certain standard of living to stay in a retirement community. They are a good source of deposits and tend to be very loyal customers.

Finally, if you want a fine, custom-tailored English suit brought right to your doorstep, just call Norton & Townsend in London. Their tailors visit busy men in their homes and offices in both London and Manhattan.

Think about ways to expand your business by reaching out to customers at home or at their offices. Consider Avon's tremendous global success: They send representatives in canoes up the Amazon River! Providing any sort of delivery service is a cost-effective way to reach more people. Not many businesses make house calls these days—maybe you should give it a try in your business!

Send Employees to a Retail Training Center

GREAT 183 IDEA

FINDING SKILLED WORKERS HAS EDGED OUT access to capital as the top small-business challenge in several recent independent surveys. Now the retail industry is doing something about it, and every consumer who waits patiently while an unskilled clerk attempts to ring up a sale can rejoice.

The nation's first "retail skills center" opened in 1997 in the King of Prussia mall near Philadelphia. The National Retail Federation partnered with American Express, Kravco Co., the mall developer, and the Commonwealth of Pennsylvania to sponsor the hands-on training program.

"I've heard from employers time and time again that they can't find workers with the skills to succeed," Pennsylvania Gov. Tom Ridge told members of the National Retail Federation meeting. "This unique partnership helps to ensure that this is not the case in King of Prussia. And for those desiring the skills to go to work, the program lends them that helping hand."

Entry-level employees are taught the basics of customer service and how to make a sale, among other things. Retail federation leaders said the center is specifically designed to help small retailers whose training resources are typically limited and who often hire the greenest, lowest-paid workers. If the center is successful, it could serve as a nationwide model. For information, call The National Retail Federation at (202) 783-7971.

Demand Great Service from Vendors

DAVID GUMPERT, AN AUTHOR, JOURNALIST, AND Web site wizard, gave me a great idea when we met in Washington, D.C., to celebrate Small-Business Week.

When he's negotiating with new suppliers or vendors that he wants to do business with, he doesn't niggle on price. Instead, he tells them, "I will pay you top dollar, if you promise to always give me excellent service."

Basically, he's very clear that he wants his phone calls returned quickly, his supplies delivered on time, and any problems resolved immediately.

He said this direct approach really works. People appreciate not being beaten up over price and are happy to respond to his demand for excellent service. He's willing to pay a few dollars more to be treated like a king.

It's similar to what happens when you need technical support from a hardware or software vendor. You can wait on hold all day by using the free side of their support team, or pay $20 to $30, speak to a real person, and get your problem resolved in minutes.

Remember, time is money. And if you're striving to give your customers and clients top-notch customer service, shouldn't you expect the same courtesy from your vendors?

Get to Know Your Customers Personally

ONE OF THE BENEFITS OF OWNING A SMALL business is being able to get to know your customers, suppliers, and vendors. When you meet people, jot down a few personal notes on the back of their business cards or on Rolodex cards. Ask for their birthdate, family members, pets, and club memberships. We all like to do business with people who treat us well and seem genuinely interested in what we do and say. When you know someone's birthday, send a card. It's a cheap and wonderful way to keep in touch.

What better way to nurture loyalty than to create a personal connection—it's important for customers to want to do business with you. That little bit of extra effort can go a long way toward solidifying a long-term contract.

Send handwritten notes to customers and clients whenever possible. The most successful, important people I know put this into practice, and it makes a tremendous, positive impression. One of my busiest friends—a person who has one of the top jobs in the country—sends me a one- or two-line note at least once a month. His notes mean a lot and always brighten my day. Of course, I quickly respond—with a handwritten note!

So spend the time it takes to make that personal connection. It's worth the effort.

Wrap It Up

ONE OF THE NICEST THINGS YOU CAN DO FOR your customers and your business is send them out the door with their merchandise beautifully gift wrapped.

It saves customers time and money, and great packaging is one of the smartest and most cost-effective advertisements for your retail business. Think of Tiffany's signature turquoise box and how much goodwill that has generated through the years.

One of my favorite stores is Felissimo, an elegant Japanese-owned boutique on West 56th Street in Manhattan. The renovated brownstone features unique jewelry and clothes, as well as gifts for home, garden, and bath. And, in addition to its gorgeous merchandise, Felissimo is famous for its perfect gift wrapping.

Gift items are swathed in layers of tissue paper and nestled into a heavy cardboard bag or box. The box is secured with a thick elastic band wrapped around a bent twig. For a few extra dollars, they will wrap your gift in a lovely piece of fabric, a traditional Japanese way to present something special. Gifts are carried out in brown bags with heavy twine handles.

No matter what you buy there, whether it be a candle or $500 earrings, the gift is even more special because of the unique gift wrapping.

Craft Company No. 6, Rochester, New York's dazzling, one-of-a-kind craft gallery, wraps gifts in custom-designed cardboard boxes. Their gift boxes feature a pen-and-ink drawing of the converted firehouse that houses the 6,000-square-foot store. While you are waiting for your gifts to be wrapped, they encourage you to sign up for their mailing list. The store also has a newsletter to keep good customers posted on merchandise, special events, and promotions.

As an avid shopper, I'm always surprised when a merchant hands me my purchases in a blank paper or plastic bag. If you can't wrap merchandise, at least invest in custom bags or order stickers with your logo, address, and phone number.

It doesn't take much to make every customer a walking billboard for your business.

CHAPTER 9

Going Global

IF YOUR BUSINESS IS FAILING, GOING global won't save it. But if your business is poised for growth and offers a product or service with universal appeal, read on.

Entering the international marketplace has never been easier. The U.S. Small Business Administration has several export development programs. There are wonderful books on how to deal with customs brokers, shipping lines, and embassies. State and federal agencies, including the U.S. Export-Import Bank, offer entrepreneurs a plethora of business development services. Major insurance companies sell insurance policies designed to help minimize the risk of doing business abroad.

Doing your homework is the first and most important step on the road to international trade. Find out everything you possibly can about the country you think you'd like to do business in.

Make sure there are consumers with cash and a business infrastructure before you book one plane ticket.

The best way to find out what's going on in other countries is to speak with other business owners already doing business overseas. Most entrepreneurs are happy to share their horror stories and victories.

Most developed and undeveloped nations have consuls and business development officials based here and abroad. You can search the Internet and collect more information than you'll need to get started.

In this section, I cover a few specific countries, and I share some tips on how not to embarrass yourself abroad.

So read it all before you pack your bags.

Expand Production South of the Border

GREAT IDEA 187

JAPANESE GIANTS SONY, SANYO ELECTRIC, AND Hitachi made headlines by investing hundreds of millions of dollars in Mexican border factories, but hundreds of small U.S. businesses are also taking advantage of Mexico's affordable skilled labor force.

"It's the big guys and the small guys—the growth is phenomenal," said Mike Patten, editor of *Twin Plant News,* a trade magazine covering the maquila industry.

Shared production plants, known as "maquiladoras," offer big and small businesses a cost-effective way to boost production. There are about 3,000 maquiladoras employing about one million workers in Mexico. Employment has doubled since the peso devaluation in 1994, according to industry experts. The majority of workers are making electronic equipment, automotive parts, textiles, and furniture. Tijuana has become the TV production capital of the world, manufacturing 14 million units a year, according to *Business Week.*

While it's easy for megacorporations to deal with government permits, customs regulations, and cultural and language problems, working in a foreign country is daunting for most entrepreneurs.

Jeff Paul had about 1,000 Mexican workers when he was working for a major blue-jeans manufacturer 10 years ago. But too many labor and financial problems made it an unpleasant experience.

About a year ago, Paul, now the president and owner of Sierra Pacific Apparel, decided to return to Mexico. His Visalia, California–based company has 400 workers in California and about 100 in Mexicali, Mexico. Sierra Pacific's Mexican workers sew jeans for Gap, Old Navy, and Sears, among other customers. Making jeans in Mexico saves Paul about 75 cents per garment, but he still faces some challenges. "Our employee turnover in Central California is 5 percent a year," said Paul. "In Mexico, we lose 5 percent a week."

Still, he said, his Mexican workers produce high-quality

jeans, and his customers are satisfied. To make it easy, Paul set up his Mexican operation in partnership with North American Production Sharing Inc. (NAPS), a small Solano Beach, California–based company that helps U.S. companies set up shop over the border.

NAPS, founded by Bill Lew and Richard Jaime in 1991, works with about a dozen U.S. companies doing everything from refurbishing telephones to making computer cables. NAPS, which has an office in Tijuana, screens applicants and hires workers, manages the payroll, helps train workers, and even rents buses to collect workers for one client's second shift. Best of all, they handle all the permits, payroll-related paperwork, taxes, and customs requirements.

But before they'll help a company move across the border, they spend quite a bit of time evaluating the company's needs and goals. "We start by helping them understand if it makes sense to be in Mexico," said Lew, NAPS vice president and a former loan officer for Wells Fargo Bank. "We make sure the client is right for Mexico."

Lew said NAPS currently manages about 850 employees, with a weekly payroll of $60,000. In exchange for its services, the 30-person company charges clients a markup on labor costs, around 50 cents an hour for a worker paid $2.

If you're considering setting up a production facility in Mexico

- Carefully calculate your current labor costs.
- Determine whether unskilled or semi-skilled workers can be trained to make your product.
- Determine whether you can wait for finished products to be shipped back to the United States or abroad from Mexico.
- Budget extra money for start-up costs.
- Find a partner who knows how to work in Mexico.
- Learn about the Mexican culture and how business deals are done there.
- Be patient.

This year, revenues will be about $8 million, he said.

The low labor cost, usually under $3 an hour for assembly line workers, is what attracts most U.S. businesses to Mexico. But contrary to popular belief, Lew said his clients are not firing U.S. workers and fleeing to Mexico. They head to Mexico to expand production. "It's not a zero sum game. Our clients are not closing down U.S. factories," he said. In fact, he cautions, "Mexico won't save a company—Mexico will help a growing company."

Ray Noble, president of Storm Products Co. in Santa Clara, California, hired NAPS because he couldn't find enough assembly workers in northern California. Storm Products makes a variety of cables. Its Mexican operation, which has grown from one to 130 employees in two years, makes computer cables for Internet access.

"Domestically, it's very hard to get people to work on assembly lines," he said. "They do an excellent job. The quality is good—we are still working on productivity."

Noble said Storm, which has a total of 500 workers in seven domestic locations, saves about 50 percent on labor costs in Mexico. NAPS found and leased a 20,000-square foot facility for Storm in the La Mesa area of Tijuana. Noble said he pays more for rent in Mexico than in Los Angeles, but the company makes it up on labor costs.

Twin Plant News, an El Paso, Texas–based monthly publication, has been covering the maquila industry since 1985. Subscriptions cost $85 a year. Their address is 4110 Rio Bravo, Suite 108, El Paso, TX 79902.

Forge an International Alliance

FORGING AN INTERNATIONAL ALLIANCE IS A quick way to expand your business without spending a lot of money. The secret is to find a partner who can share his or her contacts and also understand your vision and integrity. Entrepreneurs in the service sector often have the easiest time striking informal agreements to work together because they are selling time and talent.

A few years ago, Manhattan architect William Leeds was

introduced to Indian architect Bobby Mukherji by a mutual friend. Mukherji, founder of a five-person firm in Bombay, was interested in entering the U.S. market. Leeds was eager to tap into India's thriving economy, which is growing about 5.5 percent a year.

For several years, the two architects have designed a variety of projects, including a fabric showroom, a trendy Chicago restaurant, and a major Indian government office in New York City. They say they both benefit from sharing their clients and talents.

"To be working with somebody from a place as far away as India gives us a new perspective on architecture and a new approach to planning," said Leeds. "Bobby brings in new ideas that we wouldn't necessarily have at our fingertips."

Besides new ideas, Mukherji provides access to unique Indian building materials and a team of 25 Indian craftsman and artisans on his payroll in Bombay. Many Mukherji projects, especially his nightclubs, feature original artwork and hand-carved details.

Although they live thousands of miles apart, Leeds and Mukherji communicate frequently via phone, fax, and modem. They hope to try videoconferencing down the line.

"Something that is on our computer screen here in New York City is on his screen in minutes," said Leeds.

The firms work together on a project-by-project basis based on a handshake, not a written agreement. They split the expenses and profits depending on who does what. Joint projects with Mukherji comprise about 10 percent to 15 percent of Leeds' total billings. In 1997 his firm billed approximately $1 million.

Leeds said eventually he hopes 25 percent of his total projects will be in conjunction with Mukherji's firm. Both say one of the great benefits of the relationship is acting as each other's marketing representatives in the United States and India.

"We look out for his interests and help him to grow," said Leeds. "In India, Bobby helps us because he can usually determine who is real and who is not. Between the two of us, we can accurately target the right clients."

Do Business in India

ALL TYPES OF AMERICAN ENTREPRENEURS SHOULD be exploring ways to tap into India's thriving economy, according to Bobby Mukherji *(see Great Idea 188)*. A growing middle class of 300 million is eager to buy American goods ranging from computers to clothing. Business expansion is rampant in Bombay, New Delhi, and Bangalore, where there is a vast pool of cheap, skilled labor.

But before making a trip to India, he suggests doing extensive research into its history and culture. He said many foreigners are astonished by the massive poverty in the midst of great wealth.

"An American who has never been exposed to the Indian culture will find the conditions extremely different from anywhere else in the world," said Mukherji.

He recommends hiring a driver to get around, but there

More thoughts on India

BOBBY MUKHERJI has these additional tips for Americans interested in doing business in India:

- Learn how India's Foreign Exchange Regulation Act affects financial transactions.
- Find an accountant who is familiar with Indian accounting rules and regulations.
- Cultivate personal relationships. Bring American-made gifts that are not widely available in India.
- Make sure your Indian business partner has a good reputation, as well as good contacts.
- Learn as much as you can about the culture and what to expect before making travel plans.
- Book hotels in advance. Many, especially in major cities, are filled with foreign business people.
- Be on the lookout for torn or damaged bills. Many merchants won't accept holey money. (Banks staple the notes, and the staples often rip up the bills.)

is no need for an interpreter because most Indians speak English.

Still, be prepared for challenges. The business infrastructure is far from modern. Power outages are frequent, and there are only about 9 or 10 million phone lines for a country of 900 million people.

"India is an extremely friendly, social place," said Mukherji. "Personal relationships are very important. There is a lot of weight given to word-of-mouth agreements, and people respect that."

If there's a specific country you'd like to do business in, contact the U.S. Commerce Department and speak to a trade officer. Most officers are assigned to a particular nation or region, and they can put you in touch with prospective contacts.

You can also call the commercial attachés assigned to most embassies in the United States. Most countries want to encourage trade with the United States, so they will send a business person along with the ambassador.

You can also contact the Export Small Business Development Center in El Segundo, California. It serves business owners all over the United States: 222 N. Sepulveda Blvd., #1690, El Segundo, CA 90245; (310) 606-0166.

Explore Opportunities in Russia

IF YOU WANT TO UNDERSTAND THE CHALLENGES of doing business in Russia, consider this:

Although new ATM machines adorn major boulevards in Moscow, most people are reluctant to use them. Fear of being robbed is one reason, but that's not all. Until 1997 it was legal to drive your car on the sidewalk. In light of that, what Muscovite in their right mind would line up on the sidewalk in front of an ATM machine?

In addition to impossible traffic jams and crime, Russia's corrupt politicians, lack of a business infrastructure, and crippling bureaucracy pose real challenges. In mid-November 1997, a few weeks after I returned from a five-day trip to Moscow (to speak at a U.S. Agency for International Development–sponsored conference promoting entrepreneurship), this headline appeared in *The New York Times* business section: "Russia Punishes 11 Financial Concerns".

The story reported that Russia's central bank refused do business with 11 Western financial institutions because apparently they had failed to honor international securities deals. Chase Manhattan and J.P. Morgan were among the U.S. banks in trouble with the Russians. By the time you read this, the dispute will certainly be resolved, but it illustrates how precarious the Russian economic system is despite lip service promoting the free market.

No matter how tough it is, doing business in Russia has tremendous appeal to Western entrepreneurs. Since 1993 the Russian Federation, especially modern Russia, has welcomed Westerners and their cash. Boris Yeltsin is trying to privatize state-run institutions and attract hard-currency investors. But wanting to do a deal in Russia and actually *doing* it are two different stories.

There are myriad roadblocks awaiting the swarms of U.S. businesspeople packing Delta's daily nonstop flights from New York City to Moscow.

For instance, while standing in line waiting to board the flight home, I overheard an engineer from Illinois Power and Light describing how the Russians wanted them to build a desperately needed nuclear power plant.

After 10 years of work, however, only one cooling tower and a section of one building were complete. The Russians really wanted to do business with the utility, but had no money and apparently were hoping for a barter deal.

A few years ago, Mary Heslin, an American business consultant, opened her Limpopo drop-in daycare center in a suburban Moscow community center to protect herself and her employees from the mafia. Unlike American daycare centers, she has a highly educated staff, including a doctor and an engineer, tending kids and hosting birthday parties.

It took $4,000 and nearly a year to obtain the permits she needed to open the center, but things are going so well, she hopes to open more around Moscow.

If you have a product or service that you think will appeal

to Russians, start doing your homework now. You can call the U.S. Commerce Department and ask to speak to a trade specialist. The U.S. Agency for International Development also has assistance programs for people wanting to do business in Russia.

Officially, you need an invitation from a Russian firm or individual to obtain a business travel visa. However, there are several U.S.–based companies who can easily facilitate that. The Russia House, in Washington, D.C., for example, needs eight to 10 days' notice, a copy of the first two pages of your U.S. passport, three passport photos, and $195 to provide a one-trip visa. If you plan to go back and forth, a three-month visa is $245.

Do try to arrange for a colleague or the hotel driver to pick you up at the airport. The taxi drivers who greet new arrivals allegedly are mafia-controlled. If you go with them, you risk getting ripped off or worse, a Moscow friend told me.

Here are some resources if you are interested in doing business in Russia:

Web sites

- American Chamber of Commerce in Russia: **www.amcham.ru**
- Russian-American Chamber of Commerce: **www.rmi.net/racc/**
- Business Collaboration Center: **www.bcc.ru**

U.S–based business development groups

- Center for Citizen Initiatives: (812) 327-5599
- Citizen Democracy Corps: (202) 872-0933
- Opportunity International: (708) 279-9300
- Deloitte & Touche is working with USAID on several business development programs: (202) 879-5600. Contact: Clint Singer.

You can also contact USAID/Russia in Moscow at 011-7095 956-4281.

Learn about a Culture before Doing Business

SOMETIMES AN INTERNATIONAL BUSINESS DEAL that makes perfect sense falls apart for no apparent reason. The numbers look good, but personalities clash, or someone says something that sends the deal spinning out of control.

The problem may be caused by a breach of business etiquette, according to experts in protocol and negotiation.

"About 80 percent of all business owners going abroad fail to complete a deal because they don't do their homework," said Syndi Seid, founder of Advanced Etiquette in San Francisco.

Frank Acuff, author of *How to Negotiate Anything with Anyone around the World,* agrees.

"American culture focuses on the logical part of the deal, but in other cultures the relationship comes first," said Acuff, director of Human Resources International based in Oakbrook Terrace, Illinois. Knowing how to act in a foreign business situation is critical to your success, he said, especially since many entrepreneurs are thinking globally for the first time.

Acuff said Americans are considered too open and direct by most foreigners. "We are not widely regarded for our business savvy in other parts of the world."

For example, Americans often complain that Japanese business people do not look them in the eye. But the Japanese consider looking directly at someone to be a sign of disrespect, according to Acuff.

"Some countries, like China, have a strong need for harmony," he said. "So they may agree to do something, but not comply with the terms of the agreement."

He said Americans are often frustrated when foreigners have a totally different concept of time. Americans, Germans, Swiss, and Australians tend to be prompt and expect meetings to begin on time. But Latin Americans, for instance, usually begin meetings a half hour after the appointed time and can't understand why their American guests are so agitated.

Another common problem: Americans prefer to have about three feet of space around them, Acuff said. Yet Latin Americans and Middle Easterners often embrace their business associates, which upsets many American men.

So take the time to learn as much as you can about a country before you book your plane ticket. You'll save money and time by being a savvy traveler.

Acuff offers these tips for entrepreneurs thinking of doing business abroad:

- Before visiting a foreign country, talk to people who have done business there to learn firsthand about their experiences.
- Meet with people from the country you are planning to visit. Ask them what they like and don't like about doing business with Americans.
- Do your homework. Learn as much as you can about the culture and customs of the country you are planning to visit.

Go on a Trade Mission

"GOING GLOBAL" IS A POPULAR BUZZ PHRASE, BUT talking about doing business abroad is much easier than actually doing it.

One smart way to explore the overseas market is to go on a government-sponsored trade mission. Every year, the Department of Commerce's International Trade Administration invites selected entrepreneurs in search of new business to travel to foreign countries.

Business owners apply for a slot on the trip and pay all their own travel expenses. The government organizers find appropriate local business contacts and set up an intense schedule of meetings, tours, and receptions. A high-ranking official usually accompanies the group.

While most trade missions are co-ed, the White House has been organizing special missions just for women business owners. Missions have headed to London, Amsterdam, Paris, Milan, and Mexico City in recent years.

"The Women in Trade Business Development Missions

create a level playing field for mission members to network with each other, as well as with buyers and sellers in international markets," said Alexis Herman, former director of the White House Office of Public Liaison and current Secretary of Labor.

Herman, who escorts the business owners, said the women-only missions were created by President Clinton and former Commerce Secretary Ron Brown.

Glenda Binkley, owner of D&H Electronic Systems Inc. in Mount Juliet, Tennessee, was one of 21 women who went to Amsterdam and London with Herman in September 1995 and to Mexico in 1996.

"My objective was to gather data and look at the market potential," said Binkley.

Before making any deals or decisions, she needed to know how to adapt her security systems and other electronic products for sale and use in European countries. Other countries have different electrical systems, safety requirements, and fire codes. In addition to collecting the technical information she needed, she attended a variety of receptions and business meetings to acquaint herself with business opportunities.

"The embassies took our product brochures and matched them with prospects," she said. Since visiting Europe, she's begun modifying some of her products for future export. She is also asking the manufacturers she buys equipment from to think about redesigning their products for export.

Lori Foster, who owns a gift business and a juice business in San Francisco, went with Binkley on the mission. She returned from Amsterdam with memories, souvenirs, and a contract to sell her juices to a Dutch grocery chain.

"The business deal happened within two weeks of coming home," said Foster, founder of Creative Juices, which makes upscale beverages. Her juices are sold at Nordstrom and Neiman Marcus stores in San Francisco, as well as other outlets.

She's also looking into ways to manufacture her juices abroad to save the cost of shipping them from the United States.

"Every single minute was filled with interview possibilities, business contacts, and meeting people," said Foster, adding that because the women on her mission all made something different, there was no competition, just a lot of good feeling. "It was nonstop business in a very pleasant way from the minute we got on the plane," she said.

For more information on the women's trade missions, contact Loretta Allison at the International Trade Administration in Washington, D.C.; (202) 482-5479.

The Commerce Department sponsors trade missions for all kinds of entrepreneurs. Missions for minority business owners are organized through the "Matchmaker" program, which has taken business owners to Mexico, Canada, and South America. For information, contact Molly Costa at (202) 482-0692.

The Export-Import Bank offers various programs for business owners, including financing and insurance policies designed to protect small exporters against political and commercial risks. The bank is based in Washington, D.C.; (202) 565-3946.

A tremendous amount of information is available by calling the Commerce Department's Trade Information Center at (800) USA-TRADE. The TIC coordinates information from 19 federal agencies. Call to receive information on various countries via fax or to speak with a trade representative.

The center provides export counseling, advice on export licenses and controls, market research, and trade leads. Check out the TIC Web site at **www.ita.doc.gov/tic**.

Translate Your Marketing Materials

ONE OF THE BIGGEST MISTAKES BUSINESS owners make is not hiring native speakers to create marketing materials destined for foreign markets.

In the 1970s Chevrolet made a legendary cultural faux pas when it decided to market the Chevy Nova in Mexico. The family car was a big hit in the United States, but the Mexican advertising campaign was a total disaster. Why? Because "no va" in Spanish means "no go."

Another famous goof involved a soft drink company that

used a photograph of a happy family dressed in white clothes to push its sodas in Japan. The ads were beautiful, but white is the color of mourning in Japan, and the campaign was offensive.

If you are going to spend thousands on marketing materials, spend some more up front to make sure you are saying just the right thing. You should avoid using slang at any cost.

It's easier than you think to find people who are fluent speakers in whatever language you need. You can hire university graduate students or professional translators. Most translators charge by the project, and their fees are negotiable.

You might want to call the consulate of the country you are preparing materials for and ask if they can recommend a native speaker who freelances. Advertising agencies and marketing consultants who specialize in target marketing often have a stable of skilled linguists on call.

Above all, be sure to do your homework and learn everything possible about the culture; you don't want to end up offending the people you are trying to attract.

Abide by the Etiquette of International Trade

WITH EVERYONE BUZZING ABOUT INTERNATIONAL trade, it helps to know the do's and don'ts of conducting business abroad. I asked my friend Syndi Seid *(see Great Idea 191)* for a few specific ideas to share with you.

- **Avoid calendar confusion.** One of the most confusing things about dealing with foreign businesspeople is the way they note the date. In many countries, people put the day, month, and year, rather than the U.S custom of writing month, day, and year. One good way to avoid confusion is to write a date like this: 5 February 1998. This can save you the grief of a missed appointment or conference.
- **Bring a gift.** Many foreigners will expect you to present them with a gift before any real business can be done.

  "Consider the person's heritage, religion, and culture

before choosing a gift," advises Seid.

For instance, items made of cowhide are verboten in India because cows are considered sacred. Never give a Chinese person a clock, because if it stops, it's considered bad luck. And don't give letter openers or sharp objects to Mexicans. They consider that offensive. So what is the best universal gift? Chocolate!

If it's too hot to bring chocolate, try a well-crafted business accessory.

Don't wrap your gifts before you leave home because you may be asked to open them by picky customs officials. "Take paper and simple ribbon along to wrap it after you arrive," Seid advises.

- **Treat shopkeepers with respect.** All small-business owners will appreciate this international etiquette tip. Always acknowledge the person standing behind the counter when you visit a shop. "Americans have often been criticized for being rude because we don't say anything to the clerk or cashier," said Seid. "Most small stores throughout the world are owned by husbands and wives and often staffed by family members. It is customary for visitors to greet the shopkeeper when entering the store and say goodbye, even if you don't buy anything."

  Seid's business, Advanced Etiquette, is located at 1168 Clay Street, San Francisco, CA 94108-1406; (415) 346-3665.

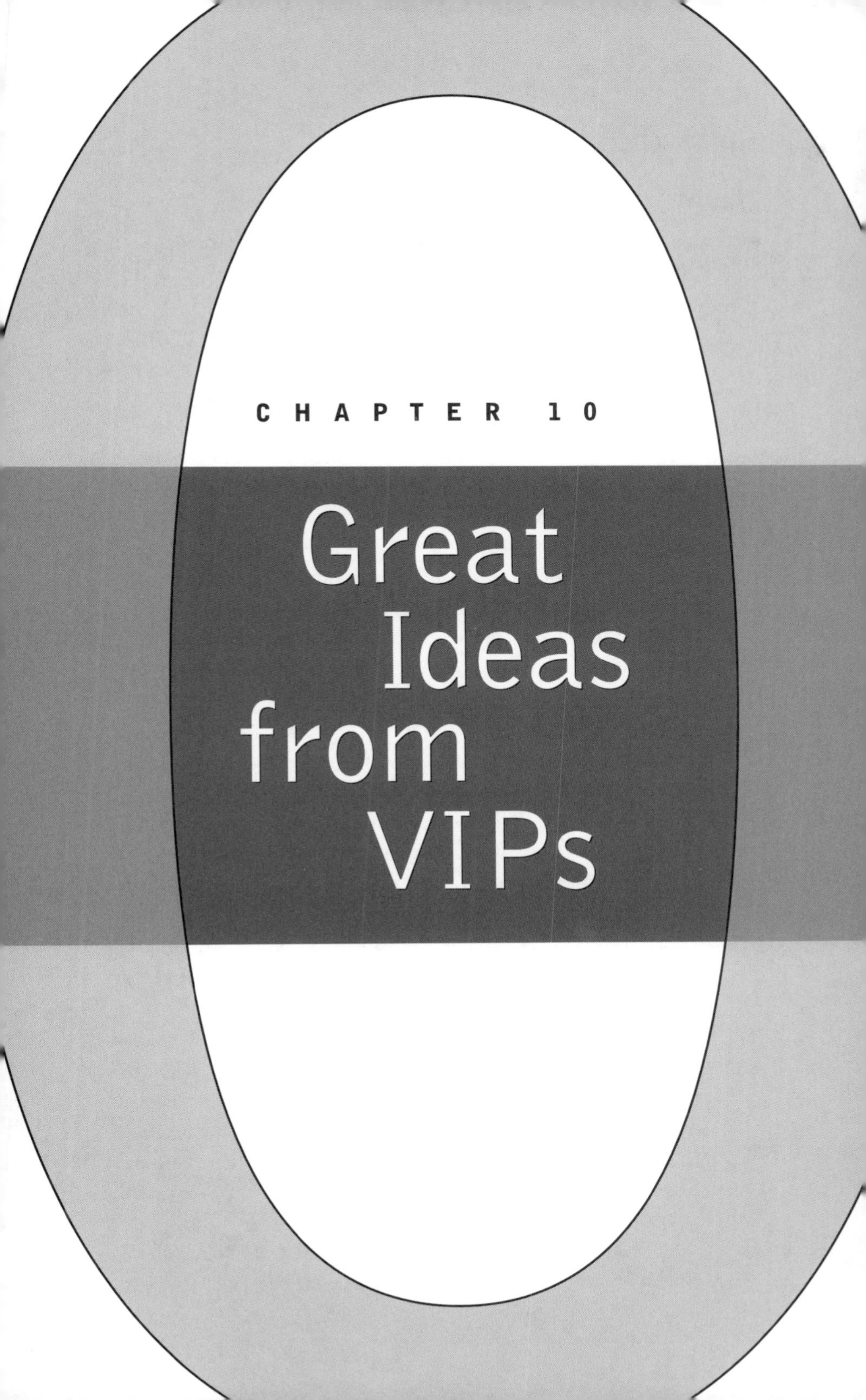

CHAPTER 10

Great Ideas from VIPs

HERB KELLEHER

Be a Maverick in Your Industry

HERB KELLEHER, HIS FRIEND ROLLIN KING, AND banker John Parker sketched out the idea for Southwest Airlines on a cocktail napkin in a bar. True story. They began with one simple notion: If you get your passengers to their destinations when they want to get there, on time, at the lowest possible fares, and make darn sure they have a good time doing it, people will fly your airline.

Kelleher, now chairman of the fifth largest U.S. airline, said he liked the idea because he had admired the way the now-defunct Pacific Southwest Airlines pioneered cheap, short-haul service throughout California.

Doing the same thing in Texas generated a firestorm of industry opposition and a tangle of government red tape. But Kelleher fought on. Kelleher, who worked in a Campbell's Soup factory as a teenager and eventually became a lawyer in New Jersey, followed his wife home to Texas.

In 1968, after much wrangling, the Texas Aeronautics Commission finally approved Southwest's plan to fly between three cities. But the next day, competing airlines went to court and got a temporary restraining order against Southwest. It took three years to clear up the legal mess, but Southwest finally got off the ground. Service began June 18, 1971. Of course, the rest is history. His formula of frequent, cheap, no-frills service has paid off. In a cyclical and often depressed industry, Southwest has been profitable 24 years in a row.

Southwest has broken so many traditions it's tough to list them. They fly only 737s to cut down maintenance costs. By not assigning seats, they can turn a flight around in 20 minutes. Southwest's quick turnaround time allows for more than 2,200 flights a day to 51 cities. They open the front and back doors to let people on and off faster, and they serve only peanuts and a few kinds of drinks.

Although it flies to only 25 states, Southwest boasts the best safety record and youngest airline fleet in the business.

Southwest was the only major carrier in 1990, 1991, and 1992 to make net and operating profits. It became a major airline in 1989 when it exceeded the billion-dollar revenue mark.

"Our people were perfectly aware that our company could cease to exist at any given time," Kelleher told *Success* magazine. "In that kind of environment, you come together as a band of warriors."

Southwest's flight attendant "warriors" wear shorts and sing the safety regulations.

The corporate culture is party, party, party. Personnel directors once asked a group of pilots to put on shorts before their job interviews. All but one did.

To land an exclusive account with Sea World of Texas, Southwest painted a model airplane to look like Shamu, the killer whale. When the deal was signed, they painted a real plane the same way. They also painted the Texas state flag across a 737 named *Lone Star One* to celebrate their 20th anniversary.

Today, Southwest Airlines is a member of the Fortune 500 and and was ranked in the "The 100 Best Companies to Work For in America" in 1993.

Kelleher has succeeded in his business by setting himself apart, by being unconventional and charismatic. Although this approach won't work for everyone, if it suits your personality and your business, why not be a maverick?

MURIEL SIEBERT

Find the Business That's Right for You

IN 1967 MURIEL SIEBERT BECAME THE FIRST woman to own a seat on the New York Stock Exchange. A true pioneer in finance, she was made a partner in a major Wall Street brokerage firm, yet was turned down when she originally sought sponsorship for her application for a seat on the NYSE floor.

Today her thriving investment management company offers discount brokerage services, online financial transactions, advice for individual investors, industry newsletters, and a lot more.

Muriel Siebert devotes her time to many areas besides finance. Her credits are far too numerous to list, but her dossier includes honorary doctorates, fellowships, trusteeships, and directorial positions in public and private sectors. She was gracious enough to contribute this sage advice:

> If you don't really know what you're good at, starting a small business is an expensive way to find out. A burning desire to be your own boss may be a necessary condition for taking the plunge as an entrepreneur—but it's not sufficient for success.
>
> The Greek sages said "Know Thyself"—that is indeed the beginning of wisdom. Before going out on your own, I recommend taking some serious time off to explore your areas of strength and weakness.
>
> I've come to identify four areas of ability which distinguish most people. In my experience, people are good at working with either words, numbers, things, or people.
>
> If you're fluent with well-chosen words, why not create conferences or training seminars in fields where you can do some public speaking? If you already have some experience in a particular field, use your strong verbal skills to share your knowledge.
>
> If you're comfortable crunching numbers and enjoy detailed analytic work, how about concentrating on the fast-growing audit business? You can analyze utility bills, hospital bills, mortgage payments, and all the other daunting documents that people hate to handle. The beautiful part is that this work can be done part-time. Or if you are at least average in handling numbers, train as a financial planner.
>
> Were you born with golden hands? If you can fix anything from leather to lampshades, a repair business may be your bag. Even in our affluent society, folks don't like to throw things away. You might want to sublease some space from a mall merchant—you'll both benefit from each other's traffic.
>
> Finally, if you are great with people, consider signing on as an independent sales rep for a company whose product you respect, especially if you are handy enough to demonstrate it.
>
> You may have noticed that entrepreneurs need to combine several strengths to launch their ships—and to avoid steering courses where their weaknesses will wreck them. Match your own strength to the opportunities popping up around you, as lifestyles change along with the economy. Test your idea. Don't commit to a long lease or expensive equipment until you are cer-

tain that the idea is viable.

No matter how favorable the financing terms may be, how glowing the prospects of the industry, if a prospective business bores you or scares you, step away from it.

This advice is born from decades of experience. Siebert proved herself to be an entrepreneurial risk-taker from the very start of her business career. To learn more about the "First Woman of Finance," check out Siebert & Company's Web site at **www.msiebert.com**.

MIKE BLOOMBERG

Stick to Your Guns and Keep Your Ideas Simple

I SHOULD TELL YOU UP FRONT WHAT YOU probably already know: The book you are reading right now is published by Mike Bloomberg and Bloomberg Press. That said, you would find Mike Bloomberg profiled in this section even if he wasn't my publisher. Here's why:

Michael Bloomberg is a genius whose success is an inspiration for all entrepreneurs. His achievements exemplify the American Dream—starting a business from scratch and earning billions.

After some sticky personality clashes and the sale in 1981 of Salomon Brothers to Philbro Corporation ended his fifteen-year career there, Bloomberg, with about $10 million in hand, set out to develop the premiere, proprietary information system for traders and savvy investors. Hence, the beginning of Bloomberg Financial Markets.

There are about 89,000 Bloomberg terminals in use around the world today, providing current data on a myriad of subjects that matter most to traders, brokers, analysts, and investors. Once focused exclusively on financial market data, the Bloomberg system of today also offers news stories, multimedia reports, apartment listings in New York City—it even lets you send flowers. The amount of financial information and general resources available on the Bloomberg system, and the level of customer service that is offered, is astounding.

I know Mike personally and was able to watch him in action on a regular basis when I was a producer/reporter on Bloomberg's small-business TV program. Of course, I took appropriate advantage of my time at Bloomberg to get into the mind of the master and ask him to share some of his ideas on business for aspiring entrepreneurs.

"Do something simple that you can really define," he said, twirling his reading glasses. "Sitting in your office, pondering momentous, abstract ideas doesn't always work." You need to keep it straightforward, particularly in the initial stages, and then you can build from there, he said.

It's also essential to share your dreams openly and stick to your game plan.

"I went out and said to someone, 'I'm going to do it,'" he said. "Then I did it."

"It" is a continually growing multimedia communications company with nearly 4,000 employees and annual sales approaching $1 billion. The company buzzes with innovation.

If you go away from Bloomberg's New York City office for three days, you won't recognize the place when you return.

As soon as a newly expanded area opens up, it's filled with people, phones, and equipment. The kitchen, known worldwide for its unlimited supply of free snacks, fresh fruit, and beverages, bustles with visitors and staffers from early morning to long past dinnertime.

Need a Coke? A raspberry truffle? A phone to call to Los Angeles?

Just hang out in the Bloomberg kitchen and reception area and do your thing. You never know who you'll meet or bump into. The structure is deliberate.

"Walls and titles act as barriers," said Bloomberg. That's why open space is the rule around the office. He sits in the corner of the 15th floor newsroom, accessible and willing to listen to anyone who catches his eye and ear.

Although it appears that the company took off like a rocket from the beginning, Bloomberg says it's taken years to build the business because "we didn't try to do everything at once."

Perfecting and updating the Bloomberg system takes top priority. Bloomberg spends about $30 million a year on research and development.

The radio network and television production are the toddlers in the Bloomberg family. Bloomberg Television provides 24 hours of news every day through national cable distribution, USA Network, DirecTV, and the Bloomberg terminal. Bloomberg News Radio is syndicated through more than 100 affiliates worldwide and airs on Bloomberg 1130 AM in New York.

"You've got to sit back and do things carefully," advises Bloomberg. "You can't jump to the endgame."

When asked about the future, he rubs his forehead and twirls his glasses slowly.

"I don't think I've had many great ideas for a long time," he admits. "I've got a bunch of people that aren't well coordinated—deliberately. I'm the one who sits and listens.

Anyway, he had his brilliant idea over a decade and a half ago—now he's running with it.

TOM PETERS

Two Great Ideas

TOM PETERS, BEST-SELLING AUTHOR, HIGH-LEVEL consultant, entrepreneur, and speaker, was in a state of transition when we met in New York City in the summer of 1997. He had just sold The Tom Peters Group, the training side of his Palo Alto–based communications business and was devoting most of his attention to his new company, a textile and bedding venture owned by his wife, textile designer Susan Sargent in Pawlett, Vermont. Previously, Peters worked for McKinsey & Company, a management consulting firm, where he eventually became a partner.

Taking a cue from the Japanese, Peters adopted management strategies which he teaches around the world. Since he's been a sharp observer of the changing business world for many years, he has offered two great ideas for small-business owners.

1 **Focus on a creative brand design.** "Produce first-class marketing materials for your company," he said. "Find an innovative, young design team on Day One to create a Starbucks/Nike kind of feel for the enterprise." Then put your very cool image on "everything from the Web site, to the nameplate, to the business cards."

Although graphics and printing are costly, "spend the money whether you are running a 12-table restaurant, a three-person company, or anything in between."

2 **Look beyond credentials.** "The great people at business love hanging around people," he said. So, when you are building your team, "my advice is, 'forget the certificates.'

He said when he and Susan began advertising for their first administrator for their textile business, "I stole the words from Steve Jobs, and I said, 'this is a company that from Day One intends on being insanely great, and if you're not insanely great—don't even think about applying."

"Well," he said with a grin, "that draws in some flakes you wouldn't touch with a 20-meter pole—on the other hand, it was great to see the responses from all over the map."

Before racing off to keynote another business conference, Peters had these parting thoughts for us:

"I think it's the halcyon years for entrepreneurial firms," he said. But "you gotta be damn good at something. Your 'it' has to be fabulously special."

HARVEY MACKAY

Benefit from Volunteerism

FROM ENVELOPE SALESMAN TO BEST-SELLING author of *Dig Your Well Before You're Thirsty*, to entrepreneurial guru, Harvey Mackay makes a big impact on the business world every day. He's always selling. Selling himself, selling his books and columns and, of course, selling his envelopes. Among his pursuits, Mackay is a founder and major partner in Cogni-Tech Corporation, a company that develops and distributes computer software.

He admits that after he completes his big-ticket, customized corporate presentations, he follows up later with the decision makers and usually lands a big envelope account for his Minnesota-based company, Mackay Envelope Corporation, founded in 1959. He's also pushing "Sharkware," his contact management software, as an easy way to keep track of all those people you meet.

But although he's known for his for-profit ventures, he also knows how to give back to the community. A veteran networker, Mackay believes strongly in the power of volunteerism.

"I've spent 25 percent of my life in volunteerism," Mackay said. "When I started, I didn't realize that I would become a better speaker because I had to lead. I became a better salesperson because I had to raise money from all my friends."

Mackay, who has served on many charitable and cultural boards, recommends joining a group you have an interest in or aiding a cause you feel passionate about. If you've lost relatives to cancer, raise money for cancer research. If you adore modern art, become a benefactor. Try ushering at your church or synagogue. It takes so little time—and it can bring you into contact with a lot of new people.

"Believe it or not, you'll become a better networker, you'll have more contacts, and you'll also be doing good." Mackay's moral: "There can be surprising rewards for thankless jobs."

WALLY AMOS

Reinvent Yourself

ON MARCH 10, 1975, AT 7181 SUNSET BOULEVARD in Hollywood, Wally Amos, showbiz talent manager, became Famous Amos, the Cookie Man.

Using his Aunt Della's chocolate chip cookie recipe, Amos sold deluxe cookies for the unheard of price of $3 a pound.

Celebrities and locals alike lined up to buy Famous Amos cookies. Sales skyrocketed. Media attention drove sales as he increased production to keep up with demand.

But the initial success wasn't enough to keep the company in Amos's hands. Looking back, Amos sees clearly why he lost control of the company 10 years later.

"I was irresponsible in the management. I really wasn't focused on the core business. I was doing audiocassette tapes, television shows, and I was focused on getting into a movie," he admitted.

After going through four management changes from 1985 to 1988, his original venture was eventually acquired by a Taiwanese food conglomerate, which still sells cookies under the Famous Amos brand.

Because he was the living brand and image of the cookie company, the new owners sued Amos to keep him out of the cookie business. He went to court and eventually won the right to use his name for other ventures, including a line of dolls named Chip and Cookie.

Although he can't bake cookies, Amos and his partner, Lou Avignone, are back in the baking business under the brand "Uncle Noname" (pronounced no-nam-eh). They sell fat-free and sugar-free muffins baked in Bohemia, New York.

"Now, I'm the muffin man," laughs Amos. "I didn't plan it. Circumstances created it. And you have to go with what works." He is determined to avoid making the same mistakes he made 20 years ago.

The muffins appear to be a big hit.

"I believe if you have an idea and focus on achieving your goal, your whole energy is focused on doing it, and ideas just come to you."

He says he finally has a great management team that keeps him busy with marketing and promotion.

"You never know what the hell is going to happen. Life is unpredictable, yet we spend much of our time trying to predict it. I have no regrets. I'm still feeling good. And for Uncle Noname, the future looks fantastic."

LILLIAN VERNON

Take Some Advice from the Mail-Order Queen

THE FIRST THING I THOUGHT WHEN I MET Lillian Vernon was, "Wow, I hope I have as much energy and look as great as she does when I'm older!"

This petite powerhouse of the mail-order industry started her business on her kitchen table in the early 1950s. She was pregnant and needed to earn money, but working outside the home was frowned upon at the time. Her father was in the leather business, and she thought she could make money by selling his fashion accessories.

Taking a risk, she placed a $495 ad in the September 1951 issue of *Seventeen* magazine: "Be the first to sport that personalized look on your bag and belt," read the ad touting a $2.99 leather purse and $1.99 belt. That ad, placed by Vernon, a suburban New York housewife and mother, garnered $32,000 worth of orders—a huge amount of money at the time. It also launched a mail order empire projecting 1998 sales of about $240 million.

"I make quick decisions based on my golden gut," said Vernon, who named her firm after the New York suburb of Mount Vernon where she lived. Later in life, she changed her name legally from Lillian Hochberg to Lillian Vernon.

In several interviews, the feisty entrepreneur told me how, despite a lack of formal business training, she turned $2,000 in wedding money into a successful mail order business serving 18 million customers.

"To this day, I don't know how to read a financial statement," she admits. "I still need help with the numbers."

She doesn't need any help selecting merchandise. Every year, hundreds of items are submitted by eager vendors. Only a fraction ever make it into her slick catalogs. Her biggest hits are the items she dreams up herself. For example, in 1996 Vernon received 120,000 orders for the Battenburg lace Christmas tree angels she designed. Not bad for a Jewish woman whose family fled their comfortable life in

Leipzig, Germany, after the Nazis threw them out of their home in 1933.

Vernon's rags-to-riches story is detailed in her amazing autobiography, *An Eye for Winners*. Vernon's book stands apart from many autobiographies because it combines intimate and often painful details of her life story with practical business advice.

Known for her sharp wit and strong support of Democratic politics, Vernon told me her company has flourished by finding the right professional managers to complement her entrepreneurial style. But the process hasn't been easy.

"At one point, I surrounded myself with experienced veterans of large corporate cultures," she said. "Unfortunately, they almost killed us—they took analysis to the point of paralysis."

Now she relies on a team of skilled managers, including her two sons, to help her manage the New Rochelle, New York–based company. Times have changed since she started the business. In the 1950s there were about 50 specialty catalogs; now, there are nearly 10,000 generating about $70 billion a year.

The tough competition keeps Vernon busy. A few years ago, she said, 89 percent of the items in her catalogs made money; today the percentage has dipped to about 79 percent.

A few years ago, mail-order industry analysts criticized Vernon for lagging behind competitors when it came to using modern technology. For example, the company, which went public in 1987, didn't install toll-free 800 lines until 1993.

Today, the company operates a million-square-foot warehouse in Virginia Beach, Virginia, and keeps close tabs on customers with sophisticated computer programs. Vernon said she sells via 180 million catalogs a year, nearly 100 editions in all.

Vernon, the queen of free personalization on most merchandise, offers this advice to small-business owners: "Risk your own money, trust your creative instincts, and find someone who can execute your vision."

Resources

Just one great idea can completely revolutionize your life.

—EARL NIGHTINGALE

A Brief Conclusion

WELL, IF YOU'VE GOTTEN THIS FAR (OR, MAYBE YOU STARTED reading here!), you deserve a short farewell. For more than a year, I collected and researched these 201 really great ideas. I set the bar very high and rejected many for being too dull or too obvious. To make the cut, these ideas had to be creative, practical, and proven effective. None were made up or embellished.

I hope you are able to use many of these ideas in your business. Or maybe some of my ideas inspired you to think a bit more "out of the box," as my publicist likes to say.

Now, I'd like to ask you a favor. If you have a great idea that has helped you make money or run your small business better, send it to me! I would like to share it in my column, or perhaps in another book.

During the final days of writing, I joked that my next book will be titled: "Two Ideas for Great Success." The ideas are simple: Rob a bank and flee the country.

But, I'm kidding. You know I'll be back interviewing more wonderful entrepreneurs just like you, as soon as I can take the Band-Aids off my fingers.

If reading this book inspires you to share a great idea with me, I'd welcome it. Please send it to: Jane Applegate, P.O. Box 768, Pelham, NY 10803. Check out my Web site to see when I'll be visiting your area on my national speaking tour: **www.janeapplegate.com**.

Agencies, SBA, and Other U.S. Government Offices

SBA OFFICES

SBA Office of Financial Assistance

(202) 205-6490

Direct loan funds are limited to businesses owned by disabled individuals; all other assistance is provided through SBA guarantees of loans made by local banks.

(*See also* "Getting Money" section, below)

SBA Office of Rural Affairs & Economic Development

(*See* U.S. Department of Agriculture, below)

SBA Office of International Trade

(202) 205-6720

(*See also* "Export/Trade" section, below)

SBA Office of Government Contracting

(202) 205-6460

SBA Procurement Automated Source System (PASS)

409 3rd Street, SW
Washington, DC 20416
(202) 205-7310

For small businesses interested in government procurement opportunities.

Service Corps of Retired Executives (SCORE)

National SCORE Office
409 3rd Street, SW, 6th floor
Washington, DC 20416
(800) 634-0245
fax: (202) 205-7636

In addition to one-on-one counseling, SCORE offers a free 19-page workbook entitled *How to Really Start Your Own Business.*

REGIONAL GOVERNMENT AGENCIES

IN ADDITION TO SBA DISTRICT OFFICES, EVERY STATE HAS A primary agency or office to provide one-stop guidance on the programs and services offered to small businesses at the state level. In each state this agency or office goes by a different name. Below are listings for the biggest states.

California Trade and Commerce Agency

Office of Small Business
801 K Street, Suite 1600
Sacramento, CA 95814
(916) 324-1295

New York Department of Economic Development
Business Assistance Hotline

1515 Broadway, 51st floor
New York, NY 10036
(800) 782-8369

Texas Department of Economic Development

1700 North Congress
Austin, TX 78701
(512) 936-0100

U.S. Small Business Administration

409 3rd Street, SW
Washington, DC 20416
(800) U-ASK-SBA
(800) 827-5722
fax: (202) 205-7064
TDD: (704) 344-6640

Most dealings with the SBA are best handled through district or regional offices. Call the toll-free number above to find the SBA district office nearest you.

FEDERAL GOVERNMENT WEB SITES

SBA

www.sba.gov

The home page of the SBA.

U.S. Business Advisor

www.business.gov

A one-stop link to government for business.

Federal Marketplace

www.fedmarket.com

The "federal marketplace" is the Internet's procurement resource gateway for firms interested in marketing and selling products and services to the U.S. government.

The Patent and Trademark Office

www.uspto.gov

The home page of the Patent and Trademark Office.

(*See* "Patents" section, below.)

CONGRESSIONAL COMMITTEES

Senate Small Business Committee

Russell Building, Room SR-428A
(202) 224-5175

or write to:

The Honorable ______________________
U.S. Senate
Washington, D.C. 20510

House Small Business Committee

Rayburn Building, Room 2361
(202) 225-5821

or write to:

The Honorable ______________________
U.S. House of Representatives
Washington, DC 20515

DEPARTMENT OF COMMERCE

14th Street & Constitution Avenue, NW
Washington, DC 20230
(202) 482-2000
www.doc.gov

Economic Development Administration (EDA)

(202) 482-5081

The purpose of this administration is to generate jobs, to help protect existing jobs, and to stimulate commercial and industrial growth in economically distressed areas of the United States.

(*See also* Trade Information Center in "Export/Trade" section, below.)

U.S. DEPARTMENT OF AGRICULTURE

THE U.S. DEPARTMENT OF AGRICULTURE WORKS TO IMPROVE and maintain income and to develop and expand markets abroad for agricultural products.

12th Street and Jefferson Drive, SW
Washington, DC 20250
(202) 720-2791

Office of Advocacy and Enterprise
(202) 720-5212

Rural Information Center
(800) 633-7701

Rural Development Administration
(202) 690-4730

U.S. CHAMBER OF COMMERCE

THE CHAMBER OF COMMERCE IS THE LARGEST PRIVATE volunteer business federation in the world. The national headquarters, below, has materials geared specifically toward small business.

Center for Small Business
1615 H Street, NW
Washington, DC 20062
(202) 659-6000
Small Business Center: (202) 463-5503
www.uschamber.org

Institute of Standards and Technology (NIST)
(301) 975-2000

Advanced Technology Program (ATP)
(800) 287-3863

Provides funds to help U.S. businesses develop new technologies that are commercially promising.

OTHER GOVERNMENT AGENCIES AND PROGRAMS

SMALL BUSINESS DEVELOPMENT CENTERS (SBDC) COORDINATE federal, state, local, university, and private resources in counseling and training small-business owners. There is an SBDC in every major city in the United States. You can find out the telephone number of the SBDC nearest you by calling the SBA's toll-free number (800) U-ASK-SBA. Some U.S. state SBDC reference lines are listed below.

CALIFORNIA

California Trade and Commerce Agency
(916) 324-5068

NEW YORK

State University of New York (SUNY)

(800) 732-SBDC

TEXAS

Dallas County Community College

(214) 860-5850

Book Publishers

Bloomberg Press

100 Business Park Drive
P.O. Box 888
Princeton, NJ 08542-0888
(609) 279-4670

The company that published my book, Bloomberg Press, is a division of the larger Bloomberg Financial Markets. This business press publishes accessible, authoritative books on small business, personal finance, investment, and professional finance topics.

Nolo Press

950 Parker Street
Berkeley, CA 94710
(510) 549-1976
fax: (800) 645-0895
www.nolo.com

Begun in 1971 by two legal aid lawyers, Nolo now publishes more than 100 titles. In addition to legal self-help books for the small business owner, they also publish software.

Directories Online and by Mail

National Directory Publishing Association

www.directory-digest.com/publishr.html

List of A–Z directory and information publishers with links to other directory home pages.

Oxbridge Mediafinder Connection

www.oxbridge.com

Targeted lists to rent, advertising sources, and subscription information from almost 100,000 magazines, journals, catalogs, newspapers, and directories.

Hoovers

www.hoovers.com

Find information about a company, any company.

American Business Directories

5711 S. 86th Circle
P.O. Box 27347
Omaha, NE 68127
(402) 593-4600

Export/Trade

OIT (Office of International Trade)

www.sba.gov/oit

Has trade terms, trade links, and trade loans. The agency offers export-related guaranteed loans. In 1996 the SBA assisted small firms with more than 1,300 export-related loans worth nearly $385 million.

International Trade Administration (ITA)

(212) 466-5222

Export Opportunity Hotline

(800) 243-7232

Speak to a trade specialist to discuss export problems and get advice; they also publish industry reports, distributor lists, country market reports, and more. The basic starter book is Exportise for $19.95; includes a list of sources.

Export/Import Bank (EXIMBANK)

811 Vermont Avenue, NW
Washington, DC 20571
(202) 565-3200

Government agency that provides export financing to large and small businesses and exporters who have had difficulty obtaining loans from commercial lenders.

Export Hotline

(800) USA-XPORT
www.exportweb.com

The export hotline and trade bank provides global business information by fax or online.

Trade Information Center (TIC)
U.S. Department of Commerce
(800) 872-8723
(Also 800-USA-TRADE)

Small Business Exporters Association (SBEA)
4603 John Tyler Court, Suite 203
Annandale, VA 22003
(703) 761-4140

A national organization representing small- and midsize exporters.

National Association of Export Companies (NAXCO)
P.O. Box 1330
Murray Hill Station
New York, NY 10156
(212) 725-3311

Can help companies searching for information on financing or trade leads.

Family Business

Family Firm Institute
12 Harris Street
Brookline, MA 02146
(617) 738-1591
fax: (617) 738-4883

Publishes a membership directory of professionals who offer services to family businesses in the United States; they also publish a quarterly journal, *Family Business Review.*

The Center for Family Business
P.O. Box 24268
Cleveland, OH 44124
(216) 442-0800
fax: (216) 442-0178

Offers books, seminars, resources.

The Family Business Advisor

A monthly newsletter on successful business management, family relations, and asset protection, $179/year.

Family Business Advisor

P.O. Box 4356
Marietta, GA 30061-4356
(800) 551-0633
fax: (770) 425-1776
www.arthurandersen.com/

Franchising

International Franchise Association (IFA)

1350 New York Avenue, NW, Suite 900
Washington, DC 20005
(202) 628-8000
fax: (202) 628-0812
e-mail: ifa@franchise.org
www.franchise.org

A resource center for current and prospective franchisees and franchisors, the media, and the government. IFA is franchising's only trade group. For their publications desk, call (800) 543-1038.

Contact IFA's International Affairs Department (202) 662-0760), for the following:

National Franchise Association—a list of 40 associations around the world that maintain their own publications and products.

International Calendar—a compilation of expos, seminars, and conferences around the world.

AAFD

(800) 733-9858
www.aafd.org

Sixty chapters, formation of the AAFD's National Purchasing Co-op to enhance members' buying power; created a set of Fair Franchising Standards; offers insurance programs. One of the leading franchisee trade associations.

Free Things

Brochure on "slamming," or getting your phone service switched without your permission. Contact Call For Action at

(301) 657-8260.

Disk from KeyCorp to help you with your financial planning from the SBA's top-ranked small-business lender for loans under $250,000 and microloans under $100,000. Call (800) 891-8918.

Getting Money

U.S. Small Business Administration

Office of Financial Assistance
(202) 205-6490

Direct loan funds are limited to businesses owned by disabled individuals; all other assistance is provided through SBA guarantees of loans made by local banks.

Small Business Investment Companies (SBICs)

SBICs are privately capitalized, owned, and managed investment firms licensed by the SBA that provide equity capital, long-term financing, and management assistance to small business. Contact your nearest SBA office. A directory of SBICs is available by sending $10 to:

NASBIC Directory
P.O. Box 4039
Merrifield, VA 22116

Office of Business Development and Marketing (SBA)

409 3rd Street, SW
Washington, D.C. 20416
(202) 205-6666

Offers free fact sheet on the basics of raising money, types of business loans, writing a loan proposal.

The States and Small Business: A Directory of Programs and Activities published by the SBA's Office of Advocacy

Available from the
Government Printing Office
(202) 512-1800

National Association of Development Companies (NADCO)

6764 Old McLean
Village Drive
McLean, VA 22203

(703) 812-9000

The trade group for Certified Development Companies (CDCs) promotes small-business expansion through the 504 loan program. This program offers fixed, low-interest loans to qualified existing businesses for the purchase of fixed assets such as real estate or machinery. All CDC funding is guaranteed by the SBA.

Partners Grant Program:

AT&T Capital Corporation and the American Institute of CPAs offer $50,000 in grants to small companies with a sound plan and a socially responsible mission.

National Association of Small Business Investment Companies

Washington, DC
(202) 628-5055

National Venture Capital Association

(703) 351-5269
www.envista.com/nvca/index.html

Membership organization of over 200 venture capital firms. The site includes a discussion of venture capital in general and what it does for the business community.

The Foundation Center

79 Fifth Avenue
New York, NY 10003
(212) 620-4230

Gathers data on foundations /corporate giving programs/contribution programs; also has grant listings.

Minorities

Office of Minority Enterprise Development (MED) SBA

409 3rd Street, SW, Suite 8000
Washington, DC 20416
(202) 205-6410

Helps foster business ownership by individuals who are socially and economically disadvantaged. The SBA has combined its efforts with those of private industry, banks, local communities, and other government agencies to meet that goal.

Minority Business Development Agency (MBDA)
U.S. Department of Commerce
Washington, DC 20230
(202) 482-1015

Management and technical assistance provided to businesses primarily through a network of local Minority Business Development Centers. Call number above to find your nearest MBDC.

National Minority Supplier Development Council (NMSDC)
15 West 39th Street, 9th floor
New York, NY 10018
(212) 944-2430

Can supply information about becoming certified as a minority contractor. NMSDC has matched more than 15,000 minority-owned businesses with member corporations that want to purchase their goods and services. Local chapters exist throughout the United States.

National Association of Minority Contractors (NAMC)
666–11th Street, Suite 520
Washington, DC 20001
(202) 347-8259

A trade association formed in 1969 to address the needs of minority contractors worldwide.

Equal Opportunity Employment Commission (EEOC)
1400 L Street, NW, Suite 200
Washington, DC 20507
(800) 669-EEOC
TDD: (800) 800-3302

U.S. Hispanic Chamber of Commerce
1019–19th Street, NW, Suite 200
Washington, DC 20036
(202) 842-1212

Represents the interests of more than 400,000 Hispanic-owned businesses. Its annual convention combines trade fair, business sections, and workshops designed to promote business opportunities.

National Association of Investment Companies (NAIC)
1111 14th Street, NW, Suite 700

Washington, DC 20005
(202) 289-4336

Provides entrepreneurs with names of investors in their area that invest exclusively in small businesses owned by minority entrepreneurs. *See also* "Getting Money" section, above.

Newsletters and Other Resources

SCOR (Small Corporations Offering Registrations) Report (Not to be confused with SCORE)

Tom Stewart-Gordon
Editor/Publisher
P.O. Box 781992
Dallas, TX 75378
(972) 620-2489

An eight-page newsletter published 14 times annually reporting on capital formation alternatives for small companies. *SCOR* is a securities registration at the state level that is simpler and quicker than the SEC process.

The PC Bible

Edited by Eric Knorr
Peachpit Press
2414 Sixth Street
Berkeley, CA 94710
(510) 548-4393

Nineteen top PC experts discuss hardware and software; hundreds of tips to sort through the tech maze.

The Money Connection: Where & How to Apply for Business Loans and Venture Capital by Lawrence Flanagan; published by Oasis Press/PSI Research

(800) 228-2275

Leadership Directories Inc.

104 Fifth Avenue, 2nd floor
New York, NY 10011
(212) 627-4140

A series of "who's who" guides in the worlds of government, finance, law, business, etc.

Six Figure Consulting: How to Have a Great Second Career by Gary Goodman; published by AMACOM Books

1601 Broadway,
New York, NY 10019
fax: (212) 903-8083

Online Resources

SMALL BUSINESS MAGAZINES ON THE WORLD WIDE WEB

Entrepreneurial Edge Online
www.edgeonline.com

Entrepreneur
www.entrepreneurmag.com

Franchise Times
www.franchisetimes.com

Entrepreneur International
www.entrepreneurmag.com

Inc Online
www.inc.com

Their archives list every past *Inc.* article; the online version of the magazine has some content the magazine doesn't. Download worksheets on finance and management.

Price Costco
www.pricecostco.com

Live weekly business chats, message board to interact with other small business owners; monthly column by Jane Applegate.

Black Enterprise Magazine
www.blackenterprise.com

Business Week Online
www.businessweek.com

WEB SITES TO CHECK OUT

Jane Applegate
www.janeapplegate.com

Everything you want to know about Jane, plus tips, columns, and news.

Microsoft smallbiz
www.microsoft.com/smallbiz

Essays, excerpts from popular business books, how-to's,

Applegate answers questions in her Microtalk column, and, of course, all the hi-tech office information you need.

CCH Business Owners's Toolkit

www.toolkit.cch.com

A great resource for small-business owners. Basically, a small-business guidebook on the Web.

Hewlett Packard's small-business site

www.hp.com

Check out Hewlett Packard's small-business site.

MCI's Web site

www.mci.com/smallbiz/

Drake Software

www.1040.com

Drake Software hosts this site for general tax questions, downloadable forms, and federal and state links.

Home Office Computing

www.smalloffice.com

Web site from *Home Office Computing* magazine.

HTML tutorial

www.webdiner.com/utensil.htm

A barebones tutorial of HTML, the computer language used to create sites on the World Wide Web.

Partners for Small Business Excellence

www.smallbizpartners.com

A clearinghouse of resources available to small businesses launched by Pacific Bell Directory. Also use to register for seminars, matching grant education workshops, or to purchase educational products.

GTE

www.gte.com.

A good site for product and service information, plus updates of the GTE/Applegate national speaking tour.

DoubleClick

doubleclick.net/general/general.htm

One of the best Web Banner placement services on the Web today. DoubleClick has gathered profiles of more than 10 million anonymous Web visitors and uses them to provide targeted marketing opportunities to clients. Good resource for Web advertising information.

Organizations, Foundations, and More Advocacy Groups

National Federation of Independent Businesses (NFIB)

Capitol Gallery East, Suite 700
600 Maryland Avenue, SW
Washington, DC 20024
(800) 634-2669
fax: (202) 554-0496
www.nfibonline.com

Nation's largest small-business advocacy group; represents more than 600,000 small and independent businesses before legislatures and government agencies at the federal and state levels. Also disseminates educational information.

National Small Business United (NSBU)

1156 15th Street, NW, Suite 1100
Washington, DC 20005
(202) 293-8830
e-mail: nsbu@nsbu.org

Join and subscribe to a weekly two-page fax of information on legislation, regulations, and news that affects the small-business world.

Alliance of Independent Store Owners and Professionals (AISOP)

3725 Multifoods Tower
Minneapolis, MN 55402
(612) 340-1568

Protects and promotes fair postal and legislative policies for small-business advertisers.

National Association of Temporary and Staffing Services (NATSS)

119 S. Saint Asaph Street
Alexandria, VA 22314
(703) 549-6287
fax: (703) 549-4808
www.natss.org

Call NATSS for information about employment and economic trends.

TEC: An International Organization of CEOs

5469 Kearny Villa Road, Suite 101
San Diego, CA 92123-1159
(800) 274-2367
fax: (800) 934-4540

More than 3,400 members worldwide; membership by invitation only.

Edward Lowe Foundation

58220 Decatur Road
P.O. Box 8
Cassopolis, MI 49031
(800) 232-LOWE
fax: (616) 445-4350
smallbizNet: www.lowe.org

American Society for Training and Development (ASTD)

1630 Duke Street, Box 1443
Alexandria, VA 22313
(703) 683-8100

Business for Social Responsibility (BSR)

A national association that provides assistance to companies seeking to implement policies and practices that contribute to their success.

1683 Folsolm Street
San Francisco, CA 94103-3722
(415) 865-2500
fax: (415) 865-2505

Corporate Alliance to End Partner Violence (CAEPV)

2416 East Washington St., Suite E
Bloomington, FL 61704
(309) 664-0667
www.caepv.org

A membership organization of employers committed to putting workplace education programs in place to end violence between partners. Relevant to businesses large and small; the costs of partner violence take their toll on businesses through increased sick leave, reduced productivity, increased medical expenses, and employee turnover.

The Grantsmanship Center

1125 W. Sixth Street, 5th floor

P.O. Box 17220
Los Angeles, CA 90017
(213) 482-9860 (list of publications catalog/seminars)

Patents

U.S. Patent and Trademark Office (PTO)
Public Service Center
P.O. Box 2089
2021 South Clark Place
Eads Station
Arlington, VA 22202
(703) 308-4357
(800) PTO-9199
www.uspto.gov

General Information Concerning Patents (stock #003-004-00659-5) can be ordered from:
Superintendent of Documents
U.S. Government Printing Office
Washington, DC 20402

Patent Database from IBM
www.ibm.com/patents

Offers free online search access to IBM's database of more than 2 million patent filings dating back to 1971.

Trade Associations

American Consultants League (ACL)
30466 Prince Williams St.
Princess Anne, MD 21853
(410) 651-4869

The Consultants League sells:

- *The Consultant's Legal Guide* ($29) by Nancy Tyeatt
- *How to Expand Your Consulting Practice, Triple Your Revenue, and Become Number One in Your Field* ($19) by Consulting Intelligence

Also try:

- *The Consultant's Kit: Establishing and Operating Your Successful Consulting Business* ($38.50) by Jeffrey Lant, JLA

Publications

American Health Care Association

1201 L Street, NW, 8th floor
Washington, DC 20005
(202) 842-4444

American Management Association (AMA)

1601 Broadway
New York, NY 10019
(212) 586-8100

American Retail Federation

325 7th St. NW, Suite 1000
Washington, DC 20004
(202) 783-7971

American Small Business Association (ASBA)

1800 North Kent Street, Suite 910
Arlington, VA 22209
(800) ASBA-911

Members are businesses with 20 or fewer employees; member benefits and services.

Custom Tailors and Designers Association of America

17 East 45th Street, Room 401
Washington, DC
(202) 387-7220

Direct Marketing Association

11 West 42nd Street
New York, NY 10036
or
1120 Avenue of the Americas
(212) 768-7277
(212) 790-1400

Direct Selling Association (DSA)

1666 K Street, NW, Suite 1010
Washington, DC 20006
(202) 293-5760

Information Industry Association

1625 Madison Ave., Suite 700
Washington, DC 20001
(202) 986-0280

International Mass Retail Association (IMRA)
1700 North Moore Street, Suite 2250
Arlington, VA 22209
(703) 841-2300

Multi-Level Marketing International Association (MLMIA)
1101 Dove Street., #170
Newport Beach, CA 92660
(714) 622-0300

Also known as "network marketing." Distributors not only sell products and services but also recruit other salespeople.

National Association of Wholesaler-Distributors
1725 K Street, NW, Suite 710
Washington, DC 20006
(202) 872-0885

National Association of Desktop Publishers
462 Old Boston Street
Topsfield, MA 01983
(978) 887-2246

National Business Association (NBA)
P.O. Box 700728
Dallas, TX 75370
(800) 456-0440
www.natlbiz.com

Assists small-business people in achieving their goals. NBA offers benefits/services that provide discounts and resources.

National Business Incubation Association
www.nbia.org/homepg.htm

The comprehensive listing of incubator programs on the Web.

National Restaurant Association
1200 17th Street, NW
Washington, DC 20036
(202) 331-5900

Professional Association of Innkeepers International
P.O. Box 90710
Santa Barbara, CA 93190
(805) 569-1853

Promotional Products Association International (PPA)

3125 Skyway Circle North
Irving, TX 75038
(972) 252-0404
fax: (972) 594-7224

Small Business Institute Director's Association (SBDIA)

Stephen F. Austin State University
Department of Management and Marketing
Nacogdoches, TX 75962
(409) 468-4103

Taxicab and Livery Association

3849 Farragut Avenue
Kensington, MD 20895
(301) 946-5701

U.S. Food and Drug Administration (FDA)

Food safety center (800) 532-4440

TRADE SHOW INFORMATION ONLINE

Event Seeker

www.eventseeker.com

Locate trade shows and events or put your advertising at the eventseeker site.

EXPOguide

www.expoguide.com

Search for trade shows, conferences, and seminars.

Video Publishers

Video Arts

8614 W. Catalpa Avenue
Chicago, IL 60656
(800) 553-0091
e-mail: videoart@interaccess.com

This video publisher is "The world's leading provider" of business training programs, founded in 1972 by Monty Python comic genius John Cleese. Video programs cover management, customer service, finance, and sales.

Women in Small Business

Office of Women's Business Ownership (OWBO)
SBA

(202) 205-6673

www.sbaonline.sba.gov/womeninbusiness

An office of the SBA; advocates the ownership and success of women-owned businesses with information and special assistance programs. Call the number above to find your nearest OWBO office.

National Association of Women Business Owners (NAWBO)

(same mailing address as NFWBO, below)

(301) 608-2590

fax: (310) 608-2596

A membership-based federation with 50 local chapters and almost 5,000 members nationwide. It works with women's businesses to expand operations and represents women's business interests to federal and state governments.

National Foundation for Women Business Owners (NFWBO)

1100 Wayne Avenue, Suite 830

Silver Spring, MD 20910-5603

(301) 495-4975

fax: (301) 495-4979

e-mail: NFWBO@worldnet.att.net

www.nfwbo.org

Les Femmes Chefs d'Entreprises Mondiales

www.fcem.org

NAWBO is a member of this international organization.

Business & Professional Women (BPW USA)
BPW Foundation

2012 Massachusetts Avenue, NW

Washington, DC 20036

(202) 293-1100

fax: (202) 861-0298

Women's Bureau of the U.S. Department of Labor

Washington, DC 20210

(800) 827-5335

TDD: (800) 326-2577

This bureau researches and promotes policies to improve working conditions for women. Find out about issues relating to sexual harassment, medical/family leave, pregnancy, and discrimination.

Women's World Banking

8 West 40th Street, 10th floor
New York, NY 10018
(212) 768-8513

(*See also* "Getting Money" section, above)

WOMEN ENTREPRENEURS ONLINE

Business Week Online for Women in Business

www.businessweek.com/tocs/womenbiz.html

Engender—For Women in Small Business

www.cadvision.com/ffap/engender/

Women's Web Magazine

http://womenswebmagazine.com

Women's Work

www.wwork.com

Women's Professional Directory

www.womensdirectory.com

Women's Franchise Network

www.entremkt.com/wfn

Women's connection online website

www.womenconnect.com

Working from Home

National Association for the Self-Employed

P.O. Box 612067
Dallas, TX 75261
(800) 232-6273

Offers health plans and free booklets for members, including the *Small Business Resource Guide Book.*

National Association of Home-Based Businesses

P.O. Box 362
10451 Mill Run Circle, #400
Owings Mills, MD 21117

(410) 363-3698

Home Business News

12221 Beaver Pike
Jackson, OH 45640
(614) 988-2331

Bimonthly magazine for home-based entrepreneurs.

Working from Home by Paul and Sarah Edwards ($14.95; published by Jeremy Tarcher Inc., 5858 Wilshire Blvd, Suite 200, Los Angeles, CA 90036; 800-631-8571).

Home Business Made Easy by David Hanania covers businesses you can run from your home and has a small business resource guide ($19.95; published by Oasis Press, PSI Research, 300 North Valley Drive, Grants Pass, OR 97526).

http://work.soho.org/SOHO
www.workingsolo.com

Working Solo: The Real Guide to Freedom & Financial Success with Your Own Business and ***Working Solo Sourcebook: Essential Resources for Independent Entrepreneurs,*** both by Terri Lonier (both $14.95; Portico Press).

Young Entrepreneurs

KidsWay, Inc.

5589 Peachtree Road
Chamblee, GA 30341
(888) KIDS-WAY

Publishes *Young Entrepreneur,* a bimonthly newsletter (annual subscription $16) that includes a calendar of upcoming events for young entrepreneurs, business strategies, and profiles of enterprising young people.

The KidsWay Foundation Center for Youth Entrepreneurship

1350 NASA Road One, Suite 101
Houston, TX 77058
(888) 488-KIDS

For consultations or assistance with a youth-owned business or a youth entrepreneurship training program.

National Foundation for Teaching Entrepreneurship (NFTE)

120 Wall Street, 29th floor
New York, NY 10005
(212) 232-3333
fax: (212) 232-2244

Business Ship

One Alhambra Plaza, Suite 1400
Coral Gables, FL 33134
(305) 445-8869

About Bloomberg

Bloomberg Financial Markets is a global, multimedia-based distributor of information services, combining news, data, and analysis for financial markets and businesses. Bloomberg carries real-time pricing, data, history, analytics, and electronic communications that are available 24 hours a day and are currently accessed by 250,000 financial professionals in 94 countries.

Bloomberg covers all key global securities markets, including equities, money markets, currencies, municipals, corporate/euro/sovereign bonds, commodities, mortgage-backed securities, derivative products, and governments. The company also delivers access to Bloomberg News, whose more than 540 reporters and editors in 80 bureaus worldwide provide around-the-clock coverage of economic, financial, and political events.

To learn more about Bloomberg—one of the world's fastest-growing real-time financial information networks—call a sales representative at:

Frankfurt:	49-69-920-410
Hong Kong:	852-2521-3000
London:	44-171-330-7500
New York:	1-212-318-2000
Princeton:	1-609-279-3000
San Francisco:	1-415-912-2960
São Paulo:	5511-3048-4500
Singapore:	65-226-3000
Sydney:	61-29-777-8686
Tokyo:	81-3-3201-8900

About the Author

Jane Applegate is one of America's most respected business journalists. She is an award-winning syndicated writer whose column reaches 10 million readers a week in newspapers globally. Her previous books are *Succeeding in Small Business* and *Jane Applegate's Strategies for Small Business Success*. The Applegate Group, her multimedia communications company based in Pelham, New York, produces television and radio reports and orchestrates strategic planning and marketing for corporate clients. She is a popular keynote speaker at small-business events.